American Voices

AMERICAN VOICES

*Five Contemporary Playwrights
in Essays and Interviews*

by
Esther Harriott

McFarland & Company, Inc., Publishers
Jefferson, North Carolina, and London

Library of Congress Cataloguing-in-Publication Data

Harriott, Esther.
  American voices.

  Bibliography: p. 175.
  Includes index.
  1. American drama — 20th century — History and
criticism. 2. Dramatists, American — 20th century —
Interviews. I. Title.
  PS352.H37 1988   812′.54′09   88-42500

ISBN 0-89950-283-0 (50# acid-free natural paper)

Manufactured in the United States of America.

McFarland   Box 611   Jefferson NC 28640

In memory of my parents

Acknowledgments

My thanks to Charles Fuller, David Mamet, Marsha Norman, and Lanford Wilson for letting me interview them, and to Reva Cooper, Pat Galloway, Gary Murphy, and Leah Schmidt for helping to make it happen.

And my special thanks to Leslie Fiedler, whose influence as a writer, teacher, and friend has been incalculable.

Table of Contents

Acknowledgments vii

Introduction xi

I. Sam Shepard: Inventing Identities 3

II. Lanford Wilson: To Vanish Without a Trace 19

III. Interview with Lanford Wilson 36

IV. David Mamet: Comedies of Bad Manners 61

V. Interview with David Mamet 77

VI. Charles Fuller: The Quest for Justice 101

VII. Interview with Charles Fuller 112

VIII. Marsha Norman: Getting Out 129

IX. Interview with Marsha Norman 148

Afterword 165

References 171

Selected Bibliography 175

Index 185

Introduction

This book looks at five American playwrights—Sam Shepard, Lanford Wilson, David Mamet, Charles Fuller, and Marsha Norman—who have come to prominence during the last two decades. There is no label of the sort that attached to the "angry young men" of the fifties, the "non-verbalists" of the sixties, or the "postmodernists" of the eighties, to link them formally as representatives of a movement or a point of view. What they have in common is simply that they are members of a generation of writers. Their birth-dates range from 1937 (Wilson) to 1947 (Norman) and they began writing within approximately ten years of each other—Shepard, Wilson, and Fuller in the 1960s, Mamet and Norman in the 1970s. Each of them has won a Pulitzer Prize for drama, which, though no infallible guarantee of merit, is nonetheless a significant measure of critical recognition. Shepard, Wilson and Mamet have each contributed a distinctive and substantial body of work to the American theater, while Fuller and Norman are two of the most promising of the playwrights to have emerged more recently, and they bring fresh points of view to a forum traditionally dominated by white males.

As members of a generation, these playwrights have shared certain formative experiences. They came of age during the social upheavals of the sixties, when traditions in the theater, as well as in society, were being challenged. Off Off Broadway was a center of theatrical activity with its new "alternative" theaters like Caffe Cino, Theater Genesis, Café La Mama, and the Judson Theater. New playwrights were influenced by the European dramatists Ionesco, Beckett, and Pinter, who subverted conventional expectations of language and behavior to express the subversion of conventional values and assumptions. Avant-garde ensembles like the Living Theatre, the Open Theatre, and the Performance Group took up Antonin Artaud's manifesto "The Theatre of Cruelty" with its call for an end to "the subjugation of the theater to the text" and experimented with a non-verbal theater, whose impact depended on visual images and physical movement.[1] Language was relegated to one component of the aural design, and scripts evolved from workshop improvisations or were freely adapted from existing texts, often manipulated into deliberately unintelligible utterance. The director rather than the playwright was the creator. The black theater, which also experienced a resurgence in the sixties, generally adhered to traditional forms as the most effective vehicle for the social consciousness of the black liberation movement, although that consciousness often led to the rejection of the European verbal tradition in favor of African ritual and chanting.

From the viewpoint of the 1980s, the rebellion in the theater was as short-lived as the rebellion in society. For whatever reasons—that the theater, which is a business enterprise, cannot oppose the establishment and survive; that the country's shift to conservatism was echoed in the theater; that in a consumer society new directions quickly become outdated fads—the non-verbal movement began to peter out in the seventies. Its legacy is seen in ensembles like the Mabou Mines or in the tableaux vivants of Robert Wilson or the theater pieces of Martha Clarke. But there is no longer the deliberate fusing of political protest with artistic experimentation—indeed, the theater of the eighties is largely one of personal and private concerns—and there has been a return to the central role of language and the playwright.

Wilson and Shepard began to write for Off Off Broadway in the sixties, and the experimentation of that period is reflected in Wilson's aural collages and Shepard's visual imagery. But it was language that distinguished their work. The excitement in Shepard's plays is in the imagination and driving energy of his speech. The long soliloquies that are his trademark have the power of dreams, creating images that are apprehended by the unconscious even when they elude rational analysis. He alternates the heightened rhetoric of these monologues with the deliberate banality of the dialogue, and the contrast makes the rhetoric seem more intense, the dialogue more comic. Shepard, despite his attention to visual effect, reads as well as he plays—frequently better: the boisterous physicality of his stage business can be wearing, like being confined for a couple of hours with hyperactive adolescent boys.

Wilson's gift is for conversation that sounds true to character but is raised to the level of performance. The virtue is that his characters are more entertaining than they would be in real life; the flaw is that they are sometimes self-consciously articulate. Wilson alone among these playwrights has created, out of the variety of speech patterns in which Americans express themselves, a gallery of characters (although he has not yet created any who have taken up an independent life in the collective imagination, as Blanche DuBois or Willy Loman have done), from the liberated black woman in *The Gingham Dog*, to the Yankee esthete in *Brontosaurus*, to the burned-out ex-hippie in *5th of July*.

Introduction

In Mamet's *Sexual Perversity in Chicago*, Deborah says, "It's only words. I don't think you should be frightened of words."[2] But Mamet's words do frighten. You wince at their violence as you would wince at a raised fist. Although his language doesn't create poetry like Shepard's or characterization like Wilson's, it satisfies the demands of the theater by being bold, funny, and authentic. When he makes his serious observations in a serious voice, Mamet's language becomes stilted. But in his comic dialogues he masterfully captures the verbal gropings and muddled sputterings of a semi-articulate society and renders them in the jarring rhythms of urban life.

Fuller's language is liveliest when he uses idiomatic black speech: the barracks banter in his army plays and the ghetto dialect in *Zooman and the Sign* have a humor and pungency that he otherwise seems to tone down. It is the moral force of his themes—especially impressive in a theater that tends to be introspective and self-regarding—rather than the sober language in which he expresses them that gives his plays their emotional power. Fuller is a careful writer who doesn't waste words, but he sometimes leaves you wishing for more.

Norman's language is stripped to its essence. It is lean, urgent, concentrated. It is also lively, even when spoken by a character who is about to kill herself, or by one who has just been released after years in prison only to find that home is another kind of prison. This is the language of people in extremis, and the liveliness is the odd buoyancy of despair.

Since the theater is the most public of the arts, with a traditional function of holding up a mirror to society, the work of these playwrights should suggest an overview of contemporary America. Perhaps it is in their dissimilarity that this society is most truly reflected. Despite the homogenizing effects of television and a mobile population, America has become increasingly fragmented, with each fragment asserting its own identity. The five playwrights are voices of the different Americas of white and black, male and female, Northern "ethnics" and Southern WASPs. Shepard grew up in California and its physical and emotional geography permeates his work. Wilson's Middle Americans live in his native Missouri or have migrated to the various places where Wilson has lived, from San Diego to a suburb of Chicago to New York City. Mamet's speech patterns and humor come out of his urban Jewish background, and Fuller writes out of the black experience, from Northern ghetto to Southern army barracks. Norman's New South WASPs living in or just outside her hometown of Louisville, Kentucky, are making a transition to the culture of malls and laundromats that has replaced their rural traditions.

Yet through the divergences of region, class, ethnicity, and gender, there emerges a consistent image of America as a violent, unstable, and perilous society. Wilson's America is a vision of rootless people on a crumbling landscape, threatened with extinction. Against this threat they seek the continuity of family—Wilson has no plays that aren't about family, even when the characters aren't literally related—and comfort each other with jaunty, constant talk. The terror in Shepard's plays is not of the physical annihilation of civilization (although there are undercurrents of nuclear paranoia) but of the psychological annihilation of identity. His heroes—cowboys, rock stars, homesteaders, outlaws—are mythic figures, but their insistent egos are also assertions of self against the anonymity of a mass society.

Mamet's America is an urban inferno inhabited by victims who victimize one another. "The only way to teach these people is to kill them," says Teach, the hapless hoodlum in *American Buffalo*.[3] The extremity of his rage, and of the rage of most of Mamet's characters, is a funny but uncomfortable reminder of the constant threat of explosiveness in American cities. *Edmond*, Mamet's nightmare depiction of urban life, has been compared to Buchner's *Woyzeck*, but the evils in Edmond's society are more frightening because they are more senseless. Unlike Woyzeck, Edmond does not attribute them to the mysterious ways of God. There is no longer the comforting assurance of a divine plan.

Because of their discontent with the America of the present, these three playwrights yearn for continuity with the America of the past. Shepard eulogizes the frontier while trying uneasily to return to his roots. "Vanish without a trace" is the refrain of Wilson's *The Mound Builders* and the preoccupation of all his plays. The men in Mamet's *Lakeboat* live in the past because the present has become unbearably banal. Fuller, however, is not nostalgic; for him the past means slavery. If the white playwrights regret the loss of the American dream, the black playwright views it as a lie to be corrected.

Yet Fuller's America is closer than theirs to the values that they mourn. His characters, although outside the mainstream of society (not because of existential alienation—they really *are* in enemy territory), still believe in social progress and reform. They are solitary, but not nihilistic: rather than withdrawing from society, they engage in it. Norman's characters, too, constricted as they are by various kinds of imprisonment, from literal jails to marginal economic conditions to oppressive families, nonetheless believe in the possiblity of change.

The America of Shepard, Mamet, and Fuller is a man's world. The strongest attachments in Shepard's plays are between the male buddies; women, subordinate or scheming moms and molls, are defined in relation to their men. When Shepard has written about sexual love, it has been more horseplay than eroticism, as in *Cowboy Mouth* or *Fool for Love*, or it has been pathological, as in *A Lie of the Mind*. Mamet's men express their hatred for women verbally in all of his plays, and physically—through rape and murder—in two of them. And a problem in Fuller's plays is that although we are told there is intensity in the relationships of his married couples, we don't feel it because the women are not sharply drawn.

Unlike these playwrights, Wilson writes women as full-fledged people and has made them among his most articulate and sympathetic characters. Still, sex is more talk than passion. Everyone discusses the details of everyone else's sex life: there is no privacy in Wilson's bedrooms. In Norman's work, love has an elegiac cast. The one sensual passage is in *Traveler in the Dark* when Sam is recalling his youthful desire for his wife; in the other plays, women grieve for the men who have abandoned them.

The advantage (or disadvantage) of writing about living playwrights is that they can speak for themselves, and the book includes my interviews with them; only Sam Shepard did not respond to my request, which was consistent with his frequently stated aversion to being interviewed. The subjects discussed in the interviews were not designed to dovetail with the essays—the format was conversational rather than choreographed—but the juxtaposition of interview and essay necessarily gives a fuller view of the playwright and the work.

Although I discuss the playwrights as individual voices rather than as exponents of a unifying thesis, I do suggest how their work seems peculiarly American: Shepard's obsession with identity and self, an obsession associated with what social historian Christopher Lasch has called our "culture of narcissism"; Wilson's fears about the impermanence of American society and his attempts to mask those fears with deliberate American cheer; Mamet's serious observations of American manners and mores expressed through his comic renderings of American speech; Fuller's examination of justice in a racist society; and Norman's stories of people who exemplify the quintessential American belief in the chance to remake one's life.

Sam Shepard:
Inventing Identities

Inventing Identities

IF THE AMERICAN DREAM is the opportunity to reinvent one's life, an opportunity less available in older societies with more rigid class structures, Sam Shepard takes it one step further to the reinvention of one's fundamental identity. The obverse side of this freedom is the fear that there is not a real self, only the performance of one. Shepard's plays are filled with these performances: his characters change roles as easily as they change clothes. They invent new identities, switch identities with other characters, metamorphose into other forms of life, or simply disappear. The tension between the desire for escape from an unsatisfactory identity and the desire for the continuity that would give an authentic sense of self is characteristically dramatized in the ambivalent relations of sons to their fathers, or father-substitutes in Shepard's male pairs, that oscillate between dreams of patricide and reconciliation.

Identities are created, transformed, and annihilated through the use of highly imaginative language. In *Red Cross* (1966), Carol fantasizes a skiing accident that ends with her disappearance into a splotch of blood on the snow, while the Maid in the same play escapes from the fear and cramps of her swimming lesson—which, itself, is imaginary—by imagining her metamorphosis:

> But once it's over it isn't bad at all. Once you get over the shock of having water all around and dragonflies and water lilies floating by and little silver fish flashing around you. Once that's past and you get all used to your flippers and your fins and your new skin, then it comes very easy. You move through the water like you were born in that very same place and never even knew what land was like....[1]

Although he never appears, the pilot in *Icarus's Mother* (1965) is the central figure of the play, a constantly changing identity whose existence depends on the verbal inventions of the five picnickers who speculate about him. In a series of increasingly feverish monologues, they spin a tale about the unseen pilot flying overhead: his identity, motives, actions, and finally, death. The last monologue of the play is a description of the real or imaginary plane crash in apocalyptic imagery that suggests nuclear holocaust:

> ...And to hear a sound so shrieking that it ain't even a sound at all but goes beyond that into the inside of the center of each ear and rattles you up so you don't know exactly or for sure if you'll ever hear again or if it actually exactly matters.... The beach sinks below the surface. The seagulls drown in flocks of ten thousand. There's a line of people two hundred deep.... And the pilot bobbing in the very center of a ring of fire that's closing in. His white helmet bobbing up and bobbing down. His hand reaching for his

3

other hand and the fire moves in and covers him up and the line
of two hundred bow their heads and moan together with the light
in their faces....[2]

These long soliloquies (this one occupies three pages of the published
play) that are Shepard's trademark have the sensory acuity of dreams and,
like dreams or poems, or like the movies that have so deeply influenced
Shepard's sensibility, they project images that speak powerfully to the unconscious even when they resist analysis. Here, the image of the pilot, whose
presence is both elusive and all-pervading, is an objective correlative for our
omnipresent bad dream of The Bomb.

Instability of identity accounts for much of the tension in Shepard's
plays. If identities are fluid, behavior becomes unpredictable, and anything
is possible. The anxiety provoked by Action (1974) comes less from the ambiguous, possibly post-nuclear setting of the play than from the unpredictability of the characters. When one of them suddenly and inexplicably
smashes a chair into pieces, it's a shocking moment. When none of the
others react, it's more shocking. The sense of menace in Shepard's plays is
not due to the violence but to the arbitrariness of the violence. A character
may do or say anything at any minute: there's no fixed identity to rely on.
This unpredictability can provide comic effects too. In Melodrama Play
(1967), Peter, a B-movie thug who has been terrorizing his victims with a gun
and club, suddenly turns to them and says: "I'd like to ask you both what
you think of me as a person. Just frankly. Don't be afraid of hurting my feelings or anything like that. Just tell me what you think."[3]

Shepard has written that "Instead of the idea of a 'whole character' with
logical motives behind his behavior which the actor submerges himself into,
he should consider instead a fractured whole with bits and pieces of
character flying off a central theme."[4] Most of the more than forty plays
that Shepard has written are like fragments flying off a central theme too,
chaotic bursts of energy with abrupt, arbitrary endings. The best of them,
like Icarus's Mother, Red Cross, The Tooth of Crime, Buried Child, are un-
matched in the American theater for originality of conception and
imaginative use of speech; the worst, like Mad Dog Blues or The Unseen
Hand, are hodgepodges of comic strip and nostalgia (although always with
at least one compelling soliloquy). Most of them are mixtures of the inspired
and the puerile. True West is a good example, with the dramatic tension and
lunatic humor of the first act deteriorating into rowdy self-indulgence in the
second. Yet, uneven as they are, all of the plays have Shepard's distinctive
voice and cohere into a chronicle of his life, not a reenactment of events
but a reflection on them, a kind of autobiography of consciousness.

It is a consciousness that came of age in the sixties, when drugs, rock music, and rebellion against traditional values changed the look and lifestyles of American middleclass youth, the prevailing view of reality came to be shaped by images on TV, and belief in endless possibility gave way to political disillusionment and the dread of nuclear annihilation. In his book *The Culture of Narcissism*, social critic Christopher Lasch calls it an "age of diminishing expectations," in which Americans, despairing of the future and society, turned to the present and the self.[5] Lasch discusses literary work that reflects that self-absorption: the autobiographical journalism of Norman Mailer, the confessional novels of Erica Jong and Philip Roth, the self-reflexive fiction of John Barth and Donald Barthelme. His description of writer Paul Zweig, in particular, applies to Shepard: "External events play only a shadowy part in his narrative. They have the quality of hallucination, a vague background of 'terror and vulnerability.'"[6] He quotes from Zweig's *Three Journeys*: ". . . the frightening feeling that at some level of existence I'm nobody, that my identity has collapsed, and deep down, no one's there."[7] Shepard's plays express this terror. His characters invent identities not in order to conceal their true selves, but because it is only through these invented identities that they exist at all.

Shepard's most striking identity invention may well be himself. He has become a mythic figure like the cowboys, rock stars, outlaws, and other loners of American popular culture who inhabit his plays. Even his all–American hero's name is an adaptation of his given name, Samuel Shepard Rogers III, a change (and a repudiation of his patronymic) that he made in 1964 when he left his family's small ranch in California and headed East, a Jay Gatsby for the sixties. Or Gatsby's creator. Like F. Scott Fitzgerald, Shepard has created a persona that has caught the imagination of the American public, and for some of the same reasons: the extraordinary good looks, the early success, the acting out of the role of bad boy in public, with Fitzgerald's Roaring Twenties carousings updated to Shepard's drug and rock music scene. There are deeper parallels between the two men: the puritanical nature under the hedonism that idealizes an abstract, moral "West"; the tormented, eternally adolescent sensibility; the inconsolable regret for the loss of America's earlier promise. It is as though Fitzgerald's "orgiastic future that year by year recedes before us" has ended in Shepard's "sound of America cracking open and crashing into the sea."[8]

Shepard arrived in New York City during the period of intense theatrical activity Off Off Broadway. His roommate, Charles Mingus, Jr. (the jazzman's son), found him a job as busboy at a jazz club, the Village Gate, whose headwaiter, Ralph Cook, was forming an experimental theater. Cook encouraged Shepard to write a play, and the result was a double bill of one-act plays, *Cowboys* and *Rock Garden*, that was the first production of Theater Genesis. It opened October 10, 1964, one month before Shepard's twentieth birthday, and was panned by every critic except Michael Smith of *The Village Voice*. But Smith's review of Shepard as an important new playwright was enough to bring audiences and launch his career.

Cowboys #2 (1967) is Shepard's rewriting of *Cowboys* (one of several plays that Shepard, whose approach to writing was casual and improvisatory, lost or discarded), and it announces most of the characteristics of a Shepard play: the images and characters of the Old West derived from Hollywood movies; a man's world (or boy's world) ambience; abrupt shifts from horseplay to menace; language that alternates between comically banal dialogue and lyrical soliloquies; the presentation of self through performances; and the view of identity as precarious. Like Shepard's other male buddies, the protagonists Chet and Stu are not individuated as characters, but function in turn as performer and audience, each using the other as a mirror in which to try on an identity. Assuming the speech and mannerisms of old-time cowboys, they act out a series of make-believe events, beginning with mudfights and stargazing, then building to a climax of marauding Indians, dehydration in the desert, and buzzards circling overhead. At intervals, two unidentified male voices are heard offstage and, as the play ends, two actors come out of the wings reading Chet's and Stu's lines from the beginning of the play. It is quite chilling. For Shepard's characters, the threat is not external catastrophe but the loss of identity.

Shepard has said that *Rock Garden*, the other play of that first production, is about leaving home. The first of its three scenes of familial interaction is a brief absurdist tableau vivant of a boy, a girl, and their father at a kitchen table. The second is a prototype of Shepard's father-son identity mergings. A boy sits in a rocking chair in his underwear listening to his mother's observations on the anatomical similarities between father and son. She ends each of her comments with a request for a glass of water; when the boy returns with it, he has put on an article of clothing to cover the part of his body that she has referred to. At the end of the scene the boy leaves, the father comes to sit in the rocking chair in *his* underwear, and the mother picks up where she left off, oblivious to the son's replacement by the father. The mood that Shepard creates here is both irrational and convincing—the logic of a dream. In the last scene, the father delivers an endless, banal discourse on the care of lawns, fences, and rock gardens, to which the son listens quietly, periodically dozing off and falling out of his chair. When his father is finished, the son exuberantly launches into a long, explicit description of his orgasms and positions of sexual intercourse. The monologue illustrates the humorous use of unpredictable identity: the character does not behave in a way that seems appropriate to his role because that role is fluid.

If *Rock Garden* recorded Shepard's first "escape," *Cowboy Mouth* (1971) recorded the second, from his wife and baby son. In 1969 he had married actress O-lan Johnson and fathered a son; a year later he left home for a much-publicized affair with rock poet Patti Smith. Shepard helped to publicize it further in his collaboration with Smith on *Cowboy Mouth*, a narcissistic exercise, compounded by their performing their autobiographical roles on opening night. It comes across as a very young, very stoned play. Slim (Shepard) and Cavale (Smith) act out a series of childish impulses—yelling, singing, playing drums at top volume, ordering food to be brought in the minute they get hungry, then throwing it all over the floor of one of Shepard's junk-strewn sets—and generally behave more like two kids who have escaped their parents than the principals in an adulterous affair. Slim complains that he is torn between Cavale, the raggedy Circe-figure who has kidnapped him to make him into a rock star, and the wife and baby he has abandoned. Besides examining and celebrating the ambivalent affair in public, *Cowboy Mouth* reflected Shepard's belief that the rock musician was the quintessential artist of the time, the new savior. Cavale exhorts Slim to:

> reach out and grab all the little broken busted up pieces of people's frustrations. . . . And then you gotta take all that into yourself and pour it back out. Give it back to them bigger than life. . . . You gotta be like a rock 'n' roll Jesus with a cowboy mouth.[9]

There is no exploration of this notion, but that's not what we expect from Shepard: he's a playwright of imagination rather than ideas. What *Cowboy Mouth* lacks is the transforming language that made *Rock Garden* transcend the autobiographical material. It is interesting primarily as another fragment in the continuing dramatic work that Shepard is writing. The playwright's recurring fantasy is expressed in the last words of the play, when Cavale explains her unusual name. "It means escape," she says (CM 216).

In 1971, Shepard returned to his wife and son and moved to England. He had wanted to get out of New York, drugs, and the theater, he told the English magazine *Theatre Quarterly*. "I was in a band in New York," Shepard said—he had been the drummer in a rock group called the Holy Modal Rounders—"and I had this fantasy that I'd come over here and somehow fall into a rock 'n' roll band. . . . I much prefer playing music really to theater, but it's hard to find the right situation."[10] This escape-transformation fantasy echoed Shepard's first move from California to New York and the changes of identities in his plays. Nevertheless, he stayed in the theater and wrote five plays during his three years in London. The best of these, *The Tooth of Crime* (1974), is Shepard's elegy to rock and to his earlier idealism about its sacramental function. In *Melodrama Play* Shepard had written about the cynicism of the rock musician's manager; in *The Tooth of Crime* he writes about the cynicism of the new breed of rock musician. But if this is its subject, identity is its obsession. Rock musicians, whose identities are invented, are ideal emblems for Shepard's preoccupation.

The action of the play is a contest between Hoss, the reigning rock star, and his challenger, Crow. It is staged as a duel. Guns and knives are provided and, with Shepard's usual playfulness, so are cheerleaders and a referee. But, after setting the scene for physical combat between two killers, Shepard turns it into a battle of style, with words as weapons. "Choose an argot, Leathers," Crow tells Hoss as the match begins.[11] The extraordinary energy of the play is in its kinetic language, written in the rhythms of rock music.

Hoss stands for authentic identity, Crow for manufactured image. "You should be past roots on this scale," he says to Hoss's insistence on acknowledging rock's origins in black music. "Fence me with the present!" (*TOC* 239, 241). Hoss is attached to history, Crow is disconnected from time and place. Yet Crow is free of Hoss's identity crisis. "I'm pulled and pushed around from one image to another. Nothin' takes a solid form.... Where do I stand!" Hoss cries.

The referee decides in favor of Crow, who then, at Hoss's panicky request, tries to teach him a new style for the new times:

> First you gotta learn yer eyes.... There's too much pity, man.... Too much searchin!... Go beyond confidence. Beyond loathing. Just kill with the eyes.... Hitch up yer shirt. Sex man. Tighten your ass.... Empty your head. Shift your attention to immediate sounds. The floor. The space around you. The sound of your heart. Keep away from fantasy.... No pictures just pure focus.... Start with a clean screen. Are you blank now? [*TOC* 245, 246, 247, 248].

Content and emotions are obsolete; gesture is everything. "I believe in my mask," is Crow's refrain, "the man I made up is me" (*TOC* 234). Hoss finally chooses suicide as the only authentic assertion of identity left to him that "can't be taught or copied or stolen or sold. It's mine. An original" (*TOC* 251).

This is the first play in which Shepard argues that there is an inextricable bond between the artist and his roots, although it is implicit in his earlier plays in the recurring presence of father figures as alter egos. Even his constant references to traditional American foods such as bacon and eggs, Rice Krispies, etc. suggest nostalgia for roots. But if Hoss speaks for Shepard in *The Tooth of Crime*, Shepard identifies with Crow, too, and shows it by giving him the best lines (he's Shepard's Iago: his amoral wit makes him a livelier character than the victim-hero). The stage directions for Crow say "He looks just like Keith Richard" [of the Rolling Stones] (*TOC* 229). In "The Curse of the Raven's Black Feather" (published in his collection of prose pieces, *Hawk Moon*), Shepard, driving alone at night, meditates on the contrast between Keith Richard and his fellow Rolling Stone, Mick Jagger, and on his attraction to what Richard represents:

> Keith and Mick. Like brothers. Like evil sisters in disguise. The left and the right hand.... The dark and the light. I've always been pulled toward darkness. Toward black. Toward death. Toward the South.... Now I'm heading in the right direction. Away from the quaint North. Away from lobsters and white churches and Civil War graveyards and cracker barrel bazaars. Toward the swamps, the Bayou, the Cajuns, the cotton mouth, the Mardi Gras, the crocodile.[12]

This pull between sensuality, primitivism, and decay on the one hand, and rationality, Puritanism, and order on the other, which has informed American writing from Hawthorne to Mailer, gives *The Tooth of Crime* its tension. It's the pull between Hoss and Crow, and between continuity and escape. Connection to the past gives Hoss his identity, but absence of that connection gives Crow his freedom. It is a constant movement in Shepard's plays, as it has been in his life.

In 1974, Shepard returned to his roots, leaving England to settle in California with his wife and son and his wife's mother and stepfather (whose pop-mythic names of O-lan, Jesse Mojo, Scarlett and Johnny Dark could be the dramatis personae of a Shepard play). Ties to the past began to dominate his plays, both in explicit theme and in the use of a more traditional structure. Before leaving England, Shepard had talked about a change in the direction of his writing:

> I'd like to try a whole different way of writing now, which is very stark and not so flashy and not full of a lot of mythic figures and everything, and try to scrape it down to the bone as much as possible. Well, it could be called realism, but not the kind of realism where husbands and wives squabble and that kind of stuff.[13]

This is a fair description of *Curse of the Starving Class* (1977) and *Buried Child* (1978), the two major plays he wrote after returning home and his two best plays to date. (He wrote them after a transitional play, *Suicide in B♭* (1976), in which the artist-protagonist dresses up in costumes symbolizing his earlier selves, then ritually kills them off one by one.) In both plays, the earlier quest for identity has been replaced by the understanding that it was there all the time and, indeed, is inescapable. The emotional center of *Curse of the Starving Class* is Wesley's identity and its ambivalent connection to the identity of his father, Weston. Shepard reminds us of this connection, this shared blood, in one image after another. The "curse" is not the menstrual blood that is the subject of Ella's opening speech to her fourteen-year-old daughter Emma, but the identity that is passed along in the blood. Ella tries to describe it:

> It's a curse. I can feel it. It's invisible but it's there. It's always there. It comes onto us like nighttime.... Even when you try to change it. And it goes back. Deep. It goes back and back to tiny little cells and genes. To atoms. To tiny little swimming things making up their minds without us. Plotting in the womb.... It's bigger than government even. It goes forward too. We spread it. We pass it on.... It goes on and on like that without us.[14]

Everything is biologically preordained in a fate as unalterable as in Greek tragedy. The destructive explosiveness in the blood that Emma calls "nitroglycerine" (CSC 153) has been passed from generation to generation. "I never saw my old man's poison until I was much older than you," Weston tells Wesley, "and then you know how I recognized it?... I saw myself infected with it.... His poison in my body" (CSC 168). Emma has inherited the poison, too. On the day of her first period, her "curse," she shoots up the bar owned by the man who is about to seize their land in payment of her father's bad debts. Near the end of the play she is killed in her father's car when two thugs blow it up with "gelignite-nitro," a semantic variation of the ingredient she had identified as the curse in the blood.

Blood is a powerful visual motif as well: Wesley's bloody face and hands after fighting with his father's enemy, his bloody arms after butchering the lamb, the bloody skinned carcass of the lamb that dominates the stage at the end of the play. But if blood destroys, it also unites. After Weston launders his family's clothes in a ritual of purgation and rebirth, according to Shepard's symbolic use of clothing as identity, he reflects on his sudden insight into the benign function of blood:

> Like our bodies were connected and we could never escape that. But I didn't feel like escaping.... It was good to be connected by blood like that. That a family wasn't just a social thing. It was an animal thing. It was a reason of nature that we were all together

10

under the same roof. Not that we had to be but that we were supposed to be. And I started feeling glad about it. I started feeling full
of hope [CSC 187].

More often the blood imagery is ambivalent in its suggestions, as in the
startling speeches that open and close the last act of the play. The first is
Weston's story of the eagle who, drawn by the smell of blood, came to the
field where Weston was castrating his lambs. Weston recalls how he tossed
the testicles of each lamb onto the roof, then watched in exhilarated terror
as the eagle swooped down to carry them off. He identified with the eagle,
he says, as he watched the bird feed on "those fresh little remnants of
manhood" (CSC 184). At the end of the play, mother and son reconstruct
the Oedipal tale in an even more grotesque variation:

> *Ella:* . . . A big tom cat comes. Right out in the fields. And he jumps
> up on top of that roof to sniff around in all the entrails or whatever
> it was.
> *Wesley:* And that eagle comes down and picks up the cat in his
> talons and carries him screaming off into the sky.
> *Ella:* That's right. And they fight. They fight like crazy in the middle
> of the sky. That cat's tearing his chest out, and the eagle's trying to
> drop him, but the cat won't let go because he knows if he falls he'll
> die.
> *Wesley:* And the eagle's being torn apart in midair. The eagle's try-
> ing to free himself from the cat, and the cat won't let go.
> *Ella:* And they come crashing down to the earth. Both of them
> come crashing down. Like one whole thing [CSC 201].

Locked in symbiotic embrace, they are both predator and prey in this
nightmare version of Shepard's male pairs. The relationships between
fathers and sons in the earlier plays, from the murderous conflict of *The
Holy Ghostly* (1971) to the loving filial bond of *Back Bog Beast Bait* (1971), are
reconciled, if imperfectly, in *Curse of the Starving Class*. Father and son are
each other's identity, and escape is impossible.

Buried Child is a more controlled variation on the theme. Vince, an
estranged son, stops at his family's farm en route to the Southwest with his
girlfriend Shelly, and finds the family in various stages of physical and men-
tal decay. Dodge, his grandfather and head of the household, is an embittered old drunk who spends his days staring at a blank, illuminated TV
screen. Dodge's wife, Halie, is planning a memorial statue to their dead son
Ansel, whom she describes as a war hero, and is about to embark on an
affair with a dim-witted parish priest. Their two living sons are an idiot,
Tilden, and a cripple, Bradley. None of them recognizes Vince.

11

The atmosphere is country-western Pinter, suggesting Pinter's *The Homecoming* not only in the funny, threatening reactions of each family member to the returning son and his mate, but in the frightening premise of both plays. Dodge, addressing Shelly, enunciates it: "Don't be so easily shocked, girlie. There's nothing a man can't do. You dream it up and he can do it. Anything."[15] While this is always true in Shepard's plays, it is especially unsettling in *Buried Child* because of its conventional surface. It has a linear plot and realistic dialogue. The characters don't suddenly switch identities or metamorphose or vanish. Their unpredictable behavior is all the more menacing because it is not in the context of surrealism.

The farm is the house of Atreus on the prairie, with the gods punishing the sins of incest and infanticide. Just before he dies, Dodge reveals the secret of the family's downfall. At the prosperous middle point of their lives, Halie became pregnant by their son Tilden. The baby "wanted to grow up in this family," says Dodge:

> It wanted to be part of us. It wanted to pretend that I was its father. She wanted me to believe in it. Even when everyone around us knew. Everyone. All our boys knew. Tilden knew.... Tilden was the one who knew. Better than any of us.... He'd walk all night out there in the pasture with it. Talkin' to it. Singin' to it.... We couldn't let a thing like that continue. We couldn't allow that to grow up right in the middle of our lives. It made everything we'd accomplished look like it was nothin'. Everything was cancelled by this one mistake [BC 124].

Dodge killed the baby; the ruin of the family and the land followed.

Buried Child continues Shepard's obsession with identity. When his grandfather doesn't know him, Vince performs a repertoire of infantile tricks from his childhood, frantic to be recognized. Shelly, menaced physically or mentally by each of the men in turn, is less upset by their assaults than by Halie's refusal to acknowledge her identity. After Vince's initial impulse to escape the mad ménage he has rediscovered, he decides to stay because of the vision of continuity that comes to him on his all-night drive away from the farm. He describes looking at his reflection in the rain-washed windshield:

> As though I was looking at another man. As though I could see his whole race behind him.... His face became his father's face.... And his father's face changed to his grandfather's face. And it went on like that. Changing. Clear on back to faces I'd never seen before but still recognized. Still recognized the bones underneath. The eyes. The breath. The mouth [BC 130].

The past, whether it is Vince's "whole race behind him" or Dodge's bitter definition of heritage as "a long line of corpses behind me," is an essential component of the present (*BC* 112).

At the end of the play, Dodge lies dead on the floor and Vince lies motionless on the sofa, his body assuming the posture of his grandfather's. As Halie calls down from upstairs to announce the miracle—the crops are suddenly growing again after all these years—Tilden appears. Against the tableau of the supine figures of Vince and Dodge, Tilden, covered with mud and carrying the corpse of the baby, slowly makes his way up the stairs. Besides the sheer sensory power that it projects, the image embodies and unifies the theme of the play. To be able to live in the present, you must incorporate the past. If one image of heredity is a mummified baby in the arms of its feebleminded father, the other is of a strong young grandson carrying on the family line. The rebirth of the family and of the crops is dependent on the rebirth of the buried child.

There are no rules of behavior in *Buried Child*, but it is less chaotic than the other plays: Shepard has more control over his material here. The play's tight construction emphasizes the constant possibility of eruption and when it does occur—Vince's drunken terrorizing of the family after his all-night drive—the shift from curbed threat to uncontrolled violence is a catharsis. In the earlier plays characters are separated from each other by their shifts of identity and their extended monologues, but in *Buried Child* they have real relationships, bizarre as they are. Shepard's surreal sensibility still pervades the drama and gives it its atmosphere of ambiguity and dream, but by providing a shape for his hallucinatory images and incantatory language, he creates a more dramatically satisfying work. The surface realism furnishes the center that many of the other plays lack, and the intersection of this realism with his poetic imagery creates a rich texture. The tension between extravagant imagination and formal structure sustains the menace and the manic humor, but keeps them from slipping into the excesses of some of the other plays. The juxtaposition of order and disorder balances and heightens both.

In *True West* (1980), Shepard's third drama of volatile accommodation to family and spiritual inheritance, the ambivalent conflict between rootedness and escape is between two brothers. Conventional, respectable Austin, a successful screenwriter and family man, has been housesitting in a suburb of Southern California for his mother, who is vacationing in Alaska. Lee, a semibarbaric loner who has been living in the desert, appears unannounced, a Caliban in suburbia. A typical exchange between the brothers ends the first scene: Austin, trying to work at his writing and no longer able to endure Lee's hovering and the submerged threat of his violence, asks

13

nervously, "You want to sleep for a while?" Lee, after a pause, stares at Austin, then answers, "I don't sleep."[16] Lee is one of Shepard's scarily unpredictable characters. Yet he yearns for another kind of identity, more like Austin's. He describes looking in the window of a home in the neighborhood:

> Like a paradise. Kinda' place that sorta' kills ya' inside. Warm yellow lights. Mexican tile all around. Copper pots hangin' over the stove. Ya' know like they got in the magazines. Blonde people movin' in and outa' the rooms, talkin' to each other. *(pause)* Kinda' place you wish you sorta' grew up in, ya' know [*TW* 12].

Lee begins taking over his brother's identity by trying to establish a relationship with the movie producer who arrives for a story conference with Austin. He incongruously suggests a game of golf and equally incongruously offers to write a screenplay. Before long Lee is dictating his Western ("I'm not a man of the pen," he unnecessarily explains) to Austin, who serves as amanuensis because he is intimidated by his brother and because he too wishes for a new identity. Lee dictates a movie chase that is also a description of their relation to one another. It is reminiscent of Wesley and Weston's symbiotic embrace-death grip in *Curse of the Starving Class*, the two aspects of one self, each fighting against and yearning to become the other:

> So they take off after each other into an endless black prairie. The sun is just comin' down and they can feel the night on their backs. What they don't know is that each one of 'em is afraid, see. Each one separately thinks he's the only one that's afraid. And they keep ridin' like that straight into the night. Not knowing. And the one who's chasin' doesn't know where the other one is taking him. And the one who's being chased doesn't know where he's going [*TW* 27].

By the early part of the second act of the two-act play, the role reversal has been at least temporarily accomplished. Lee is working hard at the typewriter and Austin is about to embark on a drunken, thieving spree in emulation of his brother (with a humorous twist: instead of breaking into houses in the neighborhood to steal television sets, as Lee did, Austin returns with a cache of toasters). Always in the background of the brothers' conversation is their father, an eccentric old loner who lives in the desert. It is the recurring father figure of Shepard's plays, who is also Shepard's real father, about whom he wrote in *Motel Chronicles*, a collection of remembrances, "My Dad lives alone. He says he doesn't fit in with people."[17] Austin tells a gripping story of visiting their father in the desert shortly after the old man had spent all his money on a set of false teeth. Austin took him out to a Chinese restaurant, but he only wanted to drink, so they ordered a doggie bag and went barhopping. The old man put his uncomfortable new false teeth in the doggie bag, and before the night was over, he had left the bag in one of the bars. Like all wonderfully told tales, the story takes on a resonance beyond its specific circumstance and suggests that the myth of the West—the heroic loner surviving gloriously on the frontier—is a sham. The *true* West is a shabby and diminished place for which an appropriate image is a drunken old man losing his false teeth in a bag of chop suey.

The play is not nearly as well constructed as the two earlier family plays, and much of the second act is frantic stage business, funny at first, but over-long—Lee bashing the typewriter with a golf club, Austin making toast in all the stolen toasters, the two of them littering the kitchen with whiskey bottles, a ripped-out telephone, toasters, smashed toast slices. The mother returns to this chaos and in a funny exchange admonishes them as though they were two slightly obstreperous boys. The play ends with the brothers locked in inconclusive struggle. "I can't stop choking him!" Austin explains to Mom. "He'll kill me if I stop choking him!" (*TW* 58). The last ambiguous image is of the two of them squared off, each brother a threat to the other's identity. It is also a conflict between the values of home and family, and the solitary, rootless life—the continuing dichotomy in Shepard's plays.

In California, Shepard lived as a semirecluse, dividing his time between his family home, his horsebreeding ranch, and the Magic Theater in San Francisco, where he was playwright-in-residence. He stopped giving interviews, refusing, for example, to speak to a reporter from the *New York Times* after winning the Pulitzer Prize in 1979 for *Buried Child*. But at the same time, he became more of a public figure than ever when he began to act in movies— *Days of Heaven* in 1978, followed by *Resurrection, Raggedy Man, Frances, The Right Stuff*—playing the kinds of loners he invents for his plays. Adding to his movie star image was his liaison with actress Jessica Lange, for whom he left his wife and with whom he co-produced and co-starred in *Country,* which opened the 1984 New York Film Festival; *Paris, Texas,* for which Shepard wrote the screenplay (about another father-son relationship) closed it. By the winter of 1986, *A Lie of the Mind* (1985), written and directed by Shepard (and memorializing his father's death in 1984), was playing in New York to unanimous critical praise, having joined Shepard's long-running play, *Fool for Love,* as well as the movie version of *Fool for Love,* starring Shepard, and a successful revival of *Curse of the Starving Class.* Shepard's picture was everywhere, dominating the popular press. The few journalists to whom he consented to give interviews wrote feature articles about him; others contented themselves with interviewing Shepard's cast members or his sisters.[18] A cartoon in *The New Yorker* showed people in line at a theater gazing up at a marquee that read, "NOW PLAYING: The Sam Shepard To Beat All The *Other* Sam Shepards Around Town."[19]

Henry Hackamore, the protagonist of *Seduced* (1978), is based on Howard Hughes, a figure whose mythic status and elusive identity make him a natural subject of interest to Shepard. Facing the end of his life, Hackamore recognizes that he has had no identity apart from his public image. Even his blood, received by transfusion throughout his years of failing health, is not his own. Together with the public, he has worked to create a persona until he no longer has a sense of real self. It is the penalty for realizing the dream of inventing one's identity. "I was taken by the dream," he says, "and all the time I thought I was taking it. It was a sudden seduction. . . . Almost like a rape. You could call it a rape."[20] Hackamore now sees that only his myth was alive: the man never existed.

Shepard and the public have made *him* into an American myth, too, a composite of Huck Finn (beginning with his running away from home and joining up with a black buddy), writer, rock musician, cowboy, and movie star. Another mythic role that has been assigned to him is as bard of contemporary America, but Shepard is really the most private of playwrights. His plays, for all their iconography of American popular culture and elegies for the Old West, express a more personal loss, as primal as an infant's separation from its parent.

Heinz Lichtenstein, a psychoanalyst known for his studies in identity theory, has observed that "narcissistic individuals . . . yearn to return to a symbiotic union with a dominant parental figure" and that it is a fantasy, like the fantasy of metamorphosis, of the relinquishing of identity.[21] Shepard's repeated fantasies of shared and blurred and transformed identities suggest this ambivalent yearning, ambivalent because it is in tension with the accompanying terror of having no real identity. The American landscapes that permeate Shepard's plays are not the focus of his imagination, but the backdrops against which to play out invented identities in order to discover his own.

Lanford Wilson:
To Vanish Without a Trace

To Vanish Without a Trace

LANFORD WILSON'S PLAYS are haunted by the notion of impermanence, of "vanishing without a trace," in the repeated phrase of his play *The Mound Builders*. His characters suffer from a lack of continuity with the past, a failure of connection with the present, and a fear of annihilation in the future. Uprooted and transient, they come together in a place of temporary refuge, where they wait uneasily for a dreaded event, mourn the loss of a more stable past (or the nostalgic idea of one), and wonder how best to spend the time left to them. To comfort each other, and perhaps their author, they chat companionably from beginning to end. Wilson masks his darker concerns with cheerful surfaces: lighthearted facades, deliberate theatricality, and constant, lively talk. This strategy engages the audience, but it also risks reducing significant statement to facile entertainment. Perhaps this is an American insistence on optimism. It is never clear whether Wilson avoids confronting the terror of his themes because he is whistling in the dark, or because he is eager to make his audience comfortable, as though he were the host and they the guests. Just as Wilson's characters need to reassure each other, Wilson needs to reassure the audience, which he often does by stopping the action for a direct address or intimate aside to them, or even a vaudeville turn. These breakaway speeches, jokes and songs sound as though the playwright is saying, "Don't be bored or alarmed. We'll have fun, you'll see."

Wilson's life has been marked by the uprootedness and impermanence that pervade his plays. He was five years old in 1942 when his father left their home in Lebanon, Missouri, and moved to California. His mother found a job as a seamstress in a garment factory in Springfield, Missouri, for the next six years, then remarried and moved with her husband and son to a farm in Ozark. After graduation from high school and one year at a state college, Wilson went to San Diego to be with his father, whom he had not seen in the intervening 13 years. He lived with him and his new family, worked part-time in an aircraft factory, and took courses in art and creative writing at San Diego State. But the reconciliation was a fiasco and after one year (the traumatic events of which he dramatized in *Lemon Sky*), Wilson moved to Chicago. He lived there for six years, working as an apprentice artist in an advertising agency and writing plays in his spare time. In the summer of 1962, he moved to New York to try to write for the theater.

It was during the height of the Off Off Broadway movement, with new playwrights putting on plays in lofts and basements, churches and coffeehouses. One of the most active of the "alternative spaces" was Caffe Cino, and in 1963 its proprietor, Joe Cino, whose help to young playwrights was legendary, produced Wilson's first one-act play, *So Long at the Fair*. Another pioneering Off Off Broadway theater, Café La Mama, produced his first full-length play, *Balm in Gilead*, in 1965. It was directed by Marshall Mason, with whom Wilson and two actors, Tanya Berezin and Rob Thirkield, founded the Circle Repertory Theater in 1969.

This was a crucial event in Wilson's career. It gave him the opportunity—almost unique for an American playwright—to work over the years with the same director and with a company of actors. It is even conceivable that without Circle Rep Wilson might have lapsed into the silence that has followed the early promise of many American playwrights. When his plays *The Gingham Dog* and *Lemon Sky* flopped on Broadway—the first closed after 5 performances in 1969, the second after 17 in 1970—Wilson's reaction was to develop a writing block. It lasted until 1972, when Mason asked him to write a one-act play to complete an evening of two of his earlier one-act plays. The result was *The Family Continues*, which was little more than an exercise, but it started Wilson writing again. The following year he wrote *The Hot l Baltimore*, his most successful play: it ran for three years, was made into a television serial, and won an Obie award for the best Off Broadway play of 1973. Since then Wilson has written a new play every few years, has won a second Obie award, for *The Mound Builders*, and the 1980 Pulitzer Prize for *Talley's Folly*.

In the avant-garde spirit of the sixties, Wilson experimented with language-as-sound but, unlike the non-verbalists of the period, didn't subordinate words to movement. His plays were closer to choral music than to dance, using musical conceptions like contrapuntal dialogue, repetition of motifs, and orchestration of voices. A few of his early one-act plays— *Wandering* and *This Is the Rill Speaking* (both 1966), and *Stoop* (1969)—were primarily aural collages, but others like *Home Free!* and *The Madness of Lady Bright* (both 1964), *Ludlow Fair* and *Days Ahead* (both 1965) demonstrated Wilson's gift for writing amusing, absorbing dialogue and for creating character. He gradually shifted to realistic speech, but rather than abandoning his early techniques, he modified them. Contrapuntal dialogue evolved into lifelike overlappings of conversation, and characterizations suggested by voice patterns expanded into characters sharply delineated by their use of language.

Balm in Gilead (1965) announced many of the themes and techniques that came to characterize Wilson's work: uprooted people converging in a temporary haven; the contrast of their misery with the diverting presentation of it; language that is both true to character and heightened for performance; and the underlying uneasiness masked by theatricality and non-stop talk. The protagonists are Joe, a small-time drug dealer, and Darlene, a young woman recently arrived in New York and dumbly drifting into prostitution. The entire cast—addicts, thieves, hookers and hustlers—are outcasts of society, and the seedy, all-night coffeeshop is their substitute for community. The humor and vitality of Wilson's language and his theatrical highjinks turn the potentially depressing material into an exhilarating entertainment.

The high-spirited tone is established by a quartet who open the show with a song-and-dance routine. The audience is plunged into an immediate hubbub created by the sheer number of verbal exchanges of the cast of 33, and by the rapid tempo of overlapping speeches. Balancing the frenetic activity are four long monologues (three of them addressed directly to the audience) that provide wonderful star turns for the actors. They also keep the audience from becoming disturbed by the gloomy subjects. Dopey, a dope addict, delivers a monologue on nuclear annihilation that turns into a light-toned meditation on cockroaches:

> They've made tests, and they found out that a roach can stand—if there was going to be a big atom explosion, they can stand something like *fourteen times* as much radio-whatever-it-is, you know, activity, as we can. So after every man, woman, and child is wiped out and gone, those same goddamned cockroaches will be still crawling around happy as you please over the ruins of everything. Now the picture of that really gripes my ass.[1]

A soliloquy by Fick, another dope addict, is an anguished cry for help, but at its end Wilson abruptly breaks the mood by having Dopey, who acts as stage manager, turn to the audience and say, "We'll call an intermission here" (*BG* 46). And when Dopey, in his second monologue, announces that Joe is about to be murdered, Fick says to him, "We ain't seen this, have we?" and he and Dopey turn towards the stage to watch Joe die (*BG* 67). In fact, they watch him die three times. This consecutive repetition of the stabbing creates an effective nightmare atmosphere and also reminds the audience that they are in the theater, that the murder is not real.

Dopey reminds them of that, too. He is Wilson's omniscient narrator who explains or predicts the action. This role establishes rapport with the audience by inviting them to take a privileged, inside look. At the same time it distances them from the upsetting events taking place. The distancing mechanism, along with the stylized structure, the songs and choric commentary, and the cast of riff-raff, are reminiscent of *The Threepenny Opera*. But Brecht uses deliberate artifice to remind the audience that life does not have the happy ending of his play, while Wilson uses it to reassure them that his play is *only* a play.

His next full-length play, *The Rimers of Eldritch* (1966), is another stylized treatment of the theme of impermanence. *Rimers* is often compared to

Thornton Wilder's *Our Town*. But Wilder's Grover's Corners, the essence of which is timelessness, is replaced here by a ghost town where the rats have taken over the granary, the streets are broken, and the buildings are falling down. Eldritch is about to vanish without a trace. The town's physical decline is echoed in the moral decline of its inhabitants, who spend their lives in prurient gossip with occasional flareups of violence. Everyone is spying on everyone else and commenting lavishly on their sexual proclivities.

The Rimers of Eldritch is an expanded, harsher version of Wilson's earlier one-act play, *This Is the Rill Speaking*, which also evoked the atmosphere of a small town through the orchestrated voices of its characters. This time there is a suspense story, complete with rape, murder, and a trial, all within a stylized structure. The characters are American Gothic stock figures: Skelly, the town pariah, accused of fornicating with sheep; Mary, a feeble-minded Cassandra, given to incantatory outbursts; Cora, the fallen woman with a heart of gold. The fluidity accomplished by overlapping scenes, rapid shifts of time and place, and the manipulation of speech into musical patterns is technically effective. But *Rimers* overdoes the melodrama and is finally less interesting than its more modest forerunner.

The Gingham Dog (1969) was the first of Wilson's realistic plays, without stylization or artifice. This time the people gathered temporarily under one roof, talking nervously as they await the end, are a husband and wife (the husband's sister and a neighbor play minor roles), and it is their marriage that is ending. Because it is an interracial marriage, the personal drama is enlarged by the social resonances; and it is not only the marriage that is about to vanish without a trace, but the young couple's earlier illusions about social change. Vincent is from the Kentucky Bible Belt, and his sixties' liberation has included moving to Greenwich Village, growing a beard, and marrying Gloria, a black woman. There are nostalgic references to their first idyllic year together (for the characters in Wilson's plays the past is always better) and their shared ideals. Now Vincent's ideals have been sacrificed to upward mobility. He works for an architectural firm, designing a highrise apartment building that will displace the present ghetto community: Wilson's theme of the destruction of continuity in the name of progress. The issue has become a principal quarrel between husband and wife, and Gloria's interjections, as Vincent explains pictures of the housing project to his sister Barbara, an unreconstructed Southern bigot, are typical of her mordant humor:

> *Barbara:* . . . Is this an apartment building?
> *Gloria:* It's a crematorium.

Barbara: A what?
Vincent: It's a section of an apartment building, put it back now.
Barbara: No, I'm interested; all those little rooms.
Gloria: Infinitesimal...
Barbara: (Looking up) What?
Gloria: I said it was the hanging gardens of Babylon.

. . .

Vincent: (to Barbara) I'm working with a company which is trying
to get a contract to build...
Gloria: (Overlapping) ...To build uninhabitable brick ovens. Hi-
rise slums. You don't prevent slums or clear them, you *elevate* them
thirty stories.

. . .

Barbara: Well, I would think that you'd be very proud of Vincent
trying to do good at his job, instead of criticizing him.
Gloria: Vincent's job has nothing to do with good. Were Vincent's
job anything at all good, I would cheer. Vince is trying to do *well*
at his job, which is another thing altogether...[2]

It is to Vincent, the less attractive character, that Wilson gives the more
emotionally charged lines. He shows the special ugliness of a marital quarrel
exploding into a racial one, as Vincent fuses the personal and social, recoil-
ing from the "otherness" of Gloria's physical person and invoking racial
stereotypes to support his attack on her:

I loathe their pompous boasting—their telling you the sexual myth
is a sexual myth, and then using it as naturally as a fox uses cunning
to get what they can out of their *petty* desires.... And Gloria, god-
damn you, I loathe you. I loathe the look of you, and the oily feel
of you and the bitter ear-wax taste, the sour orange-rind smell of
you. You disgust me in every way—your strength and muscle and
firm round stomach disgust me, Gloria, and your single narrow-
mindedness. I loathe you because you made me hate. Everything
else. And everyone else. You destroy. It's all you know. And you've
not got a goddamned thing to rebuild with. Certainly not love. Not
in one of you. For all your popularized warmth!... [GD 40].

The play takes place during the day and night of Vincent's moving out
and is an exchange of the couple's recriminations (Act I) and regrets (Act
II). Structurally it is Wilson's weakest play—the tension and energy slacken
by the end of the first act and are never recovered in the second—but it is
one of his most honestly charming. That is, the charm comes from the
freshness of the dialogue and from the vitality of the character of Gloria;
there are no ingratiating asides to the audience and no palliatives. Indeed,
the outlook of the play is a pessimistic one, suggesting that there is no
possibility of understanding between the races in America. They are

doomed to be as irreconcilable as the gingham dog and the calico cat of the nursery rhyme.

In *Lemon Sky* (1970) Wilson resumes his use of the stage manager-narrator and of chatty speeches and asides to the audience. Alan, Wilson's alter ego, simultaneously participates in and reflects on events in this autobiographical play, a dramatization of Wilson's attempt to reconcile with his father when he was 17. Wilson is less interested in the events themselves than in his retrospective response to them: Alan-Lanford acknowledges to the audience at the outset that "if it happened this way or that, who knows?"[3] Then he introduces Douglas, his father, with the disclaimer that "If he's nothing, I mean *But nothing!* Then the fact that he comes off the short end of the stick shows something" (*LS* 7). Unfortunately, what it shows is that in the case of his father, Wilson had difficulty separating art from life. Douglas, depicted as a lecher and bully of repugnant machismo, is the only character in Wilson's plays who is unredeemed by the playwright's usual compassion. Alan goes on to tell the audience what will take place: he will live with his father and his father's family—a second wife, two sons age 8 and 12, and two teenage foster daughters; there will be conflict culminating in a quarrel with his father, after which he will leave; and six months later Carol, one of the foster daughters, will die.

The failed reunion, and to a lesser extent Carol's death, are the focuses of Wilson's preoccupation with impermanence in this play, and his authorial intrusion through Alan is a method of dealing with it: as the omniscient narrator, Alan can exercise control. He manipulates the proceedings like a puppeteer, switching back and forth between past and present, summoning and dismissing the characters, annotating their lines, forecasting and interpreting events. One way to fight against the vanishing that so terrifies Wilson is to freeze time, and the theater, as he exuberantly illustrates, can do this. When Alan sings a line of a popular song, Carol says to him, "You couldn't possibly have said that, that song didn't come out for ages," and Alan replies, "That's all right, you aren't even alive. You've been dead ten years" (*LS* 42). But Carol isn't dead so long as she is alive in the play, and so she thanks "the . . . management for the magic of the theater which enables me to be continually young and alive and beautiful and current" (*LS* 42). The illusion is brief, however, and a few lines later Wilson pulls the rug out from under it. Carol, no longer willing to be "locked in your goddamned sideshow," tries to run off stage but is summoned back by Alan (*LS* 42). When she rails out against him, it is like our railing out against God. Carol's anguish as a character in the play is not mitigated after all by her knowledge that it is only a play. Before this all gets too serious, Wilson moves to one of his playful distancing devices: Alan greets

Carol's return to the stage by singing a commercial jingle of the period ("She's back and she's better than ever before/ Campbell's Pork and Beans"), joined by Carol and Penny, her foster sister, in three-part harmony (*LS* 43). The moment sacrifices thematic development for theatricality and character development for charm.

There is something jittery about these performances and asides, as though they were designed to hold the audience's attention during the slow stretches. Early in the play, after a fair length of time spent in chitchat with his newly found family, Alan turns to the audience to say, "It can't go on like this, of course, there'll be a scene soon" (*LS* 17). It's a kind of promise of something more exciting than what's happening now. Or, near the end of the first act, Alan tells the audience that "In six months I'll be sleeping in a park in Chicago with a letter in my pocket telling me that Carol is dead. But who would know that now?" (*LS* 34). Giving away this bit of the story creates its own kind of suspense: as with Joe's pre-announced death in *Balm in Gilead*, the question becomes How will it happen? instead of What will happen? But it is an easy shortcut, appealing to our sympathy for Carol on the grounds of her anticipated misfortune rather than earning it through the development of her character.

A far more serious problem is the character of the father. The play revolves around Alan's relationship with him, but Douglas is portrayed as a monster whom it is impossible to take seriously. Nor do the other characters carry the play very far along. Alan's stepmother, the patient, long-suffering wife who does not want to rock the boat, is no more than a blandly pleasant figure. His two half-brothers are in the play for no discernible reason except (presumably) autobiographical accuracy and (unfortunately) sentimentality. They win Alan's and the audience's hearts not for the way they have been conceived dramatically, but for being cute little tykes. The foster daughters are more expressive characters, and contribute to the emotional texture.

The burden of the play, however, falls all too heavily on Alan. He dashes back and forth between his functions as actor and narrator, all the while chatting the audience up. The effect, besides busyness, is an attempt at "poetic realism": the presentation of realistic subject and dialogue within an unrealistic form. But poetry depends on words, and these characters (unusual for Wilson) are no more articulate than they would be in real life. No amount of narrator's mediation, crosscutting of dialogue, flashbacks and flash forwards, or Pirandellian self-consciousness can supply the poetry that is missing in the language. It's as though in this play Wilson's imaginative powers have been inhibited by his fidelity (perhaps unconscious) to his real life models, and his attempts to break out of the constraints of conventional form ultimately draw attention to how conventional the substance of the play is.

Elegy is again the prevailing mood in *The Hot l Baltimore* (1973), which mourns vanishing hotels like the Hotel Baltimore, scheduled for demolition (the "e" has already vanished from "Hotel" on its marquee), vanishing trains, vanishing great houses, and vanishing cities of America. "Baltimore used to be one of the most beautiful cities in America," says one character, and another retorts, "Every city in America used to be one of the most beautiful cities in America."[4] The play is dominated by Wilson's fear that everything in American life, including the theater, will vanish. In his otherwise matter-of-fact stage directions he writes, "The theater, evanescent itself, and for all we do perhaps itself disappearing here, seems the ideal place for the representation of the impermanence of our architecture" (*HlB* 7).

Once more a group of characters assembled in a temporary community—the crumbling residential Hotel Baltimore—spend their time invoking an idealized past as they face an uncertain future. The Girl romanticizes the heyday of American trains, all of whose schedules she has memorized; Paul is trying to locate his grandfather in order to recover a past familial relationship; Millie lives in her memories of better days in a grand house; Mr. Morse hoards his dead wife's and mother's possessions, the remnants of his past. Only Jackie, the hippie health food faddist, believes in the future, but her dream of establishing roots on the land is foiled when she discovers that she has been swindled into buying a piece of desert. The play ends with April, a prostitute, teaching Jamie, Jackie's younger brother, how to dance. "Come on," she urges, "they're gonna tear up the dance floor in a minute. The bulldozers are barking at the door" (*HlB* 68).

Amidst all the nostalgia is the considerable vitality that comes from Wilson's imaginative grasp of how people sound—the Girl's unadorned, breezy Midwestern speech, the hotel manager's Jewish cadences, Jamie's little mannerism of chiming in with the ending words of other people's sentences—and his ability to transform these speech patterns into lively dialogue. Here is Jackie, the evangelist of ecology:

> *Jackie:* ...You know those plants out past Fort McHenry? You know what they do?
> *Girl:* They're sugar plants, I thought.
> *Jackie:* Refining. Sugar refining. They take natural sugar and turn in into shit. And then they pollute the atmosphere doing it. You can't get people to care about the environment. Of their own planet.... You know the great discoveries? Like the discovery of bacteria; and the discovery of uranium; the discovery of sulfur drugs? Like that?
> *Girl:* (*Serious, nodding*) The discovery of penicillin...

Jackie: Right. Well, the next major discovery—scientists are going to find this out, they're going to be researching this... *(Pause)* Garlic.
Millie: What?
Jackie: Garlic. It's biodegradable [*HlB* 43].

The guests at this dying hotel are society's flotsam but, as in *Balm in Gilead*, Wilson presents them as lovable eccentrics who charm and entertain us. His decision not to probe is more diminishing in this realistic play than in the earlier one where his characters were figures in a stylized setting. *The Hot l Baltimore* is an attractive play because of Wilson's ear for American vernacular and because of the sureness of his craft: he knows how to enliven a stageful of characters. But because there is no looking beneath the surface, it is also a safe and sentimental one.

It is in *The Mound Builders* (1975) that Wilson gives full expression to his concerns about impermanence. He resists dipping into his bag of theatrical tricks and achieves a gripping play. The set represents the two locations and time periods of the action: the present in an archeologist's study in Urbana, and the previous summer in a house in rural Illinois near an excavation site. Slides are to be projected throughout the play, and Wilson writes directions for them in imagery of the deluge: "The house is seen from August Howe's memory of the wrecked expedition and may be represented as he sees it— not in photographs but in his mind's eye: a house that lifted up like an ark as the lake flooded the valley and floated down some great flood-struck current, wrecking in another place."[5]

The play opens with August running his slides and dictating a tape for his secretary, which provides an exposition of the past summer's events and takes us into the reenacted flashbacks. Their expedition was to uncover the ruins of an Indian village, and the archeologists were racing against the flooding of the area that would be converted into a resort island. The play is a variation of *The Hot l Baltimore* theme: the flattening of the ancient Indian mounds in order to build highways over them symbolizes the transformation of a rich past into a banal present. Dan, August's assistant, explains that the Indians of the Mississippian culture built these mounds for protection from floods and sacrifices to the gods. But there were less concrete reasons, too: "Every society reaches the point where they build mounds. As the society becomes more sophisticated, the rationalization for building them becomes more sophisticated" (*MB* 22). He would have built mounds, too, he says, "For an accomplishment . . . to bring me closer to Elysium; to leave something behind me for my grandchildren to marvel at. To say I'd built something!" (*MB* 22).

What makes the theme more interesting than in *The Hot l Baltimore*, where the issue was black and white—the fine old architecture threatened by the wrecking ball—is that Wilson shows both sides here. If the developer's bulldozer and artificial lake are destructive, so are the excavator's digs. Chad Jasker, whose family owns the land, points out that the archeologists are in fact pillaging. And when they tell Chad that they have succeeded without his knowledge in persuading the government to reroute the planned highway, we feel his betrayal. He too would build "mounds," and who are the archeologists to say that his dream of immortality, predicated on a Holiday Inn, driving ranges, and tennis courts, is less worthy than theirs? Wilson, always sympathetic to the underdog, makes us aware of the archeologists' arrogance. Chad has been doublecrossed by his summer companions. "Boy, you're pretending to be my friend," he says, "you're listening to me talking about soul food and grilled bass out of the lake; what are you saying behind my back?... Where do you get off thinking you're better than the people around here and can take over and take away everything we hope for ... laughing about my goddamned island.... Millions! You're trying to steal from me!" (MB 133).

Which is the greater good: to hold on to the past or to get on with the new? The theme comes up early in the play when Cynthia, August's wife, describes her schizophrenic existence of "adjusting to a life stripped down to what I can carry on my back" each summer at the site, then returning for the rest of the year to "eleven rooms of memorabilia" (MB 39). And Delia, August's sister, travels all over the globe, alternately collecting and mislaying: "the world's unclaimed-baggage departments are crammed with my paraphernalia" (MB 39). Delia is a writer, and she sees herself and the archeologists as "compulsive compilers" (MB 102). Artists, like archeologists, try to find coherence in life by ordering its fragments. They assert and verify their existence by collecting the artifacts of their past or by creating them for the future.

The fear is to have one's existence vanish without a trace. Dan's long speech is on this theme (MB 107). The Mississippian Indians did not vanish without a trace, he says, because they crafted a bone awl, and the archeologists, having found a fragment of it, can bear witness to and celebrate an existence as palpable and holy as their own. The repeated variations of the phrase "vanish without a trace" add to the musical resonance of his speech and tie it to Chad's desperate act of murder-suicide at the end of the play. Chad's and Dan's bodies are never recovered from the lake; they have vanished without a trace.

Wilson reminds us here of the theater's unique power, not shared by movies or TV, to make language the principal dramatic medium. A movie

28

on the subject of *The Mound Builders* would have special visual effects: the descent into the cave, the flooding, the drowning. But Wilson's special effects are words. The dialogue is absorbing and convincing, it creates distinctive characters who charm without playing to the audience (the lapses into self-conscious or arch language are few) and, as in Dan's speech about vanishing without a trace, it is heightened into dramatic utterance. In *The Mound Builders*, Wilson uses his theatrical craft to illuminate, rather than to divert from, his central themes.

It is always startling to remember that Wilson's plays are death-ridden, since their surfaces are so merry. *Serenading Louie* (1976), a play about two charming, successful couples, ends in a blood bath when the protagonist kills his wife, his daughter, and himself. Again, people at a turning point in their lives—in this case, two couples approaching middle age—recall the past with regret and face the future with dread. One stage set used for both homes emphasizes the boring standardization and the shared predicament of their lives. It also enables Wilson to employ his favorite format of gathering his characters under one roof.

The couples, friends since college (the title comes from a line in "The Whiffenpoof Song"), have been living out the American dream and finding it empty. Carl, the college football hero who married the homecoming queen, became a self-made, successful businessman and expected to live happily ever after, discovers that his wife, Mary, is unfaithful. Alex, a lawyer on the threshold of a political career, regards his wife, Gabby, with sexual disgust and is trying to recover his youthful optimism by having an affair with a college student. The men feel estranged not only from their wives, but from everything around them. Carl "can't get involved with anything . . . can't galvanize any concern," and Alex drily suggests that *his* "real life will begin any day now. This can't be it. This is just temporary."[6] Their wives are equally alienated. Mary, who finds herself "becoming an emotional recluse," questions whether she has really ever loved Carl, despite the storybook trappings of their college romance. "I don't actually think . . . that I loved him then," she says, "but I love him then now" (*SL* 37). If she loved only the illusion of loving Carl then, as she seems to suggest, she now loves only the memory of an illusion. As for Gabby, she speaks to Alex in the nervously self-deprecating manner of the unloved wife who has no identity apart from her marital role.

This is familiar stuff—the mid-life crisis, the existential angst, the ennui of affluence—but Wilson rescues it from cliché with his lively, witty, and convincing language. Finally, though, the people in this play do not arouse strong feelings of compassion in us. Perhaps it is because their despair seems too much like the petulant dissatisfactions of the indulged. Yet Chekhov (to whom Wilson is occasionally likened) writes about spoiled people too, and they move us deeply. The difference is that Chekhov penetrates past the external signs of class and privilege to the essential humanity of his characters. We become involved with them as people rather than merely observe them as exemplars of their social condition.

The characters in *Serenading Louie* are single-faceted. Wilson shows us their pain, but he does not show us the idiosyncracies and contradictions, the complex mix of pathos, foolishness, gallantry, and comedy that make Chekhov's characters come fully to life. Nor is there a feeling of dramatic movement in the play. Carl's jealousy of Mary's adultery, his outrage at the disruption of his American dream, his need for a desperate act to break through his feelings of anomie and withdrawal—all are there from the beginning. There is not a series of impalpable inner events, gradually revealed, that we follow with pity and terror to their inevitable conclusion. When Carl slaughters his family at the end of the play, we feel the horror at one remove, like the reaction we would have to the account of a respected family man gone berserk: melodrama instead of tragedy.

If in some of his plays Wilson's charm vitiates his themes, in others it makes them more arresting by presenting them through the voice of an especially attractive character. This is true of *Brontosaurus* (1977), another play with the motif of impermanence. The protagonist is a Wilsonian heroine: talkative, witty and self-conscious, edgily charming, sympathetic and self-absorbed, wrestling with how best to live her life, and puritanical about work. She is identified only as the Antique Dealer, a suitable profession for the relic of a generation that, she says, is about to become obsolete:

> . . . that last generation, we honorable brontosaurs who are the last to die . . . who knew only that at the very least their lives would have a form: a shape, a beginning and a middle and, for those who cared for it, a progeny, and finally and blissfully or regrettably, an end.[7]

She tells this to her seventeen-year-old nephew, whose counterculture values create the dramatic conflict. Wilson presents the nephew's viewpoint sympathetically too, and the boy's aria-like speech describing the shaping experience of his childhood—a religious-physical feeling of union with all sentient beings—is deeply felt. The Antique Dealer's closing soliloquy echoes but counters it. Like her nephew, she yearns for belief, but she is reconciled to a life that vanishes without apparent meaning. She and her fellow brontosaurs have lived their lives, have made their "migration"

...purely for the sake of the journey, being fully aware of the ab-
surdity, the biological accident, or if you would, the biological
miracle of it all. And we made the migration to its no doubt ignoble
end for the sake of experiencing the miracle...[B 19].

There is nothing more than existence and experience. That is all we can
know, and our task is to decide what to do with that knowledge. The Antique Dealer concludes her speech by opposing a retreat into transcendence
and declaring her faith in work and in simply keeping on. It is Wilson's
American existentialism, preferring pragmatism and the Puritan work ethic
to philosophical probing.

Wilson's use of the family as an emblem of continuity is most explicit
in his trilogy about the Talley family of Lebanon, Missouri: *5th of July*
(1978), *Talley's Folly* (1979), and *Talley & Son** (1981). *5th of July* takes place
on the evening and day after Independence Day 1977 and brings together
the remaining members of the formerly powerful and numerous Talley family, reduced now to Ken, the grandson who has inherited the homestead,
and his recently widowed Aunt Sally. These are paradoxical survivors—a
barren woman and a crippled, homosexual Vietnam veteran. Both are
of the breed of Wilson's beloved outcasts: Ken is planning to sell the
homestead and move away because he feels too sensitive to the gossip of the
townspeople to continue his job as a schoolteacher there, and Aunt Sally
was ostracized by her family 23 years ago for marrying a Jew. She has come
home to scatter the ashes of her dead husband on the land, not as an act
of defiance, but as an affirmation of continuity. The conflict of the play
turns on that notion of continuity. Ken's sale of the house is opposed by
Aunt Sally and by Ken's lover, who has been turning the property into a
garden showplace. Eager to buy it are Ken's former college friends (and present houseguests)—a rock singer, burned out by drugs, and her manager-
husband—who want to use it as a recording studio. Joining this group (the
typical arrangement of people congregating under one roof as they discuss
where their lives will go next) are Ken's unmarried sister, her illegitimate
adolescent daughter, and a young rock guitar player. The older guests are
nostalgic for their counterculture past and Berkeley in the sixties, but
Wilson is too much in the Puritan grain, devoted to the efficacy of work, to
feel sympathy for hippies and their stoned activism. The past that he honors
is the establishment of the family symbolized by the Talley homestead. Ken
and Aunt Sally may be the last of that family, but by the end of the play
they have chosen to continue its presence there by planting hedges and

*The original version was called A Tale Told. The title was changed for the revision used
in its 1985 revival.

future blooms on the land, rather than selling it to rock musicians who will turn it into an airplane landing strip.

The other two plays are flashbacks to the night of July 4, 1944, when Aunt Sally eloped with Matt Friedman. *Talley & Son* introduces us to the Talley clan, an assortment of schemers and villains whom Wilson manages to rescue to a degree (in a way he did not or could not rescue Douglas in *Lemon Sky*) with energetic and sometimes witty language. It is finally a melodrama, however, and interesting principally for its narrative function as background for the Talley history. *Talley's Folly* takes place during the same evening as *Talley & Son*, shifting the scene to the Talleys' boathouse and focusing on Matt's wooing of Sally.

Its two characters are sweet and likable, but the play caters entirely too much to the audience. It opens with an address to them by Matt, whose tragic past and present forebodings are sweetened here, and throughout the play, by his repertory of jokes, impersonations, and stories. As he sets the scene for *Talley's Folly*, he chattily reminds the audience that they are in the theater: "There's a rotating gismo in the footlights . . . because we needed the moon out there on the water."[8] And although he touches on Wilson's central concerns—fear of apocalyptic destruction; regret for the hopeful American past, contrasted with present disillusionment and a growing apprehension that the American system no longer works; a preoccupation with the brevity of life—his cute, jokey manner keeps things light. Immediately after the darkest section of this speech, Matt says, "Now I know what you're thinking. You're saying if I'd known it was going to be like this, I wouldn't have come" (TF 5). This soothes that part of the audience who want nothing more taxing than what he has charmingly promised at the outset: "If everything goes well for me tonight, this should be a waltz, one-two-three, one-two-three; a no-holds barred romantic story . . ." (TF 4).

It is interesting that the only two plays in which Wilson puts romantic love at the center are about exogamous love: between black and white in *The Gingham Dog* and between Jew and Gentile in *Talley's Folly*. In *The Gingham Dog* he explores uncomfortably but honestly the tragic cultural and psychological impediments to such a relationship, but in *Talley's Folly* he glosses over them. Matt tells us that, just before he came to the boathouse, the Talleys ran the "Communist infidel" off their property with a shotgun. This would suggest that there are many issues to consider in a marriage between the daughter of a bigoted Ozark clan and an immigrant Jew orphaned by the Holocaust. But instead of exploring them, Wilson turns the action of the play on Sally's refusal to marry Matt because, we finally learn, she can't have children. Luckily for the match, Matt has decided earlier never to bring children into this cruel world. Boy and girl thus discover in a simplistic denouement that they are made for each other.

The first line of the play is Matt's comment to the audience: "They tell me that we have ninety-seven minutes here tonight—without intermission" (TF 3). The last lines are:

> Matt: (*Looks at her for a long while, then his gaze drifts to the audience*) And so, all's well that ends . . . (*Takes out his watch, shows time to Sally, then to audience*) . . . right on the button. Good night. (*They embrace*) [TF 60].

If we felt moved by Matt's observations about World War II, or by his terrible past as a European Jew, or by his presentiments about the American future, Wilson pacifies us. It's only a play, he says, and look how well I control it. This deliberately transparent control, like Alan's in *Lemon Sky*, may come out of his own fear. But to tailor the play to a precise 97 minutes is annoyingly slick. We can admire the perfection of his craft, but we are not emotionally or intellectually enriched by it.

The themes of *Angels Fall* (1982) are the familiar ones of apocalyptic fear, continuity, and the redemptive uses of work, and the structure is once again the converging of a group of troubled people in a temporary haven. This time it is an adobe mission in New Mexico, where six characters wait out a "nuclear accident" that has trapped them there. The convention is an ancient one: a band of travelers huddle in a common shelter, telling their tales in turn until the danger passes. But Wilson creates characters whom we care about and lets us listen to their good conversation. The point of the play is made by Doherty, the mission priest, who reads from Revelation:

> The day of the Lord will come as a thief in the night; in which the heavens shall pass away with a great noise, and the elements shall meet with fervent heat, the earth also and the works that are therein shall be burned up. Seeing then that all these things shall be dissolved, what manner of persons ought ye to be in all holy conversation and godliness?[9]

Doherty's answer, and the playwright's, in this most literal of Wilson's apocalyptic visions, is work. Work is the one certainty in an otherwise unstable world. Niles, an art history professor who is careening in and out of a nervous breakdown, is questioning the importance of the academic calling that has been the center of his life; Doherty and Don Tabaha, a young Indian doctor, quarrel over Tabaha's decision to leave the practice of clinical medicine on the reservation for a research position at a posh clinic in San Francisco. He will be forsaking his calling, the priest insists. Similarly, Niles cannot just give up. He is a teacher, "one of those professions," says Doherty, that "one is called to. As an artist is called, or as a priest is called, or as a doctor is called" (AF 2:13). Zap, the tennis player, expresses Wilson's notion of "calling":

> I hit that first ball and I said "This is me. This is what I do. What
> I do is tennis." And once you know, then there's no way out. . . .
> Once you know what you are, the rest is just work [AF 2:32].

Only once does Wilson lapse into sugarcoating for the audience. Niles, explaining his professional and intellectual crisis as the "disturbance in my willful suspension of disbelief," says bitterly (and wordily) that:

> whereas we have assumed the artistic expression of a culture was the
> mirror of the people's soul . . . or at least . . . an expression of how
> they thought, felt, and spent their spiritual existence; and that from
> that mirror, or expression, we can posit an esthetic for our own
> enlightenment . . . it is also possible that the expression of an artist
> tells us nothing whatever about the people and from it we can
> posit—nothing (AF 1:30).

Marion Clay, a character who has been established as intelligent, sophisticated, at home in the art world—she has even read the professor's books—immediately responds, "I *think* I followed that" (AF 1:30). That gets the audience off the hook if *they* haven't. Vita, the professor's wife, adds, "There'll be a quiz later," goodnaturedly confirming that his statement was pedantic, and completing the message to the audience that if they found it hard to follow, they are not inferior to the clever people in the play (AF 1:30). Niles is suggesting here that his principal belief—that art leaves a permanent legacy—may be wishful thinking and that, in fact, art is as impermanent as the rest of life. A terrifying possibility for the professor, and for Wilson. But the grief of it is diluted by the cozy reassurances.

For the most part, however, Wilson uses charm of expression to emphasize his serious points rather than to distract from them. Doherty's exchange with Vita is an example:

> *Vita:* What time is Mass? . . . If we're still here we'd like to see the
> service.
> *Doherty:* No, no, nothing to see. I'm afraid there isn't anything to
> watch. Not even picturesque, I don't imagine. Twelve, fifteen stoic
> Navajos shuffle in, kneel, I mumble sincerely, and they shuffle out.
> Nothing to see. Nothing on their faces, probably nothing on mine.
> In and out. Shuffle, shuffle.

Vita: It must be something to them, though. And to you.
Doherty: Oh, it's what we live for, but there's nothing to see... [*AF* 2:3, 4].

Doherty creates a humorous picture, but the offhanded "Oh, it's what we live for" reveals the priest's fervor for his calling. And we listen attentively to his views because of the engaging way that he presents them to Vita.

If *Angels Fall* lacks the technical virtuosity of some of Wilson's earlier plays, the very absence of verbal and theatrical pyrotechnics may be a sign of the maturing of his craft. Here he uses that craft for a larger purpose than to dazzle us, and he does not give in to the impulse to wink at the audience and say, "Watch this!" In a straightforward, even old-fashioned way, he gives us sympathetic characters made distinctive through apt, amusing, and, at times, moving speech, a satisfying sequence of events, and a lucid expression of his deepest concerns: impermanence and continuity. They are symbolized in Vita's and Marion's reminiscences about moving and breaking up households. Vita says that she felt guilty about burning her father's mementoes after he died. "All that crap belonged to the race, not to me," she tells Marion. "You never know what one shard left unburnt would tell the tale" (*AF* 2:5). It is the theme of *The Mound Builders* again: if we erase the marks we make, we ourselves will be erased. And so we collect things and tell stories and write plays to prevent our vanishing without a trace, or at least to make ourselves forget that we will.

Interview with Lanford Wilson

I met with Lanford Wilson in December 1982 at the offices of the Circle Repertory Theater in New York. Wilson was a co-founder of the theater in 1969 and has been a resident playwright there ever since. Every room was in bustling use, and Wilson suggested that we walk to a café in the neighborhood.

Thin and handsome and dressed in jeans, T-shirt, and a black leather jacket, Wilson looked much younger than his 46 years. He was tired, and at the beginning of the interview when I asked questions about his affiliation with Circle Rep — questions that he has apparently been asked many times — he was politely impatient. But when we began to talk about his plays, he warmed to the conversation. He is seldom asked to discuss his work seriously, he said afterwards. Wilson is a shy but animated talker who, appropriately for a playwright, often frames his answers in anecdotes composed of dialogue. Sipping wine at our minuscule table, he talked volubly and with charm until my three hours' worth of tapes ran out.

ESTHER HARRIOTT: Are you in an enviable position as a playwright because you're in a repertory company?

LANFORD WILSON: It's not enviable unless you want to work that way. I've created an atmosphere in which I can work, and other playwrights would envy that only if they can work in that kind of atmosphere. We have a bunch of them — I'm not the only one. We have twelve resident writers and a workshop of probably 24 or 25 writers and the actors are available to any of them, to read scenes so that the playwright can hear his work spoken by the person he's writing for. That's just what I needed — working in a group and not being completely isolated, and having the feeling that the play is going to get on, rather than writing in a vacuum for some producer's secretary to read or not read, and ship them out in the mail. I've never mailed a script to anyone and I'm awfully happy about that — at least not since 1968. I suppose my agent does though, so that doesn't really count.

HARRIOTT: You started with Caffe Cino and then moved to Circle Rep?

WILSON: Yeah. I did a one-act play for Circle called *The Family Continues* and then *The Hot l Baltimore*. That was the first full-length one.

Interview

HARRIOTT: *The Family Continues* is like a piece of music, isn't it?

WILSON: I was writing like that for a while. It was an experiment to get back to work and I wasn't even thinking that I was writing. Well, it was a story more interesting than that. When we started Circle Rep I gave them *Lemon Sky* to do and they couldn't do it because they didn't have a "father." And Marshall [Mason] at that time was only casting within the company. At the time I was writing *Serenading Louie*, and *Lemon Sky* was finished. *Lemon Sky* got on in Buffalo and *Serenading Louie* almost simultaneously — just before the Buffalo show — opened down in Washington, D.C. Then *The Gingham Dog* was done on Broadway and *Lemon Sky* moved to Broadway, and I was having a lot of activity outside Circle. Of course they bombed, or to various extents none of them ran. *Lemon Sky* was fairly well received but it didn't run any longer than *Gingham Dog*, which was fairly badly received.

HARRIOTT: I wanted to ask you about that, because I think *Gingham Dog* is a fine play. It's so true.

WILSON: It wasn't a very good production, actually. The actors could do it, but for some reason Alan Schneider's production was just not very good. He had them arguing from the very top. They were screaming at each other from the very first line, and all the humor and nuance and life got washed right away. The second act was done more or less correctly, but it was too late. So what happened then was logical, since I'd been fairly well received but not run. But that didn't matter because I thought commercial theater was absolutely abominable at the time and so I would have been embarrassed if I'd had a hit. But I thought I had to write the Great American Play next. And it is impossible to set out to write the Great American Play. I mean, you write "The Great American Play" across the top of the page and you'll never write another word. And so I went into this enormous decline and didn't write anything for about a year and a half.

HARRIOTT: That's a short period of time, as playwrights generally write in America.

WILSON: Not for me, because I've been very, very prolific, as you know. I mean, I don't feel I'm prolific, but other people say I'm prolific, and I do keep turning work out where other people keep not turning work out. So what I did just in order to remain sane is I started going to the office at Circle Rep where all my friends were. They were all in the midst of overwhelming activity, doing all these plays and all these shows.

HARRIOTT: Actor friends?

WILSON: Mostly actors at the Circle Rep. We didn't have nearly as many playwrights then. And since I was a member of that group, I hung around there and answered the phone and helped clean up and helped

37

build sets and wasn't writing at all, because I couldn't write, but I was reading scripts. And Marshall decided he wanted to do two one-act plays of mine—*The Great Nebula in Orion* and *Ikke Ikke Nye Nye Nye*. And I said, "But you've got this company of actors, and you'll use two in the one play and two in the other. And that's only four. They're both short, so why don't I do another little thing that will use more people?" And so that play was written as just an exercise for eight to ten people. I just was doing something for the Circle Rep actors to do. I took what is basically my play *Wandering* and wrote it in a different way. It became very musical, and also I wanted to use some of the exercises that Marshall was doing—exercises in trust. And I finished the damn play before I knew I had written something. It was the first thing I had written in about a year and a half.

HARRIOTT: That sort of answers the question that I didn't really ask but had at the back of my mind, which was, does the fact that you've been in a repertory theater have something to do with the fact that you've continued to write?

WILSON: I think so, because they keep needing work. And naturally if they're doing six plays a year I want one of them to be mine. I've skipped a few years. It sometimes takes longer to write. I always tell Marshall to have an alternate selection in mind and not to tell me, so that he can have it ready in case I don't get my play finished on time. And with *The Mound Builders* I didn't.

HARRIOTT: That's a wonderful play.

WILSON: I like that play, too. It's one of the only times I've written what I intended to do. You have an idea, and when the play is all finished, you say, "That isn't what I intended to write at all." But when I finished *The Mound Builders* I said, "That is exactly what I intended to do." It's lovely for that to happen. I didn't know the specifics but I knew that there would be something outside that's going to get you. And when I was about three or four months into the play, I said, "I think this is about work." Why people work and what is the impulse to work and why do we strive to do good work.

HARRIOTT: It's a play, like a lot of your plays, about waiting for the end—that "something outside that's going to get you"—and what do you do in the meantime.

WILSON: Yes, what do you do in the meantime and that was answered—you work. That was what I had intended to write, and that was so thrilling to me.

HARRIOTT: I'm surprised to hear you say that, because I always get the feeling that you're in complete control of your material.

WILSON: Not always. Things slip away and characters get out of hand

and you have to slap them around a little more than you intended to. They take off in their own direction and it surprises me and leads me into slightly different areas from where I had intended to go. And I say, well what do you know? This turned out to be *that*. Like, *Hot l Baltimore* is so much sweeter than I thought it was. I thought I was writing the first filthy play. I was teaching Ron Tavel how to write a dirty play. And I got the first two acts finished and people were reading it to me—because I was going around saying, "What in the hell happens in the third act? I don't know how to end this play." I thought I had written this uncommercial, unproducible, filthy play. And they finished reading the first two acts and I said, "My God, that's *charming*." I called my agent and I said, "You know that filthy play I'm writing? It's charming." She said, "Charming? With all those whores and all those dykes and all that?" And I said, "I know. It's charming." I couldn't believe it. I was so disappointed in a way.

HARRIOTT: Did you think *Balm in Gilead* was going to be a filthy play?

WILSON: No, I didn't even know *Balm in Gilead* was a *play*. I was sitting in a café writing down things that people said.

HARRIOTT: Oh, you *do* do that? I asked myself that question, because your dialogue sounds so real.

WILSON: It was dictation. But not all of it. It's orchestrated and I was doing all sorts of sound patterns. I was just playing. I was doodling with sound.

HARRIOTT: And with time.

WILSON: Yeah. And then I started playing with the idea of monologues that I got directly from James Saunders' play *Next Time I'll Sing to You*. There are four shaggy dog stories that are told to the audience—he has just one, but I swear it must be 15 minutes long. When I got it all finished and put in those shaggy dog stories, I said, "You know, this is looking very much like a full-length play." I hadn't written a full-length play. I divided it and wrote the long monologue at the top of the second act.

HARRIOTT: In *The Hot l Baltimore* and *Balm in Gilead* and in all of your plays you show a lot of compassion for the outsider. And in *The Gingham Dog* you pay the most attention to the feelings of a black character, which is rare for a white playwright.

WILSON: Well, of course, there's Athol Fugard.

HARRIOTT: Yes, but he's living in South Africa where that issue is the central fact of his life.

WILSON: That came about because at that time [1969] everybody was writing these wild, hate-filled, screaming plays. It didn't jibe with what I was seeing and I wanted to do something very different. Matt Friedman [the hero of *Talley's Folly*] came about the same kind of way. I got so sick of the stage Jew. The way those Jewish writers write themselves and their mothers and their fathers—I just hated it. And even the novelists.

HARRIOTT: Like Philip Roth?

WILSON: Philip Roth and others. And I said, O.K. That's fine, that's one aspect of it, and we've suddenly discovered our Jewish hate. But that my Jewish friends aren't like that at all. I wanted to see if I could write a Jewish stage character that doesn't have all of those clichés. One of the strong attempts in that play was to write a Jewish character as he might really be—a Jewish hero, rather than all those Jewish villains that were being written and all those ghastly women.

HARRIOTT: That suggests a couple of questions that I want to ask you. In *Brontosaurus* you have the nephew say, "I felt myself thinning out." He talks about feeling himself a part of all kinds of people. And it seems to me that you're like that. That is, you seem to sense how a lot of different kinds of people from different classes and different regions feel. I don't know how you do that—whether it's just instinctive.

WILSON: I had that experience exactly as he describes it, which is what Allen Ginsberg would call having a satori experience, I think. I had that when I was 11. It's an indescribable experience, so I said O.K. let's try to describe it. I could have become a minister from having had that experience. I did not. It was interesting to try to recall it and write it as clearly as I could. And Zappy's monologue in *Angels Fall*, the one about tennis. When I was working in Fuller, Smith & Ross, I was an apprentice in the art department there and I thought I was going to become a graphic designer. But I was writing a lot of stories. And working in an advertising agency wasn't as interesting as I thought it was going to be.

HARRIOTT: This was before everything—before you wrote plays?

WILSON: This was before everything, yeah. I was 20. I was writing stories—I started writing stories when I was very small and kept writing stories. But I was really an artist. I was just writing stories on the side, and because friends of mine at San Diego State were writers, and I wanted to be in a class with them, so I took a writing class. I kept writing stories on my own after I left San Diego. It was very good relaxation from this stupid job I had—the closer you get to advertising the more you realize you don't really want to be a part of it all.

HARRIOTT: Morally, you mean?

WILSON: And also you don't want to go through the hassle. I thought it would be great fun designing a logo. And you design about 20 of them, but the account executive won't show 15 of them to the client, who hates them all anyway. It's all just such compromise that it's not design, it's something else. That was very disheartening. Anyway, I thought of a story and I realized it wasn't really like a story. It was like a play, like *The Glass Menagerie*. The narrative in all of my stories had been awkward and the dialogue had been good. The dialogue in the stories was almost better than it was supposed to be. It was more speakable than dialogue that you see in stories. So I started writing just dialogue and trying to get my ideas straight. And by the middle of the second page—they were big pages—I said, I'm a playwright. Forget all the art I'd been studying for 20 years. I'm a playwright. I write plays. It was like a thunderbolt. That experience is translated into Zappy's "Since I hit that first ball, I said this is me. This is what I am."

HARRIOTT: And once you decide who you are, "the rest is just work."

WILSON: "The rest is just work." I knew I had a specific talent for writing plays. And I knew then I was better at it than 99 percent of the people who were working at it already. That was what I was given. And as Zappy says, once you've been shown that, you can't just say you weren't shown that. So the rest is just work. You were asking about the characters, and this was all to answer that most of those things, I've experienced. They've happened to me or I've seen them and empathized with someone else having that experience.

HARRIOTT: I said that your remark about wanting to write about Matt Friedman not as a stage Jew, but as a sort of redeeming act, suggested *two* questions. The other one is about *The Gingham Dog*. You make a point of having your male protagonist say that he's disillusioned, that when he grew up in a small town in the South he wanted to be large-spirited about Jews and about blacks. But when he came to New York he found that these stereotypes were, in fact, vindicated, and it's upsetting to him.

WILSON: That is one whole side and the other whole side is completely different. He does say that, yeah. And you do see it. You do see Jews and blacks behaving in a terribly unattractive, stereotyped way from time to time. And you say, oh please don't do that, oh God, that's terrible, that's awful! Lord, you're behaving in exactly the way . . . you see it with Ozark hillbillies too. And ten minutes later, if you stayed with them, they'd be behaving in a way that completely denied that. Or else there are some that the stereotype is based on and there's nothing you can do about that.

HARRIOTT: Do you know the critic Leslie Fiedler?

WILSON: No.

HARRIOTT: He says that in every stereotype there resides an archetype.

WILSON: Yeah. Oh, there are some who are exactly . . . you know, there are some lazy, slovenly blacks who think of nothing except sex, and your stereo's not safe with them. But then there's Gloria Foster. Or any number of other people.

HARRIOTT: Why wasn't *A Tale Told* published?

41

WILSON: It was done here and then I rewrote it a great deal. It was not completely successful. By that I mean it wasn't exactly what *I* wanted it to be—or what any of us wanted it to be, what Marshall wanted it to be. It was a gorgeous production but it just wasn't the play yet. And so I rewrote it and we did it at Mark Taper Forum in California, where we do a lot of them. And it was vastly improved. It was so much improved that in some of the audience discussions that we had, I began to realize what the play had to be, and said, "Oh my God, have I got a lot of work to do on this yet! But not now." Because I had to write *Angels Fall*—that was a commission. So I postponed the Broadway production because it was just not what it should be yet, and I didn't have any time to do it then. Also, I was exhausted on the damn thing—you burn out on them after a while. So that's the next project, to go back to *A Tale Told* and rewrite that play the way it should have been.

HARRIOTT: You said that you began writing stories and then found that the dialogue was coming off the page. The sad thing is that very few people in this country start off by writing plays. Most people who want to be writers think of fiction and poetry. There are so many more obstacles for a playwright.

WILSON: You have to be bit. You have to be stage-struck. You have to like theater in some way to begin with. I saw a college production of *Death of a Salesman* and in the middle of the monologue when he remembered the past before all those buildings had been built, and they all faded into green trees—the backdrop changed from solid brick buildings to these bright, shining green trees—and I was hooked from then on. The next thing I saw was *Brigadoon*. Oh, my God, when that village appeared? I was gone.

HARRIOTT: You're talking about technological things.

WILSON: That was *magic!* It was what hooked me. It's not what I'm trying to do. Magic, yes. But in who knows what different kind of way. Magic with words and time and juxtapositions and light.

HARRIOTT: How did you know in, say, *Balm in Gilead*, that by dimming the light on the characters very briefly, that it would be so effective?

WILSON: Yeah, I think it is. We got it down to a flash of—bang!—about that long. The reason I did it was because in this cacaphony I wanted to point out the person that you're going to have to watch.

HARRIOTT: It does something else too. It changes the perception of time.

WILSON: It does all kinds of other things that I hadn't even intended at the time. It was just a good experiment. There are others in that play that don't work as well. But there are some very nice experiments in it, too. I haven't read that play in years, but the last time I did, I said, "Why don't I still write like that? My God, that's very inventive."

HARRIOTT: When they repeat the stabbing of Joe three times, that's very chilling.

WILSON: That *is* very chilling, really scary. We'd be going on with all this noise for the entire length of the play. It builds, and then he's stabbed as those kids go flying out. I was thinking of the play as music all the way through, and I wanted to have a musical climax. And also, even though this was a climax, it looked insignificant because there's been so much brutality and so much carrying on, that it almost isn't any more important, and did it three times for those reasons. And just repeating that almost for the physical impact. And boy, is that scary! Boy, does it work! Also the way Marshall did it was astonishing, because Joe falls back over the table and slumps down the first time, as the kids are going out, and someone pulls him up. And they stab him again and he falls back exactly the same way, and the kids are going out again. And people pull him up again. And the third time he falls down and the table collapses—one beat later.

HARRIOTT: It reminded me of a nightmare. It had that quality of relentless repetition.

WILSON: It was supposed to have. I was for all practical purposes a Missouri farm kid. You couldn't surprise me too much. You've seen an awful lot. You've seen horses die and you've seen cows die and you've seen birth and all of that. And your or someone's uncle's a drunk. You know how people are and it's not really a shock to you. But to see in New York so much of it and carried to such extremes, and the poverty and degradation and where people had put themselves. Of course, I had lived in Chicago for a long while. But it was just more intense in this place. And I had never been around the drug scene much. That was new to me.

HARRIOTT: You seem to know an awful lot about the drug culture.

WILSON: Strictly research. I'm not a druggie and never have been. So it's strictly how does that feel and what is that like and how much does it cost—strictly asking questions. And seeing people on it.

HARRIOTT: That play is sort of Brechtian, too, isn't it? That pretty tune with those bitter words, and the cast of characters—outcasts and hustlers.

WILSON: Well, I had not read a single play of Brecht's when I wrote it. Of course, I knew the songs from *The Threepenny Opera*, but I wasn't thinking it was like that. New York was so new to me, I was just writing down what it was like. I was, to a large extent, like the character Darlene coming to this city.

HARRIOTT: In a lot of your plays, like *Lemon Sky*, you insist on reminding the audience that this is theater. Just as it gets drawn in, you have a character speak to the audience in an authorial voice, describing or commenting on what's happening.

WILSON: I haven't been doing that very much lately. I haven't done it in the last few plays. It was in *Serenading Louie,* and I cut it out, and it's not really in *The Mound Builders.*

HARRIOTT: There's a tiny bit still in *Serenading Louie.* You have a couple of addresses to the audience.

WILSON: I have a couple of addresses to the audience, yeah. But I mean, in *Serenading Louie,* they did say in the first draft, "Even when you're actors like us, hired on the stage to do a part, and everything is perfectly planned out and you know all your lines, still there's that awful feeling that, tonight, goddam it, I may just run amok with the meat cleaver." And I cut that out and just had them speak that in character, so it's the character, not the actor talking to the audience. It's just very natural for me to have the character talk to the audience. In *The Mound Builders* I don't have the character talking to the audience, but to the tape recorder.

HARRIOTT: I don't mean just talking to the audience. That's part of it, I guess. But, for example, in *Lemon Sky* the young son, the protagonist, gives the audience a lot of hints about what's going to happen in the rest of the play. He's the playwright in a way.

WILSON: Yeah. It's autobiographical and it's my story, and he's a playwright. He's saying how he's organizing the play. That line, "A year from now I'll be in a park in Chicago with a letter in my pocket from Ronnie telling me that Carol is dead. But who would know that now?" was such a surprise to me when I wrote it. But I just was trying to give the audience the perception of the character that I had, that knowing what happened to that character, Carol, made remembering her incredibly painful. I was just trying to have them see her in a very different light. So everything she says after that, you say, "My God, this is the last time..." I always started out saying, "This is the stage, what can you do on it?" And I like real people better than abstract idea plays. I was very interested in the way people behave. So, given characters in more or less a set, or at least a setting, like platforms that represent an entire town, what can you do on that? How can you mess it up? I'm not doing that much any more because I'm not sure I believe that any more. Am I just doing it to make it interesting? Is it getting too tricky? And is it taking away from the character development—would the characters be deeper and more true if I was going through real time with them, rather than cutting around like that? I went through a long period of not trusting it. Then when I got to *The Mound Builders* it became the logical way to write, because they're examining shards and pieces and seeds and little bits of things and putting them together to make a story. So I thought it was trickily endemic to the piece to have it in shards and fragments and pieces that you put together yourself.

HARRIOTT: Do you read a lot of science and paleontology?

WILSON: I used to have a subscription to *Scientific American* and *Sky and Telescope*. I still do some, but not as much as I did. I used to read science a lot.

HARRIOTT: And were you very religious at one time?

WILSON: Yeah, I was converted in the black Baptist church in Lebanon, Missouri. Me and Patsy Johnson. The only white kids there, at the Bible school.

HARRIOTT: You have quite a few characters who want to believe in something, like Carl in *Serenading Louie*, for one.

WILSON: What Carl believes in, of course, is that American dream, where the college quarterback falls in love with the homecoming queen and they get married and have two kids and live happily ever after. That's his religion, that's what he believes. And when that is not true it washes everything his life has built on out from under him, and he no longer has anything to believe in at all. If that's not true, he cannot function. Everything's been based on that. He goes to work every morning and makes a million bucks, and can deal with all that jangle that he has to deal with, based on that. And that base goes and he can no longer deal with anything. He's a tragic character, Carl. I like him a lot.

HARRIOTT: But he does believe . . .

WILSON: Yeah, he does have that first speech about the church. I'm sorry. You were getting at something else.

HARRIOTT: I was getting at the saddest thing about him, that he doesn't really feel anything any more. Or so he says. There are two things happening there. He says he doesn't feel anything any more and compares himself to primitive people making sacrifices in order to have some feeling about something, and says that his wife is exposing their marriage to danger so as to feel something. But yet he really does feel so much.

WILSON: He feels so much, but he can't let it get to him because it'll destroy him. And he does, and it does. He's so obsessed with Mary and what is happening to the foundation of his life, and he is not feeling many other things that he feels he should.

HARRIOTT: But he claims he's not feeling that much even about Mary.

WILSON: But he certainly is. He has that outburst that denies it at the end of the first act. He says, "I see all of these things that go by like it was all happening in the movies and I say I don't feel anything but I do. But I don't understand it—why is she doing this? I want it back the way it was"—in other words, the way it was in fantasy.

HARRIOTT: The people in that play are very familiar.

WILSON: *Aren't* they familiar?

45

HARRIOTT: The play wasn't very well-received by the reviewers here, was it?

WILSON: In Washington it was well-received. All of the mature people are blown away by it. It's John Bishop's favorite play of mine, it's Marshall favorite play of mine, it's everyone's favorite play of mine.

HARRIOTT: Is it your favorite play of yours?

WILSON: No, because there are a few technical things that don't quite work toward the end of the play. We finally got it working in Chicago — there's a new version of it — there's a few little technical fudgings around that work much better. It's not mine because it was so painful to go there and I very nearly went crazy writing that play. I kept losing it and I must have been in some very bad place. I kept damn near going crazy because I kept discovering things that I didn't want to know, and once I discovered them I didn't want to deal with it.

HARRIOTT: Is this one of the cases where the characters started to take over?

WILSON: Oh, God, yeah! I started examining, "Why do you do that? Why do you feel that?" As I said, much of this was me. I was probing what I felt in four different areas, and the four different areas of me are the four characters. I wasn't trying to write myself. I just said, "How is that true to me? What do I feel about this?" And then I would check it out with friends of mine. I would say, "Would you read this and tell me if this is true to your experience?" And then they'd read it and go, "Oh, Jesus Christ! Oh, my God! Yeah. Oh Lord!" And I'd say, "O.K. Thanks very much. I just wanted to make sure it wasn't too incredibly weird and private." I was working this way on that play, and it led into some areas that I hadn't really intended to go into — all those weird, dark, black areas of Carl.

HARRIOTT: Do you mean the primitive person under the veneer?

WILSON: Yeah. And that to destroy this marriage if it wasn't true was the absolute only recourse that he had. He had thought about just killing the child to bring them together, but for any number of reasons that wouldn't really work. It was very strange territory to be getting into. That all just started out with these two guys, when I was living in Glen Ellyn and coming in on the commuter train.

HARRIOTT: Where's Glen Ellyn?

WILSON: It's a suburb of Chicago — way out and rather rich. Me and another guy had a very poor house in the woods. I worked at some art personnel service, and handled their correspondence, and wrote stories most of the time on their typewriter. So I came in looking like this [indicating his jeans and T-shirt] with all the advertising guys in their grey flannel suits at seven in the morning. And I was still living there when I worked at

Fuller, Smith & Ross. I usually stayed very late in town, until eight or nine o'clock. Once I had nothing to do and was exhausted, and I went with some of the guys into this bar that they always went to, that I knew nothing about. They were all in their thirties and I was twenty. And they would down the martinis and get their ride home to the suburbs. It was the first time that I was in that crowd that was just one hour and three martinis away from closing time, on their way home to their wives. I saw those two guys, they had their arms around each other and their heads smashed together, so drunk, and they were talking, both in their three-piece suits. And they stood and held hands. And they were saying, "I love you, you know what I mean?" "I know what you mean. I love you too." "I really love you, you know what I mean?" This was very embarrassing, they were both so drunk. And they split, and one went on one train and one went on the other. That's when I started thinking about these men relationships—this football with the boys on Sunday afternoon and all that. That was the genesis of that play. Men relationships where they talk so weird and so honestly and unguardedly and such bullshit.

HARRIOTT: And they fear and hate their wives.

WILSON: Fear and hate their wives. Fear and hate and love their wives. And I thought, when have they ever expressed anything like that to their wives, even drunk? During orgasm is the only time they would have an experience that large, even if then.

HARRIOTT: You were 20 when you saw this image and then you wrote a play about it when you were 32?

WILSON: I had been trying to write it. The bar where I sat with those account executives and layout artists—it was the first time I had ever been in it—was one of those midtown bars. It was so chic and quiet and fancy and has only the old standards like Ella Fitzgerald on the jukebox, and it's so low you can't hear anyway. Everything is carpeted and behind the bar they had these little Italian twinkle lights all in white, flickering off and on. I sat there listening to these people I worked with every day get progressively drunker and expose the most hideous things, being appalled at what was happening to these people and just learning altogether too much about them. Consequently, I thought for a long while that the play was going to take place in the bar on Christmas Eve. In that quiet, muted, uptown, dark, dark bar.

It took a long time to write that play. The first start of it was years earlier, before I did *Lemon Sky*. I had been working on *Lemon Sky* for years too, but one day I was trying to work on *Serenading Louie* and all of *Lemon Sky* came to me and I sat down and wrote it in a very short period. Then I went back to *Serenading Louie*. One of the starts was they've gone to one bar and it closed at six and now they've gone to one that closed at seven. Those midtown bars closed at what I used to think was the middle of the afternoon because their clientele was just the executive crowd. Their big season is lunch and from five to seven. It started with them coming in already pretty too high and the guy saying, "Wait. Wait. Hold it. Nobody moves." The guy can't find his wallet. "Wait." And then he finds it. I remember that very clearly, whatever happened to that note. It ended up not in the play. And gradually it started forming itself into *Serenading Louie*.

HARRIOTT: It's interesting. You have so much compassion and psychological insight and sensitivity, but there's one unredeemed character in your plays, I think, and that's Douglas [in *Lemon Sky*].

WILSON: Might well be. I had more facts to go on there than in most of them. I said at the beginning of the play, "If I can't write this character honestly, then it tells you more about me than if I could." What does Alan say? "If he comes off a shit, I mean *nothing*, but nothing, then that tells you more about him than if I could tell you more." Because he wasn't all that bad.

HARRIOTT: But he seems horrible.

WILSON: Well, he was fairly horrible. Maybe I was just closer to that particular villain—as far as I'm concerned—than to any of the others. Maybe I should have more unredeemed characters. I'm beginning to think they're too nice. But, see, the reason for what you call compassion and all of that, in my work and in things I saw, at some point I'd see an out-and-out villain, and I'd say, "Oh, come off it. No one is that black and no one is that white. Let's grey them out a little bit." I'd see someone who was essentially evil and I'd say, "What do they want? And what are their redeeming qualities?"

HARRIOTT: You mean you'd ask yourself quite systematically?

WILSON: Yeah. It can't be that black and white. What is under that, and what causes that? As soon as you investigate where some horrible behavior comes from, then the character begins to round out and everyone sort of rounds out till there are no villains.

HARRIOTT: Carl, for example, does the worst thing that anybody could possibly do...

WILSON: Oh yeah, Carl is a mass murderer.

HARRIOTT: And yet you can feel pity for him. But Douglas...

WILSON: Oh, well. That's one of the best characters I've ever written, Carl. I've written about eight really good theater characters and Carl is one of them.

HARRIOTT: I was going to say that Douglas is so overwhelmingly repulsive that...

WILSON: Is he? Oh, good. I'm not feeling particularly kind to him today.... I wrote that as best I could, and couldn't go back and do it any
different.

HARRIOTT: Who are the other seven or six good characters?

WILSON: I think Gloria in *Gingham Dog* is a wonderful character. She's
a very beautiful, well-rounded character. I think you know that person.

HARRIOTT: Yeah, I agree.

WILSON: And Matt Friedman in *Talley's Folly*. It's almost a better *role*
than he is a character, but I think he's really a very good character too. Who
else? There are three or four really good roles in *Hot l*, but they're not really
characters.

HARRIOTT: Who in the latest one, *Angels Fall?*

WILSON: There may not be one that I consider that. But right under
that is all of them. Certainly the professor.

HARRIOTT: I was very moved by his speech doubting his academic
calling.

WILSON: That comes from one term of teaching summer school, and
talking to the professors in the professors' lounge.

HARRIOTT: How long ago?

WILSON: Just about four years ago. I think he's a terrific character.
Doherty is too. But I really think Niles...

HARRIOTT: He's harder to make sympathetic.

WILSON: Yeah. It's really a deeper examination of a character than
Doherty. Doherty has a simple life. It's pared down and by design simpler.
Still it could probably be more interesting than that. But Niles is very close.
I don't know if he's quite that good or not. There are some others.

HARRIOTT: There's a kind of bonding, isn't there, between Niles and
the Indian?

WILSON: Oh, yes. Oh, yes. A kind of bonding is exactly right. There
are very strong similarities. There are strong similarities between so many
of the characters, and one aspect of one character is very sympathetic to
another aspect of another character. I like that very much—where Doherty
and Niles and the Indian all sympathize with certain areas of Zappy and
Zappy reflects all of them in one way or another.

HARRIOTT: Leslie Fiedler has a thesis in an essay that's become a classic
of literary criticism, called "Come Back Ag'in to the Raft, Huck Honey"
and...

WILSON: He wrote that? I know that essay.

HARRIOTT: His idea is that the central myth in American literature is
of homoerotic love between two men of different races. And also that
women are not at the passionate center of American literature.

49

WILSON: We've certainly seen that, the bonding of two disparate men. It's true, there's a very strong thesis. We've seen it in all those movies—*The Sting, Sundance Kid,* and all of that. It's a very interesting essay.

HARRIOTT: You know it?

WILSON: Yeah. I'm from Missouri, don't you know—Mark Twain territory. I've been to Hannibal, I've seen that river there.

HARRIOTT: Is there anything that anybody can do to get playwriting out of its position as stepchild of the literary arts in this country?

WILSON: We're so easily dismissed at the time. We're only considered at the time. All of the literary critics are into something very different from my work, that's for sure. They're into Pinter.

HARRIOTT: I don't think they're really much into any contemporary dramatists.

WILSON: They're into things they can write about. It's almost a vested interest. Our plays are interesting to them years later. But when they see them they can dismiss them. Who said—Gide, was it, who said, "Don't understand me too quickly"? I think we're being understood too quickly and on a very superficial level. Some of the plays that we're working on take as long as novels. Some of the plays that I've written have taken four or five years, and they've been worked out very carefully. And they're dismissed in a short paragraph in the *Partisan Review*. The academic mind is analytical and I don't think it can cope very well with current events, with things that are happening now. Like, the behavior at that table [Wilson indicates nearby table of people in the café] is more interesting than all the plays of Shakespeare, but they couldn't possibly cope with that. They can spend their life analyzing Cleopatra, but they can't cope very well with the present moment. Theater is the present moment. That's happening now. And I think when they see it they dismiss it. They're not really seeing what has been put into the work.

None of us are taking the risks we should be. It's never chancy enough, never risky enough. You're never out on a limb. While you're working on it you think you are, and you're trying to go as far as you can with something. And when you get it all finished, you say, "It's so safe."

HARRIOTT: Is that because of concern for the box office?

WILSON: No, no, God no, you don't think of that at all. I'm in an insulated situation where it doesn't matter at all. I don't care if they go uptown. Going uptown's such a hassle, because right away they start replacing people and then you don't have what you worked so hard to create in the rehearsal. You don't have that magical ensemble.

HARRIOTT: I meant are you concerned that you won't get put on?

WILSON: Oh, see, I'll get put on. I'll get put on and run for the subscribers. I guess we always feel this about ourselves: I want to *not* be put on. I want to have people get up and leave. No one gets up and leaves. They only leave out of boredom. Of course, they always say it's boredom. You know, 16 people take off their clothes and stab each other, and people get up and leave because they say they're bored. And it's not really bored at all. They unplugged and therefore are not hearing anything. Not nearly risky enough. Some of my earlier things were riskier.

HARRIOTT: In what ways?

WILSON: I can't say it. It just seems so tame. The reason I wrote *Hot l Baltimore* is that I'd finished writing *Serenading Louie*, and aside from not wanting to write another tragedy, the one thing I was dissatisfied with was they're so goddam suburban. They're so pale, they've got no color to them. They're all beige. They're beige and the're chic and they have well-rounded sentences, and we're trying to get to the underbelly of them. Just such chic people. I want to write the way Dickens did, I want to write outrageous characters. And that's how *Hot l Baltimore* came about. I was trying to write more outrageous characters. The characters in *Serenading Louie* were just too damned socially acceptable.

HARRIOTT: What might be both your glory and your handicap is that you're always charming. Is that what you mean?

WILSON: That's even more insidious. That I feel after *Angels Fall*. It's certainly true of *Talley's Folly*. They're funny and they're warm and they're human and they're in love. And, damn it, they're charming. I am very pleased with Don Tabaka in *Angels Fall* because people say, "Well he's just so belligerent, I didn't like him." Wonderful! Great! I've actually written a character, then, that maybe didn't have charm. I don't think he has much charm. Every once in a while a little bit of something cracks through, but not in that same charming kind of way. I'd like to think I've written at least one character in the last six years that wasn't completely charming, because Zappy is charming and Marion is charming and all the others are charming in one way or another. But Don is a little more abrasive.

HARRIOTT: Is that charm one of the reasons you're sometimes compared to Chekhov? Or is it the elegiac note?

WILSON: Do you know, I hate being compared to Chekhov? It's because we're both trying to concentrate on character and theme and story — although they say we aren't — and action be damned in a way.

HARRIOTT: And atmosphere?

WILSON: Yeah, action be damned, but atmosphere all over the joint. And I love him a lot and can't come up to his ankles, but one day . . . . I'm after Chekhov's and O'Neill's ass, right? Chekhov is charming. Couldn't write a negative character that wasn't charming in some way if he had to.

If that's my heel, then I'll limp on it. But I haven't thought that. At the same time I had wanted to write a negative character. I would like to write an Iago. I would like to write a son of a bitch. You say Douglas is. That gives me great hope. I'm going to try to do it again, either in *A Tale Told* or in the one after. The next original play—if I ever write again: I worked too hard, too continuously on the last one *[Angels Fall]*—is going to be a play for Lindsay Crouse. She's one of the best people in our company, and the only play she's been in of mine is *Serenading Louie*. She played Gabby. She and Tanya Berezin are the two ballsiest actors I've ever worked with. Tanya plays Marion in *Angels Fall*. Now, that's ballsy. In *Brontosaurus* she damned near cracked the antique chair—I would have killed her because it was my chair—gripping the back of it in that last speech when she says, "Get out of my house."

HARRIOTT: In *Brontosaurus* she says, "Maybe the reason I don't live with anybody is that I don't want anybody to foul up my nest." That's the *Craig's Wife* syndrome, but in *Craig's Wife* she's horrible. In *Brontosaurus* the Dealer is a very sympathetic figure.

WILSON: Yeah. What about the other character, the nephew? He is very strange, isn't he?

HARRIOTT: I felt a lot of menace in him and you're not supposed to, are you? But he scared me.

WILSON: No, I think there is. Do you know, it's interesting you should say that, because I said once and I'm toying with this—I have a thought for a thriller, and if I write it, it's going to be another *Serenading Louie* and I'm going to be sorry I ever touched it, right? But I said, "What if that nephew, instead of being, theatrically at least, passive, were active? What if he were a terrorist?" Instead of a benign terrorist, what if he were an active terrorist? Of course, he's antithetical to everything she believes in, though there was a speech that I think I did not get in. She says, "How can I relate to someone who thinks that the most perfectly crafted Louis Quinze chair is just waiting for the time when that wood decays back into the earth and becomes useful?" And that's his philosophy. That didn't get in there, but...

HARRIOTT: The feeling did.

WILSON: The feeling's in there. You certainly know that those are the two points of view. So I said, what if he were an active terrorist? And had at least one sidekick and got maybe another one during the course of the play. What if they were not in New York City but way out somewhere, like in Montauk, where the houses are a quarter of a mile apart in some of those areas. And then I put an architect buddy into it, who is 70, and the two people are so weak, they would essentially be held hostage and would have to get out of it in some way. It's very exciting to me. The thing that isn't exciting to me is that it's one of those plays—it's *Desperate Hours* or any of those others. But still, with her, and this architect, and the other guy. He is threatening in some way, you know, and maybe if he were just insidiously threatening, strangely threatening, so that you didn't quite know, rather than being overt. I think there's a perfectly fabulous thriller in that, and with all of my potential dialogue I'll be able to fuck up, right? I'll be able to completely ruin a great commercial idea.

HARRIOTT: But you won't start with a plot. Even when you talk—you have a great plot for a thriller, and you end up talking about a character.

WILSON: It's not a plot at all, it's character. And I would have to, I guess, in that kind of play. I've sat in front of those plays in awe. I sat in front of the first act, at least, of *Deathtrap* in awe. Shocked and thrilled and so excited. I couldn't believe my eyes. How on earth can anyone do that? I think it's one of the most perfect things that's ever been written—the first act of that. And finally, at the very last line of the act, you understand what everything is. Everything has been a hoax. Then, of course, the second act has the reaction from that, and that's not so effective. That's miraculous, and you have to be excited about it and in awe of it, because I could not possibly do that. I could sit down with numbers and a chart and a book telling me how to do it, and I couldn't do it.

HARRIOTT: But that's Sardoodledum, too, isn't it?

WILSON: That's Sardoodledum, yeah. But I'm in awe of Sardou, of all those people. I love it, because it's something that I couldn't do if I tried. And I'll probably have to steal someone else's plot if I ever write that kind of a play. I'll have to take a Sardou. Wouldn't that be nice? And the audiences will be bored out of their minds and say, "Nothing happened!" which they always do anyway.

This is another aspect of everything that I write I've experienced in one way or another. When I had *The Gingham Dog* typed up by Studio Duplicating Service, the first time I'd ever had anything professionally typed, I went in to pick it up and they said, "seventy-three dollars" and I wrote out a check and gave it to them. And I had this box of scripts. I wasn't even excited about seeing what they looked like anymore because he didn't say, "That is one hell of a script." He hadn't liked it. Probably hadn't even read it, you know, but he didn't say, "The typist said this is really..." Nothing. They were the first people to read the script and they said nothing about it. I was destroyed. I couldn't believe it. I went home and sat around and smoked a lot of cigarettes and drank a lot of coffee and didn't open the thing. I had opened it in the cab and looked at it and said, "That really looks professional." I didn't take them out of the box for about two days. Didn't show them to anyone.

HARRIOTT: You know, all writers are like that. They're saying, "Love me, love me."

WILSON: *Like* it! Love me, slove me, you know. Like the *work*, respond to the work. Say, "I know that," or "You said it in a way that I couldn't have said," or "I understand that, you're talking about me, you're not alone." And that is the speech in *The Mound Builders* when she says, "I had a little typist come in and type it up for me. And I gave her the check and she left and I threw it in the closet and got drunk for four days and wouldn't answer the door." And he says, "Because it was finished?" and she says, "Because I thought she hadn't liked it." Two lines that got gasps from the audience, and Tanya Berezin said both of them. That's one. The other one is in *Serenading Louie*, they're talking about how wonderful it was, Mary and— Tanya's all wrong for Mary but she played Mary here. She played her brilliantly, but Mary should look like a homecoming queen and Tanya just does not.

HARRIOTT: What was the line?

WILSON: Oh, this works out of context. The other line in [The] *Mound Builders* works in context. They're talking about how wonderful it was when they were serenading Louie "back then" at the beginning of their romance and how wonderful it was sleeping together when he went back to school to get his degree. There's this long description of sex with Carl, waking up and having sex again in the morning. She turns to the audience and says, "I don't really think I loved him then. But I love him then now."

HARRIOTT: That's a wonderful line, and a wonderful idea too.

WILSON: The audience went "Oh!" en masse. The other one was "Because I thought she hadn't liked it." And the audience, en masse, went "Shiiit." It was really something when she hit it right.

HARRIOTT: You don't write these plays in isolation, do you?

WILSON: I work well with all of this energy around, and I write in the office often. But I'm cutting out, you know, I'm using the energy and I'm not hearing anything when I'm working. It's just me and the characters and the time, and then I unplug and hear everyone. And I work like that until they begin to get on my nerves. Then I go out to Sag Harbor and I work in isolation until I say, "I am so lonely I can't stand it. Is anyone involved in the theater any more?" Then I go back and everyone's rehearsing for things and I'm very excited and energized again, until I say—and it's usually three or four weeks—I say, "I can't stand all of this damned irrelevant noise." Usually it's because I've plugged into something very strongly and I'm trying to develop a new character or a new idea, and I can't with that much noise around. So I go back out to Sag Harbor and work out in isolation again.

But I don't work in isolation, do I? I have them read me a lot of the scenes, over and over and over again as I'm trying to get them, and then other scenes I don't at all. They never see them until they see the whole script.

HARRIOTT: You have specific actors in mind.

WILSON: Oh, yeah, I don't work in a vacuum. I have actors in mind. The character comes first and then I say, "Who could play that?" and "Oh, God, that would be perfect for . . ." Then I have that actor in mind to play the part so that I can say, "You're awfully tall to keel over in that way," because I know Fritz Weaver is awfully tall. And that line played by someone who's perfectly all right for the part, but isn't tall, will have to be cut. It can certainly be cut without losing anything.

HARRIOTT: Has anyone been in your plays as long as Tanya Berezin?

WILSON: Michael Warren Powell—I came to New York with Michael and a guy named Dean Morgan. And Michael was in a number of plays of mine. He was in *So Long At the Fair* and *Home Free!* and . . .

HARRIOTT: Speaking of outrageous, *Home Free!* is pretty outrageous.

WILSON: But those are so early. You know, I go back and look at those and say, "Oh, my God, why aren't I outrageous anymore!" I thought I was going to be more outrageous with the professor [in *Angels Fall*] but he's so civil. He's just so socially acceptable. Even if he is flipping out. I have to get a little more unacceptable. Good Lord, if we were happy with ourselves, what would we do?

HARRIOTT: You wouldn't be an artist.

WILSON: No. Well, we wouldn't be able to do the next one. We'd just rest on the old laurel.

HARRIOTT: Is *The Mound Builders* your favorite?

WILSON: Yeah. *The Mound Builders* is my favorite, *Serenading Louie* is Marshall's favorite. *The Mound Builders* is just damn old deeper than anything I've done. It also does what I intended to do. As I said, I started out to write something and finished it and said, "By God, I wrote that. I really did do that." There are things in *Mound Builders* that I didn't know. They say things I didn't know until I wrote them. I don't know where they came from. And there are fun technical things in *The Mound Builders* that I just jump up and down about, that are invisible to an audience. There's one section where—I say the play is about work—within a page, a scene has been going on and another scene has been going on and then they all come back through the room, and within a page everyone's work has been mentioned. August goes off to raise money with the kid—he's going to meet some bank president. "Just tell him we'll name it the First Bank of Carbondale Village, that might do it." He goes off to raise money. Dan goes back out to the dig, Cynthia starts to go back out to the dig, and has this cutting conversation, the only one, with the gynecologist, Jean. She's saying, "Get back to your own work and stop doing his," and Jean says something like, "Well, it didn't bother you"—Cynthia has her photographic equipment all around—"you're still working." And Cynthia says, "Yeah, I have several thousand pictures of Kirsten" or something like that. She implies that she had intended to be a photographer, I mean, to be an artist. And Jean says, "Had you thought about a photographic career?" and Cynthia says, "No, no, forget I ever mentioned it." Anyway, in that tangle of people going through, the work of every single person on stage is mentioned, bang, bang, bang, bang, bang—like that [knocking table], and I had been leading up to it for 15 minutes, to get them all into that position. Well, I just jumped up and down. It's just this ganglia of the theme of the underbelly of the play. Would anyone notice that? Of course not. But what a thrill that was to get that in.

HARRIOTT: People don't write about work, do they?

WILSON: Well, certainly not why we work. I do it a whole lot.

HARRIOTT: I remember reading an essay by George Orwell, saying that Dickens wrote a lot about working classes but he never wrote about what they did. He never really wrote about the working.

WILSON: Interesting. My very first thought, of course, was *Our Mutual Friend* that begins with the man and his daughter collecting bodies off the Thames, which is what they do. That's their work. And sell them to the hospital for experimentation.

HARRIOTT: In both *The Mound Builders* and *Serenading Louie,* for some reason, which you say are your favorites...

WILSON: I like *5th of July,* I like *Hot l.* I think they're very entertaining and important in saying things I'd always wanted to do. But those are the two best. Both commercially unsuccessful.

HARRIOTT: Were they? I'm thinking about the bull mask and the godking mask in those two plays.

WILSON: Interesting. Hadn't thought of it. Only two times I've used masks. That cow mask that he thinks is a bull mask is very scary. And nothing like that flashlight flashing on him when he turns around like this, and has that gold mask on. He's in shorts, has on very little. It's very scary. All that is very scary.

HARRIOTT: *That's* a thriller.

WILSON: Oh, that's a thriller. But that's what the other one would end up like, and that's not what I had in mind at all. That's what I mean when I say I map out a thriller, and then it'll end up being another *Mound Builders* and everyone will say, "I thought he was going to write a thriller." That's not a thriller the way anyone understands thrillers. It would be a thriller for me.

The plots of many are just as banal—I'm thinking of the Huxley book. What's the name of it—*The Genius and the Goddess* or *The Genius and the Showgirl? The Genius and the Goddess*, I guess. Bo-ring! Stupid little story. With that accident out on the...? Oh, give me a break! Talk about ridiculous coincidence. The same people who would write an essay on *The Great Gatsby* and take it terribly seriously would dismiss *Angels Fall* completely, because I had used the same format that William Inge used for *Bus Stop*.

HARRIOTT: You mean the idea of people clustering together?

WILSON: Caught in a trap like a rat, yes. It's funny. When I realized the kind of play *Angels Fall* was, I said, "Oh, shit, I hate that kind of play. Oh, I don't like that sort of thing—trapped in a trap like a rat. God, I hate that sort of thing."

HARRIOTT: It's a classic device though.

WILSON: Yeah, of course it is. You know, it's *The Tempest*. Shipwrecked on an island. And a dozen other shipwrecked plays. But do they bring those up? No. They say *Petrified Forest*—you know, where you're at gunpoint—*Petrified Forest* and *Bus Stop*. Anyway.... Of course it is. I don't really mind it. I say, "Oh Lord, it falls into a category," and you don't really like to do anything that you know is going to fall into a category. But you can't worry about that. You have to rise above it. I mean, you're writing about the characters and the world we live in, and if the peg falls into that particular hole in one aspect, you just have to be damn sure that you write as honestly and as uncomplicatedly as you can. And to say, "Well, that's not a bad hole to fall in."

HARRIOTT: Do you mind when they compare you to Tennessee Williams?

WILSON: Well, I grew up loving Tennessee Williams and I worked with him a couple of times and I liked him. You know, if they liked Tennessee Williams better, I wouldn't mind them comparing me to him. But they hate Tennessee Williams, so why should.... Oh, they hate everything he did in the last fifteen years since *Night of the Iguana*. Do I mind? I don't like being compared to things, because it's a way of dismissing something. As soon as you can say, "Oh, that's like something," then you don't have to look into what it is. It's like something else. Therefore, everyone else has already analyzed all of this, so everything that they say applies to this. Bullshit! It doesn't at all. It's very different.

HARRIOTT: It's a way of getting a handle on things, like stereotyping.

WILSON: Yeah, like stereotyping. It's grabbing a handle, grabbing a quick handle and dismissing it for that. I'm not at all like Tennessee Williams. I'm very different from him. I think we both are concerned about theme and language and time. But I don't think I write any more like

Tennessee Williams than I write like Dickens or James Saunders or Faulkner or Fitzgerald or any of those.

HARRIOTT: Are your characters based on specific people?

WILSON: Sometimes it's people I've seen, then I've seen someone else that's very like that, and the second time reinforces and finally it imprints it. Like the professor, and like Gloria in *Gingham Dog*. And any number of people for Matt Friedman [in *Talley's Folly*]. He's made up of about six very specific, different people.

HARRIOTT: Speaking of stereotypes, when I started to read your plays I thought, "He must be a Southern writer. He tells stories."

WILSON: And there are people who say I don't know how to tell a story. Every time I write something there's one reviewer who says, "Oh God, I wish Lanford Wilson would collaborate with someone who could write a good play, because his characters and dialogue and sense of place are always better than anyone could touch. But he doesn't know how to write a play." I'm incapable of writing the sort of play that he wants.

HARRIOTT: What *does* he want?

WILSON: Tight action. This happens and then that happens. What they're really asking for and don't know how to say it, is what E.M. Forster said you have to have in a novel. This happened and then that happened. They want event, event, event, event, event. In some of the collage plays I do that. I hope I still have the ability to do that, because I'd like to do an event play again. It would be interesting to see how I could get event, event, event with a deep character development. I'd like to do a picaresque play again too. I haven't done that in a while.

New York City
December 1982

David Mamet:
Comedies of Bad Manners

Comedies of Bad Manners

MY INTRODUCTION to the plays of David Mamet was the 1977 Off Broadway production of *A Life in the Theatre*. It had been highly praised by the critics, who alluded to such themes as the evanescence of the theater and of life, illusion and reality, rites of passage, and Oedipal struggle. I wondered what they were seeing that I wasn't: it seemed like the emperor's new clothes to me. A few years later when I saw and enjoyed a modest college production of the play, I realized that my negative reaction to the New York production had been the result of having approached it, thanks to the critics (and to Ellis Rabb's portentous interpretation as director and principal actor), as Serious Drama. Seen on its own terms, *A Life in the Theatre* is an engaging play.

Those terms are modest. The structure is a series of conversations between two actors in a repertory theater, interspersed with scenes that they perform for an unseen audience. The thread of plot traces the course of the relationship between Robert, an aging actor on his way out, and John, a young actor on his way up. It is a superficially presented relationship, occasionally touching because its premise is touching. But it is primarily a device to connect the 26 short scenes or "bits" into a play and, rather than suggesting themes like the evanescence of the theater, it suggests a nightclub routine with John as Robert's straight man. This is not intended to be pejorative: Mamet is a talented, frequently inspired writer of comic scenes, whose theatrical antecedents are not Beckett and Pinter, as some critics have suggested, but Mike Nichols and Elaine May. Like them and like other parodists at the Second City cabaret of the Goodman Theater (where Mamet worked as a busboy when he was growing up in Chicago), he observes American manners through American speech. His structures and plots are minimal, his characters broadly sketched types. In *A Life in the Theatre*, for example, not only do the actors perform old chestnuts of the theater, they *are* old chestnuts of the theater: Robert, the old-fashioned ham declaiming grandiloquent platitudes, and John, the cool, monosyllabic Method actor. The life in Mamet's theater is in its language, in the funny-pathetic dialogues that capture the American idiom. But it was as if the critics, properly impressed by his talent, and hungry for substance in a theater largely filled with trivia, wanted Mamet to be the great American playwright. By the time they reviewed *A Life in the Theatre*, his fourth play in New York, they looked at an engaging spoof and found timeless themes. Mamet chimed in with them, telling a *New York Times* interviewer that *A Life in the Theatre* was about "aspects of artistic consciousness."[1] Robert's analysis of his script could be a parody of the search for profundities in Mamet's plays:

Robert: ...Salt. Saltwater. Eh? The thought. He lets you see the thought here.
> *(Pause.)*

John: Mmm.
> *(Pause.)*

Robert: Salt! Sweat. His life flows out. *(Pause.)* The *salt*water! Eh?
John: Yes.
Robert: To the *sea.*
John: Yes.

> . . .

John: "It's gotta rain."
Robert: The motif, eh, the leitmotif. He takes the descant through the scene.... "It's got to rain." You look at it, he does the same thing through the play.
> *(Pause.)*

John: Mmm.
Robert: "Kid, we haven't got a chance in hell." *(Pause. Musing.)* "We haven't got a chance in hell. We're never getting out of this alive." *(Pause.)* Eh? He tells us that the sea is life, and then we're never getting out of it alive. *(Pause.)* Eh?
John: Yes.
Robert: The man could write...[2]

Robert's fatuous musings lead into the actors' performance of the script, a parody of that theatrical staple, the lifeboat melodrama. It is great fun, but if expectations have been raised for a penetrating exploration of human relationships and weighty themes—or aspects of artistic consciousness—it's like being promised *Hedda Gabler* and being given *Mary Hartman, Mary Hartman.* The genre, more than the worth of the play, has been misrepresented.

Critical hyperbole is a disservice to the audience, to the play, and, above all, to the playwright. It is hard to imagine that Mamet, who was then only in his twenties, could have been totally unaffected by criticism that was pointing to profound meaning in his work. It may have influenced him to turn away from the funny vignettes that he did so well and to attempt a more serious kind of drama, resulting in the strained writing found in *The Woods* and, in part, in *Edmond.* Then the critical response became as exaggerated in its scorn as it had been in its praise.

A less secure young playwright might have lost his direction, but from an early age Mamet seems to have been singlemindedly determined to succeed in the theater. As a teenager he worked both at the Goodman Theater and at a neighborhood playhouse. In spite of his father's urgings to study law, he chose to study drama at Goddard College in Vermont. After graduation in 1969 and a few months as an actor on the straw hat circuit, he applied for a short-term teaching position at Marlboro College in

Vermont. One of the requirements was to have written a play that could be staged by the students. Mamet listed a nonexistent play on his application and, after he was hired, wrote one. When the teaching position ended, he returned to Chicago for a few months, working at odd jobs until he found a post as drama instructor and playwright-in-residence at Goddard. There he wrote plays and organized his best acting students into an ensemble group, the St. Nicholas Company, to perform them. When he went back to Chicago, he arranged to have two of the plays, *The Duck Variations* and *Sexual Perversity in Chicago*, produced in experimental theaters. In 1974 *Sexual Perversity* won the Joseph Jefferson Award for the best new play in Chicago, and Mamet and three friends founded the St. Nicholas Players, named after his Vermont ensemble company and devoted to the same repertory—Mamet and the classics. At the same time, he was sending plays to producers in New York. In 1975 *The Duck Variations* and *Sexual Perversity in Chicago* were produced in a showcase theater Off Off Broadway, and in 1976 at the Off Broadway Cherry Lane Theater. The double bill ran for 273 performances, and Mamet's career was launched.

Mamet's personal life has been closely connected to the theater too: in 1977 he married actress Lindsay Crouse, a member of one of America's most distinguished theatrical families. That year he was invited to teach at Yale and the following year he was named associate artistic director and playwright-in-residence at the Goodman Theater in Chicago. (In an interview in the *New York Times*, Mamet said that he was "trying to force myself to relax.")[3] The rest of his success story in the theater has included winning Obie awards for *Sexual Perversity in Chicago*, *American Buffalo*, and *Edmond*, a Drama Critics Circle Award for *American Buffalo*, and the 1984 Pulitzer Prize for *Glengarry Glen Ross*. Mamet has had three plays produced on Broadway, over a dozen plays Off Broadway (including their premieres at the Goodman Theater), and two London productions. Two of his one-act plays were chosen to re-open the Vivian Beaumont Theater at Lincoln Center in 1986.

Mamet's first play, *Lakeboat* (inexplicably never produced until the Milwaukee Repertory Company unearthed it in 1979, nine years after he wrote it for Marlboro College), is one of his best, announcing all of his characteristics at their strongest: the unerring ear for the American vernacular and the ability to shape it into dialogue; the minimal structure of conversations broken into short scenes; the striking aural impact and the negligible visual one; the abundant use of obscenities; and the energy of the writing.

The play celebrates the rite of passage of Dale Katzman, a college student with a summer job on a merchant ship out of Chicago. It is a parody of the classic shipboard mise-en-scène of the youth-into-manhood ritual:

instead of adventure on the high seas, the *T. Harrison* offers bureaucracy on the Great Lakes. Nothing happens. But in this play it doesn't feel like a deficiency of invention. It's part of what the playwright is saying about life on a Great Lakes merchant ship and perhaps about the drabness of working men's lives in general. Mamet establishes the contrast between the legend and the reality at the start, when Dale's intoning of romantic clichés about the ship ("The floating home of 45 men. . . . A small world. . . . A steel bulk-freight turbine steamer registered in the Iron Ore Trade") is juxtaposed with a crushingly mundane exchange about razor blades.[4]

As a playwright primarily concerned with language, Mamet uses these circumstances to advantage. Because the men's lives are devoid of event, they do nothing but talk, and since nothing of interest has happened in years, their memories, like those of the old, are more vivid than the present. "Collucci lost two fingers in the winch," one of the sailors tells Dale with urgency. When? "This was a couple, four–five years" (*L* 100). Their musings, fantasies, and anecdotes are divided into scenes that are like movements of a musical piece. It is not a labored device, nor necessarily a conscious one, but it gives the otherwise structureless play a formal shape based entirely on the subjects, styles, and rhythms of speech. It is language as language that provides the interest: the drunken rhapsody on the delights of drink, the tall tale (appropriately for this floating factory, the sailors spin yarns about monsters of industry—Cadillacs and Buicks—rather than of the deep), the overheated imaginings about what has befallen a mate who has not returned from shore leave. The comedy isn't in funny lines that can be excerpted, but in the men's unintentionally funny verbal constructions: for example, Fred's use of trendy euphemisms (he calls the Mafia "a very property-oriented group") or Stan's drunken repetitions ("I know my alcohol, boyo. I know it and you know I know it. And I know it.") (*L* 58, 30).

Even in this relatively calm play there are the frequent outbursts of obscenity that have become a Mamet signature, but they are appropriate for these men as a release from their boredom and as a mask for their feelings of powerlessness. Fred's tale of sexual prowess is in the tradition of Lenny Bruce, both in scatological shock and in being truthfully and offensively funny. The truthfulness is in its assaults on phony genteelisms (in this case, the high school prom) that camouflage basic or even brutal drives; the offensiveness is in its misogynistic view of sex, a view held by most of Mamet's male characters (and most of his characters *are* male).

Mamet's next play, *The Duck Variations*, is another series of movements based on sound, as the word "variations" suggests. Its form is spare—two old Jewish men sit on a park bench and talk about the ducks in the park—but the talk is sufficiently amusing and touching to make this tiny structure into a satisfying play. When they discuss the ducks, they are discussing their own lives, but Mamet avoids heavyhanded anthropomorphizing. George's speculations on the pattern of succession among ducks—the "lead duck" dies and another one takes its place, becoming the new "lead duck"—and its theme of mortality and continuity of the species is a potentially sentimental subject for two old men, but Emil rescues it by his summation, "It's boring just to think about it."[5] The abrupt comment that punctures flights of rhetoric is one of Mamet's effective comic devices.

There are shades of the nightclub routine, particularly in the Fifth Variation, which sounds at times like the Mel Brooks–Carl Reiner invention, "The 2000-year-old Man":

> *George:* ...They're finding ducks with lung cancer. I was reading about this hunter in the forest and he shot a bunch of ducks that were laying down...
> *Emil:* Yes.
> *George:* And he missed. *But!* as he was walking away he heard this hacking, and he went back to investigate. And there were these five or six stunted ducks sitting in a clearing hacking their guts out.
> *Emil:* No!
> *George:* And he says instead of running off they all came up and huddled around his feet with these rheumy, runny eyes. Looking quite pathetic. And he says he couldn't get it out of his mind...
> *Emil:* What?
> *George:* I'll feel silly to say it.
> *Emil:* Tell me.
> *George:* That they looked like they were trying to bum a smoke.
> *Emil:* ...That's ridiculous.
> *George:* I know it.
> *Emil:* I think someone is putting you on.
> *George:* Very likely.
> *Emil:* You aren't even *supposed* to smoke in a forest.
> *George:* Go fight City Hall [*DV* 72, 73].

This is a comic routine for the sake of comic routine. The Eighth Variation says more about the two men. Emil contrasts his city living ("Joyless. Cold concrete. Apartment. Stuff. Linoleum. Imitation.") with an idealized picture of life in the country (*DV* 77). What is of interest here is the delight that the old men take in language. Beginning his discourse on rural abundance with the cliché "Enough to feed the nations of the world," Emil warms to the subject:

> *Emil:* Enough to gorge the countless cows of South America.
> *George:* Did you make that up?

Emil: Yes.
George: I take my hat off to you.
Emil: Thank you.
George: "Feed the many"—how does it go?
Emil: Um. Stuff the nameless—it'll come to me.
George: When you get it, tell me (*DV* 77, 79).

The forgetfulness supplies a couple of funny lines, but it is not just a joke: it reminds us of their senescence.

If *The Duck Variations* is a tender duet, its companion piece, *Sexual Perversity in Chicago*, is a brutal quadrille, a parody of the mating dance, performed by four characters. There is a tiny plot—boy meets girl, girl moves in with boy, girl moves out. There is no romance, though: sexual perversity is sex with love withheld.

Danny and Deborah are the young couple. The other two characters are Bernie, Danny's office buddy, and Joan, Deborah's roommate, each of whom regards the friend's new lover with the hatred of an abandoned spouse towards a rival. Bernie is the kind of obnoxious loudmouth that people would try to avoid in real life but, through Mamet's language, he becomes the colorful center of the play. For all his flamboyant extroversion, it's obvious that he is miserable: his heartiness is too exaggerated. Like so many of Mamet's male characters, Bernie is always exploding into obscene, misogynist torrents. Yet underneath the raunchy anecdotes and sexual obsessiveness is a Puritan trying to be hip. He is bewildered and frightened by the continuous barrage of sex and sexual expectations in contemporary life, and he shows a fear of female sexuality that is shared by many men. Their opposition to the E.R.A. might be expressed more politely than in Bernie's diatribe, but it would come from the same determination not to augment women's sexual power with legal power:

> Equal rights amendment? Equal rights amendment? I'll give you the fucking Equal Rights Amendment. Nobody ever wrote *me* no fucking amendments. Special *interest* groups, okay—but who's kidding who here, huh? (*Pause.*) We got baby seals dying in Alaska and we're writing amendments for broads? I mean, I'm a big fan of *society*—but this bites the big one. I'm sorry.[6]

Joan, like Bernie, is a voice of sexual distaste, telling Deborah that: "of course, there exists the very real possibility that the whole thing is nothing other than a mistake of *rather* large magnitude, and that it never *was* supposed to work out" (*SPC* 37). This view is consistent with the sexual anger that is in all of Mamet's plays (although, like everything else, it is more powerfully and colorfully expressed by his male characters; so far, Mamet's acute ear has not been tuned in to women). It is a serious issue for him: you feel the emotional intensity.

The vignettes in *Sexual Perversity* are even shorter than in *Lakeboat* or *The Duck Variations*. Some scenes consist of only a few snatches of conversation, others of one speech. The fragmented effect echoes the discontinuity of the characters' lives as they jump from bed to bed in the familiar modern pattern of alternately seeking and fleeing relationships. And the language of Bernie's sleazy bravado, Joan's sad wisecracks, and Danny's and Deborah's irritable intimacies creates not only a biting comedy, but a convincing contemporary sensibility. The last vignette is of Bernie and Danny at the beach, ogling women, being aroused, and hating the women for arousing them. It is a suitable ending for this play about sexual desire and sexual fear.

American Buffalo, Mamet's third play to be produced in New York, was taken more seriously than its two predecessors by the critics, perhaps because it looked more like a real play. Instead of loosely connected short scenes there were two linear acts, a plot of sorts (a junk shop owner, his errand boy, and his crony plan the heist of a collection of American buffalo nickels), and a central metaphor: the expansive past of this country gone the way of the American buffalo, contrasted with the constricted junk shop of contemporary American society. Yet there is a much greater sense of movement in his earlier plays, because their lack of action is compensated for by the vitality and humor of their language. There are occasional flashes of that humor in *American Buffalo*, as in this definition of free enterprise, expressed by Teach, a petty hood who likes to theorize:

> *Teach*: You know what is free enterprise?
> *Don*: No. What?
> *Teach*: The freedom . . .
> *Don*: . . . yeah?
> *Teach*: Of the *Individual* . . .
> *Don*: . . . yeah?
> *Teach*: To Embark on Any Fucking Course that he sees fit.
> *Don*: Uh huh . . .
> *Teach*: In order to secure his honest chance to make a profit. Am I so out of line on this?
> *Don*: No.
> *Teach*: Does this make me a Commie?
> *Don*: No.
> *Teach*: The country's *founded* on this, Don. You know this.
>   . . .
> Without this we're just savage shitheads in the wilderness.
> *Don*: Yeah.
> *Teach*: Sitting around some vicious campfire . . .[7]

Embroidered with Teach's flourishes of political clichés and malapropisms, it is nonetheless a statement of uncomfortable truth. Teach's excesses of rage can be funny, too ("The only way to teach these people is to kill them," he fumes.), and his explosions of obscenity are convincing as the disproportionate violence of macho impotence (*AB* 11). But finally they become repetitive and unrelieved, as do the banalities of the two sidekicks. The three men are not only unpleasant to listen to, but boring. Missing here are the comic sensibility and verbal music of the earlier plays.

Most critics praised the play. Martin Gottfried in the *New York Post* was reminded of *Waiting for Godot*, perhaps because two characters wait for a third who never arrives.[8] But a crucial difference between *American Buffalo* and *Waiting for Godot* is that we care deeply about Beckett's characters. They are not simply the slow-witted inhabitants of a seamy world: in their vulgarities they convey the playfulness and the ache of the sad clown. Above all, there is the difference in the language. In *Godot* it seems natural to the characters, yet it is poetic and suggestive of layers of meaning. In *American Buffalo* the language is flat, but self-conscious — you are always noticing what Mamet has done with the syntax — and neither the banalities nor the pauses suggest, as Beckett's do, a subtext that resonates.

Ross Wetzsteon in *The Village Voice* praised the play's language at length, calling it "at once idiosyncratic and universal," but went on to say that it was more than language that made the play a work of art: it was "the relationship between money and business and violence."[9] The academic critics took up the theme of the play's indictment of capitalism. Robert Storey wrote in *The Hollins Critic* that *American Buffalo* "harks back to two American Enlightenments, one conferred by Reason, the other by the frontier."[10] John Ditsky wrote in *Kansas Quarterly* that "the barb in all of this, the hump in the buffalo (as it were) is the direct correlation between dishonest enterprise and American rugged individualism."[11] Jack V. Barbera pointed out in *Modern Drama* that "Mamet got the idea of an identical ethical perversity existing at both ends of the urban economic spectrum from Thorstein Veblen." (A footnote acknowledged a letter to him from Mamet, referring to Veblen as his source.) And so, Barbera advised, "in considering the relation between Veblen's thought and *American Buffalo*, one should start with Veblen's *Theory of the Leisure Class*."[12]

Harold Clurman, reviewing *American Buffalo* in *The Nation*, cautioned against the dangers of hyperbole ("Mr. Puff"), noting that "David Mamet is a talented young American writer. He is not yet a complete dramatist, but may become one."[13] But the critics continued to look for deeper meanings. Their reviews of Mamet's next full-length play, *The Water Engine*, were even more baffling in their seriousness. Originally written for radio, *The Water*

Engine is a campy version of a 1930s radio melodrama, with the stock figures of that genre: the brilliant inventor and his devoted spinster sister, two greasy lawyers connected to the Mob, the hard-boiled newspaperman and his girl Friday, the kindly proprietor of the candy store and his good little son who will grow up to be a great scientist. The plot seems deliberately corny, too. The inventor refuses to give his invention, an engine that runs on distilled water, to the Mob, so they rub him out. But before they do, he mails his plans to the storekeeper's good little son, to carry on the work when he grows up.

The stage adaptation of the radio play put a radio studio on stage, and the actors played some scenes "on mike," as in a radio play, and the rest "off mike," as in a stage play. This divided the original play in two, with one part deliberately artificial—the actors reading into microphones, the sound effects man interrupting the action, and so on. Interwoven throughout are snippets of overheard conversation (and Mamet is a playful and accurate overhearer); a voice-over, comic in its doomsday sonorities, exhorting participation in a chain letter and warning of the terrible consequences of refusal; a Communist street orator; and the announcer of The Century of Progress Exposition, the 1934 World's Fair in Chicago. But while there are levels of stage business, there aren't levels of meaning. It is a radio adventure for kids or a cabaret sketch. Nonetheless, many critics found in it mythic content and social commentary—greed in America, past innocence seen through present cynicism, and so on. The inventor's death at the hands of the Mob inspired Richard Eder of the *New York Times* to write seriously that, "We want to see Lang prevail, and when he doesn't the tragedy seems considerable."[14] T.E. Kalem's unfavorable review in *Time* magazine emphasized his moral objections: "Mamet, 30, who was unborn at the time he writes about, does not realize that resilience, fortitude and fellow feeling were the sustaining forces for the Depression years. It was the teenagers of the '30s who forged, fought and won the U.S. victory of World War II. For the flabby, self-centered, alienated lot that Mamet has assembled in his radio studio, that formidable deed would have been a manifest impossibility."[15] This denunciation implied the seriousness of *The Water Engine*. It was as though the critics could not allow Mamet simply to write an agreeable little spoof.

The reviews of *The Woods*, Mamet's next play to be produced in New York, changed abruptly in tone. Richard Eder of the *New York Times* had said, after seeing the Chicago production of the play in 1978, that Mamet "has never written better," and had suggested that "if this process of intensification and refining continues—he might just possibly become our first true verse dramatist."[16] But a year later he reversed his opinion. In his review of the New York production, Eder wrote rather defensively that "It is a disconcerting critical experience to see a play that had looked wonderful in a first production look so poorly in a second one."[17] Edith Oliver in *The New Yorker*[18] and Michael Feingold in *The Village Voice*[19] suggested sympathetically that the play may have been spoiled by a poor production. Mamet agreed, and staged a second production of it in 1982. This time the critical reception was worse.

Like *Sexual Perversity in Chicago*, *The Woods* is a play about sexual alienation, but it has none of the earlier play's quirky ribaldry and no comic character like Bernie to liven things up: just two colorless young people on a failed—and extremely boring—romantic outing in the woods. The paradox is that out of the collection of comic bits in *Sexual Perversity* there emerges an accurate picture of contemporary sexual mores, while out of the two full acts, sustained dialogue, and careful structure of conflict, climax, and denouement in *The Woods* emerges nothing more than an encounter with no resonances beyond its slight occasion. Worse, when Mamet turns from comic to serious, his ear turns to tin. The dialogue, a good deal of it written in stanza form, is not poetic but stilted; for example, "It will be wet but we will not be getting wet" (as a more typical Mamet character might say, "This is American speech?"), or this:[20]

> Nick: We do not know what goes on.
> Ruth: I know we do not.
> . . .
> Nick: All we have are insights.
> (Pause.)
> Who *knows* what's real?
> Ruth: Yes.
> Nick: They exist all independent of our efforts to explain them.
> Everything does. (Pause.) We cannot know it. (Pause.) [TW 27].

While it is true that this could be a sendup of philosophizing—it has some of the vacuous quality of Robert's reflections in *A Life in the Theatre*—it is not funny enough, and it goes on at too great a length throughout the play for us to be sure. Compare it to the philosophizing of the two old men in *The Duck Variations*, where the reductio ad absurdum of their platitudes leads to this kind of amusing exchange:

> Emil: . . . Everything has got a purpose.
> George: True.
> Emil: Every blessed thing.
> George: Oh yes.
> Emil: That lives has got a purpose.

70

George: Ducks...
George: Yeah.
Emil: We don't sweat for nothing, you know.
George: I know it.
Emil: Everything that lives must sweat.
George: It's all got a purpose.
Emil: It's all got a rhyme *and* a reason.
George: The purpose of sweat is, in itself, not clear.
Emil: Yes...
George: But ... There it is.
Emil: A purpose and a reason. Even those we, at this time, do not clearly understand [*DV* 68].

In *The Woods* Ruth is given to the following kind of speech. The question is: to what end? It is neither lyrical nor necessary to the action nor, God knows, interesting:

> Drip drip. Rain comes down, drip. It makes rings. It makes these circles.
> *Ripples.* Plop. A fish comes up. Fishes come up. They make the same ripples from underneath [*TW* 50; typography Mamet's].

We feel sorry for the hapless Ruth, towards whom Nick, feeling trapped by her importuning him for "commitment," turns mean, then violent, finally attempting to rape her. But it's hard not to agree with him when, after endless passages of these observations of Ruth's, he turns to her and says, "Will you shut up one second, please? You talk too much, Ruth" (*TW* 63). Nick is no foil for Ruth, though. For example, Mamet has Ruth say these lines:

> The gulls fly. Caw Caw Caw. And Winter comes and they go somewhere else. Do they go somewhere else when Winter comes? [*TW* 83].

Nick could answer in a way that would cause her to question some purpose beyond its apparent inanity. But all he says is, "I don't know" (*TW* 83). Ruth is presented as blithering, Nick as brutal. Why then should we care about them? Later in the play, when Nick decides that he doesn't want Ruth to leave after all, he matches her vacuousness in his recollection of childhood days at the cabin in the woods:

> And many times we'd come up with a friend. With friends. We'd ask them here. *(Pause.)* Because we wanted to be with them. *(Pause.)* Because ... *(Pause.)* Wait. Because we loved them [*TW* 101].

There are some vapid conversations between Deborah and Danny in *Sexual Perversity in Chicago* (though never so silly as these), but they are surrounded by the hilarious dialogues between Bernie and Joan, Bernie and

Danny. When Joan pontificates, Mamet makes it broad enough so that there is no question about the comic intent, which is to expose the pretentiousness and incoherence of a certain kind of contemporary pseudo-philosophizing:

> Joan: . . .It's a puzzle. Our efforts at coming to grips with ourselves . . . in an attempt to become "more human" (which, in itself, is an interesting concept). It has to do with an increased ability to recognize *clues* . . . and the control of energy in a form of *lust* . . . and *desire*. . . . (And also in the form of hope.) But a *finite* puzzle. Whose true solution lies, perhaps, in transcending the rules themselves . . . *(Pause.)* and pounding the fucking pieces into places where they DO NOT FIT AT ALL. *(Pause.)* . . . Some things persist. *(Pause.)* "Loss" is always possible. . . [*SPC* 29, 30].

Mamet is a serious writer with a comic voice. *The Woods* demonstrates what happens when he abandons that voice: the life of the characters and of their speech is eliminated, and as a paradoxical consequence, so is any possibility of taking the play seriously. When Mamet tries to be serious, he is only solemn.

By the time Mamet's next play, *Edmond*, was reviewed in the fall of 1982, there were no equivocations about faulty productions. The critics who didn't like the play savaged it, none more than Frank Rich and Walter Kerr of the *New York Times*. Rich criticized its language (Mamet gone tone-deaf), its characterizations (everyone sounds alike), its social message (fortune cookie-deep). Worst of all, he found it boring, apocalyptic vision and all. "If Mr. Mamet [has his] way," he wrote, "the world is not going to end with a bang but a long nap."[21] Kerr did not bother to discuss the play in critical terms. He simply gave a tongue-in-cheek outline of Edmond's descent into urban hell, beginning: "[Edmond's] wife remarks that the maid seems to have broken their antique lamp and he remarks that he is leaving her for good because 'I can't live this life.' Inasmuch as the only thing we know about their life together is that the maid has broken the lamp, he is apparently unable to continue living a life in which the maid breaks lamps all the time, and off he goes into the wilds of New York City. It's a jungle out there."[22]

There is a lot in the play that leaves itself open to this kind of ridicule. But where Kerr's review, and to a lesser extent Rich's, was misleading was in discussing *Edmond* as a realistic drama instead of a surreal one. It is Mamet's vision of New York, or of urban life, as nightmare, and it is not just a theatrical conceit: you feel his urgency. That may be the source of the play's power. There is so little sense of personal pressure in the theater today that when you find it, even in a play as flawed and awkward as *Edmond*, you are stirred by it.

The story is primitive, serving primarily as the occasion for a hallucinatory projection of scenes of urban terror. Edmond, a middle-aged, middle-class New Yorker, leaves his wife and home and plunges into a carnival of horrors, most revolving around sex and money. Finally, he picks up a waitress and, after making love to her, kills her in an outburst of rage that has escalated into near-madness. At the end of the play, Edmond is in jail, charged with murder.

The most serious problem in *Edmond* is that Mamet does not make clear what he feels—or what we should feel—for his protagonist. When Edmond is active, he seems psychopathic; when he is contemplative, he seems soft-headed. He is an exemplar of the psychopathology in everyday urban life, but he is not a character with whom we can become involved. Once again, it is during the "serious" parts, when Edmond reflects on the human condition, that the play falters. The stilted cadences of his ruminations contrast with the buoyant language of his encounters in the city's lower depths. The obscenity is jarring, but not gratuitous: like Lenny Bruce, Mamet makes his serious points about American society through funny, dirty talk and through confronting taboos. When Edmond is held up by a black mugger, it is the realization of a white middle-class urban dweller's nightmare; and when his fear and fury unleash a litany of racial epithets, our empathetic reaction to his emotions suggests that we are empathetic to his epithets, too. The implication that we are all racists is more unsettling than the violence.

Another uncomfortable, powerful scene is between Edmond and his black cellmate. Here, Edmond's habit of vacuous philosophizing is used to advantage. As he holds forth, the cellmate hears him out, apparently with sympathetic understanding. Then just when Edmond reaches his big epiphany—that every fear hides a wish, and that in jail he feels at peace for the first time—the cellmate pulls the rug out from under him by saying, "Now you know what? . . . I think you should just get on my body . . . now."[23] Edmond's preceding windy musings contrast with the laconic brutality of the cellmate's demand and make it more shocking.

Mamet also uses Edmond's incoherent stammerings to advantage. When the chaplain asks him why he killed the waitress, Edmond answers:

I . . . *(Pause.)*
I . . . *(Pause.)*
I don't . . .
I . . .
I don't . . . *(Pause.)*
I . . . *(Pause.)*

I don't... *(Pause.)*
I don't... *(Pause.)*
I don't think... *(Pause.)*
I... *(Pause.)* (E 97).

This halting speech creates a surprisingly affecting moment in the theater:
I think it is because Mamet has grasped the rhythms of inarticulate speech.
Edmond's inability to express his agony becomes part of his agony. It adds
to the nightmarish feeling, too—when you open your mouth to say the
words that will save you, and you are unable to speak.

The play ends with the two men, now friends and perhaps lovers, lying
on the their bunks, conversing gently with each other. (The tableau suggests critic Leslie Fiedler's observation that the passionate center of
American literature is the homoerotic bonding between two men of
different race. Edmond and his cellmate on their bunkbeds are Huck and
Jim in a society gone berserk.) What they say in this closing dialogue is not
interesting; what *is* interesting are the abrupt rhythms of their counter-
pointed sentences that create a peculiarly urban music.

Glengarry Glen Ross, Mamet's next full-length play[24] has all of the intensity of *Edmond* and none of its lapses into clumsy earnestness. Here
Mamet has resumed his comic voice to examine his serious subject. That
subject is salesmen: not decent, inept little men struggling for human dig-
nity, like Arthur Miller's Willy Loman, but crooks who sell worthless tracts
of land (with toney names, like Glengarry Glen Ross, that vaguely suggest
pastoral stability) to the gullible. They are embodiments of the free enterprise credo voiced by Teach in *American Buffalo*, with profit as their goal
and whatever will secure it, their means. Everything else, including friendship, is expendable. They cheat each other as readily as they cheat their
customers.

And yet they excite our pity. They are so desperate in their venality,
so powerless in their grandiose schemes. These aging men have no security
or peace; their only future is the next sale. Mamet portrays them without
sentimentality, but with affection. Their daily Darwinian rigors produce a
street verve that is exhilarating to them and to us. The one unsympathetic
character is Williamson, the office manager, not only because he is the
coldly vicious tool of the boss we never see, but also because he is the only
one of the men who doesn't live by his wits. Williamson is of the "world of
clock watchers, bureaucrats, officeholders ... there's no adventure *to* it,"
while the salesmen, for whom each day is a fresh exercise in survival, are
of "a world of men ... the members of a dying breed."[25]

Act I is Mamet at his best, using the structure of funny-pathetic vignettes that he used in his other strong plays—*Lakeboat, The Duck Variations,*

Sexual Perversity in Chicago. It is composed of three dialogues set in a Chinese restaurant, each of them a combination of performance, dissembling, and confrontation: the elements of a sales pitch. In the first, Levene, an aging salesman on a losing streak, tries to cajole, bluff, shame, and finally bribe Williamson into giving him some of the "leads," the office's coveted listings of likely prospects. Levene is like a hyperactive boxer, verbally sparring, jabbing, thrusting, and dancing around his opponent, who remains impassive until the end, then demolishes the old salesman with one verbal blow. In the second dialogue, Moss, a dyspeptic bully, speculates with Aaronow, his timid colleague (for whom the word "wimp" was invented) on how they could avenge themselves on their exploitative employers by stealing the leads to sell to a competitor. Moss is reminiscent of Teach, not only in his quixotic projects and volcanic temper, but in his penchant for casuistry. "I mean are you actually *talking* about this, or are we just..." Aaronow asks anxiously, as he realizes that Moss may have serious plans. "No, we're just ... *speaking* about it," Moss replies, making a nice distinction between fantasy and felony through his choice of verb (GGR 39). In the third dialogue, Roma, a greasily beguiling con artist, softens up a stranger for a sale by delivering a pseudo-philosophical discourse that is as mesmerizing as it is meaningless. It's the apotheosis of flimflam.

The second act takes place the following morning. All the characters converge on the real estate office which, having been ransacked the night before for the leads, is now under investigation by a detective. It is a lively, noisy free-for-all, a bravura chorus after the first act's intense duets. The consequences of the previous night's encounters in the restaurant are resolved in this act but, as usual, the real interest is in the language. Levene, who has finally made a sale earlier that morning (which turns out to be to deadbeats who make fake bids for sport), retells it verbatim as though it were a drama he had written. Roma swindles his customer and betrays his associate with equal brio; his morals are unconscionable but his linguistic energy is irresistible. In *Glengarry Glen Ross*, where manhood is defined by "closing the sale," an activity that depends on words, the hero is verbally virtuosic Roma, and Williamson, the monosyllabic manager, is the villain.

Out of the most unlikely material—a group of shady, middle-aged real estate salesmen talking about their work—Mamet simultaneously entertains and horrifies. He gives a sense of the daily lives of these men as they scramble to survive in a pitilessly competitive world and, in so doing, he leaves us (as he failed to do in *American Buffalo*) with a powerful indictment of American free enterprise.

The characters in Mamet's plays express their muddled ideas in uncompleted sentences and sputtered obscenities, decorate their language with ornate malapropisms, pronounce their platitudes with the triumph of fresh discovery. The desperation of their lives is echoed and intensified in their desperation to be understood. Part of their suffering comes from the state of their language, and Mamet is writing about the state of that language, in that language. It is an interesting paradox: to compose a spoken art form about the failure of speech.

Mamet is rich and famous now and can ignore the critics. But in an interview with *The Wall Street Journal* in 1982, he spoke bitterly about them,* calling them "thought police."[26] He was talking about their effect on audiences' minds, but perhaps he meant on his mind, too. Who knows which was more potentially destructive: the critics' premature praise or the abuse that followed when Mamet failed their specific expectations? A talented young playwright doesn't need instant canonization: he needs time and room to nurture his talent. He must find his own direction before everyone else tells him where he has been and where he is headed.

As he did in his interview with me in 1984, which follows.

Interview with David Mamet

Although David Mamet immediately agreed (through his agent) to my request for an interview, it took a year and a half to accomplish it. During that time he was busy with projects in Western Canada or Hollywood or Vermont, or London for the rehearsals and premiere of Glengarry Glen Ross *at the National Theatre, or Chicago for the play's American premiere, or New York preparing for its Broadway production. After* Glengarry Glen Ross *won the 1984 Pulitzer Prize, Mamet's life became even more hectic and everyone was after him for an interview. We kept arranging tentative dates that then had to be cancelled. His agent suggested to him that it might be kinder to simply refuse.*

Finally, when it turned out that he and I would both be in London in late August 1984, he suggested that we do the interview there, thinking he'd be relatively free. He was not, of course, but we did meet for an hour and a half at the Atheneum Hotel, where he and his wife and little daughter were staying, and conducted the interview over tea in the lounge. Mamet, who is short, compact, and boyish-looking, seemed rushed, although whenever I offered to end the session, he assured me he had the time. His manner was a combination of nervous energy, impatience with the kinds of questions I asked, and a desire to be helpful.

ESTHER HARRIOTT: Have things changed for you since you won the Pulitzer Prize for *Glengarry Glen Ross*?

DAVID MAMET: No, not really. I've been writing for a long time.

HARRIOTT: Are you very much affected by what critics say? You've had your share of adulation and then some of the critics gave you a rough time with *Edmond*, unreasonably, I thought. I just wondered which is more damaging—excessive praise or excessive...

MAMET: It's just words, you know. It's just words. One way to look at it is that the theater is a study in stoicism. You might not feel like training yourself to discount lavish, undue praise or vicious, undue criticism. But nonetheless, if you recognize that's the correct path, you have to live in a world where you can do such a thing, and endeavor to train yourself to discount them.

David Mamet

HARRIOTT: When you say it's a study in stoicism, do you include other things, such as the difficulties of getting the play produced?

MAMET: Of course. It's all a study in stoicism. What it finally comes down to is that it doesn't matter what I feel. I have to abide by my first principles, and those first principles should be very, very few and very, very simple. And to learn to live according to those principles takes a long, long time. It takes forever.

HARRIOTT: Are you talking about first principles in living or first principles in the theater?

MAMET: It's the same thing. It's really difficult to practice your craft two hours a day or three hours a day, and try to become an excellent human being, and to live like a doodoo-head, you know, for the remainder of the day. It doesn't conduce to those two hours being happy.

HARRIOTT: What are your first principles?

MAMET: Well, I think the idea is, as Stanislavski said, the theater is the place we go to hear the truth. The task of the theatrical worker is to bring to the stage the life of the soul. Reasoning from there to technical principles and to esthetic principles, the play is the study of one single action on the part of the protagonist, and everything which contributes to that action must of necessity be included, and everything which does not contribute to that action must of necessity be excluded. Those are a couple of real simple principles.

HARRIOTT: So that some wonderful lines, for example, must be excluded if they don't...

MAMET: Well, they can't be wonderful in general, you know. They can only be wonderful to the point that they're going to put forward the play. If they don't put forward the play, however "wonderful" they are, and the more "wonderful" they are, the more they impede the play.

HARRIOTT: Are there certain themes that you're trying to get across in your plays?

MAMET: Well, one is drawn to certain things, you know. A fellow goes to a party and his eye is drawn by a certain type of girl. It doesn't do any good to point out that there are other women there perhaps equally or more attractive. His predilections are not subject to his own intellectual recall or understanding. There's something much deeper. And it's the same thing in playwriting. The things which one is drawn to write about don't stem from intellectual prejudice or even affection, but rather from something much deeper.

HARRIOTT: I'm interested in some of the things that you're drawn to, because they're not directly out of your own background, are they? I know you worked in a real estate office, but the real estate salesmen in *Glengarry*

Glen Ross are examples of the kind of people whom you feel a particular interest in, and compassion for. They're the same people in a way as the people in *Lakeboat.*

MAMET: Right. What they are is the lumpen proletariat. Sure. America's increasingly becoming a corporate society, a bureaucratic society, a rigidly stratified and very, very unhappy society. And those people who are involved in the aboveboard aspects of that society are uninteresting to me.

HARRIOTT: I must tell you that during the intermission of the English production of *Glengarry Glen Ross* I heard an American woman say, "He certainly has a good ear for street language." An English woman next to her said, "Do Americans really speak that way in the street?" and the American woman thought for a minute, then said thoughtfully, "Yes." (Laughs) I don't know if the language as you present it is *accurate,* but it sounds *true.*

MAMET: If it *sounds* true, it *is* true. I mean, would it increase your enjoyment if I told you that I actually grew up in a house where they sold real estate, or would it decrease your enjoyment if I told you that I had never been in a real estate office in my life?

HARRIOTT: No, not at all. That wasn't what I was getting at. What I was getting at was that when I say it sounds "true" I don't know if that's your imagined, and authentically imagined, idea of how those kinds of people talk, or if that's something you've listened to very keenly.

MAMET: See, the important thing is that it's a play. The important thing in a play is that it be internally consistent, because finally there's no such thing as objective truth. If you really look at people who are called realistic writers over the course of 50, 60 years of American dramaturgy, retrospectively they don't seem so very realistic. What they do seem is *true.* What they do seem is dramatically and internally consistent. When one is writing for the theater, what one is writing finally is dramatic prose or dramatic poetry, that is to say, language which is so direct that the actual rhythm of the line carries the intention of the speaker. That, in any given time, to someone who is not very, very well trained in dramatic analysis and analysis of their own perception, is going to be characterized as real or true, much like O'Neill was, or much like Odets was or much like Inge was. Retrospectively you say, well it's really not that—quote—realistic. What it is, is dramatically correct. Right? Just like at the introduction of perspective, people said, "My God, that's so real." Well, it's still a painting. It still takes place in two dimensions. It's just one more technique.

HARRIOTT: Does it irritate you when people talk about your uncanny ear for American speech?

MAMET: Well, the truth is I do have an uncanny ear for American speech, and it's certainly served me in good stead and saved me from the ravages of many professions in which I might not be as happy as the one in which I find myself. There's also nothing I can do about it.

HARRIOTT: Is it just that you have this uncanny ear or do you also dissect the language? It seems to me that you use certain constructions that I would never have thought of as being parts of speech, and then when I heard them, sort of laughed with recognition. Do you analyze...

MAMET: I just make it up. I just absolutely make it up as I go along. It's just a gift. You don't have to have a gift for dialogue to write plays, as Mr. O'Neill proved conclusively.

HARRIOTT: You don't?

MAMET: You don't, no. I mean, if you think about it, we read great plays in wretched translations and the plays still work.

HARRIOTT: Like Ibsen.

MAMET: We read wretched translations of Ibsen. Terrible. And we read translations of Chekhov. And as good as they are, how could they ever be as good as Chekhov?

HARRIOTT: Then what is it?

MAMET: What it is, is that the actions of the characters are so irresistible, that we are won over by the action—which is what the play is. The play is nothing other than the action of the protagonist, what the protagonist wants. As Mr. Aristotle so aptly demonstrated in the *Poetics*, that's it, period. Obviously it's not going to hurt to have dialogue which is by its very rhythm, its very sound, going to help the protagonist to achieve his end and therefore help the audience to understand. But you *can* do without it.

HARRIOTT: I'm interested when you talk about Ibsen in translation or Chekhov in translation because, yes, there *is* something more than language, and language in itself isn't going to do it. But a play after all does depend on the dialogue.

MAMET: Yes, but obviously that which demonstrates it is the fact that drama can be translated and work. Obviously the things which you said in the one language are not said in the other language. The connotations, the overtones, the associations which the language has are by no means the same, the rhythm of it is completely different. Yet the play succeeds anyway.

HARRIOTT: Sometimes when your characters are especially inarticulate, I'm aware of the rhythm. I think the most noticeable instance for me is that scene when the chaplain asks Edmond why he killed the girl and Edmond answers with a series of I's and pauses. It is very affecting, and I think it's because you've grasped the rhythms of inarticulate speech.

MAMET: Well, that's the trick. The other thing is the speech is not inarticulate.

HARRIOTT: It's not?

MAMET: No. None of it's inarticulate.

HARRIOTT: Maybe that's the wrong word.

MAMET: It's definitely the wrong word, because the idea is that the intention of the character is expressly conveyed to you. You understand exactly what the character is saying. So how can it be inarticulate?

HARRIOTT: Yes, but I also feel that the characters have difficulty in making each other understand what they're saying. When Edmond talks to his cellmate and holds forth at length, and the guy seems to be sympathetically listening to him, and then says something very threatening, I thought that was an example of Edmond's words finally being useless.

MAMET: Yes, but the two things are very, very different—the words being unavailing on the one hand, and the words being inarticulate on the other hand. Don't you think?

HARRIOTT: I'm not sure I understand that distinction.

MAMET: He was perfectly articulate. He was capable of using words to express exactly what he wanted them to say, which is being articulate. Now, the other fellow didn't agree with his point of view and so didn't accept it. He put a different value on the speech than Edmond did, but the words were never inarticulate. You can't have a drama with inarticulate people in it.

HARRIOTT: So that you consider really all the characters articulate?

MAMET: Of course. I mean, that's the essence of drama. The character is only going to say that which puts forward his or her objective. They're only going to say those things which at that moment, to the best of their ability, help them to achieve their end.

HARRIOTT: How is Aaronow [in *Glengarry Glen Ross*] articulate?

MAMET: He's looking for help the best way he knows how. That's why his character is so precisely understandable. It's why the character of Aaronow wins people over immediately, because they recognize exactly what he's doing.

HARRIOTT: That's the people in the audience.

MAMET: Yeah. The people on the stage recognize what he's doing, too. They just don't have any time for him.

HARRIOTT: What keeps you in the theater? You could have a successful and easier time of it, presumably, writing for the screen.

MAMET: Well, I do have a successful time of it writing for the screen. Easier, I don't know.

HARRIOTT: I mean, you could say, "To hell with the theater."

MAMET: Yes, but why?

HARRIOTT: Because it's an obstacle course.

MAMET: Well, that's what I do. There's a joke that Herbie Gardner tells about himself. His agent said, "Why don't you write this television show." Herb Gardner said, "I don't want to write this television show." His agent said, "Just write this and you'll never have to write another word."

HARRIOTT: (Laughs) But, you know, a lot of playwrights do stop after one or two plays. It *isn't* so unusual.

MAMET: And a lot don't. It depends on what your objective is. Anyone who went into the theater as a playwright to make a lot of money probably didn't make a lot of money and certainly didn't have a good time.

HARRIOTT: I don't think anyone would go into the theater for that reason, would they?

MAMET: Well, some people do. I just never took a view of life as involving a great chain of being, that one tried to jump from the theater to the movies, and from the movies to politics, and from politics to . . .

HARRIOTT: I don't mean that. I just think it's so difficult that . . .

MAMET: Writing plays?

HARRIOTT: The whole thing, as you were talking about it.

MAMET: Sometimes it's difficult and sometimes it's not difficult. Are you married?

HARRIOTT: I was.

MAMET: Well, you know, sometimes it's difficult and sometimes it's not difficult. Somebody said of marriage that it's intermittently bearable. Sometimes the theater is like that. But trading doesn't get you anything, just like in marriage, you know—to fly to troubles that we know not of. You're going to encounter the same troubles. You encounter the same troubles in the movie business as you do in the theater.

HARRIOTT: Will *Lakeboat* ever be produced in New York? I love that play.

MAMET: Thank you. I hope so. I have another play called *Prairie de Chien*, which should make a real nice companion piece and it's never been done on the stage. I kind of hope that someday it might be done in New York.

HARRIOTT: Aren't you in the position now, if you want to, to just *say*, "I want to"?

MAMET: If they were going to be done on Broadway, I'd have to be in the position to say to somebody, "Why don't you give me three quarters of a million dollars?" It also takes a lot of time to mount a play, to work during the rehearsal period, and work with the actors, and worry about it, and blah, blah, blah. Those are old plays. There are a lot of things I would rather be doing. I kind of hope they will be done eventually. All of this stuff will be done eventually again. It's not the prime thing on my list.

HARRIOTT: What's the prime thing on your list? The next play?

MAMET: Writing, yeah. They called me up from the National [the National Theatre in London] — Bill Bryden — and he said, "Well, we have a slot for you in October of '85." I said, "Yeah, but I don't have a play." He said, "Yeah, but we have a slot, and it's easier to write a play then to get a slot." So I'll probably finish one of the many things in my trunk.

HARRIOTT: Is *Glengarry* the first play you've had produced in England?

MAMET: No, *American Buffalo* was done in England with great success. A couple of my other plays were done for shorter runs. *A Life in the Theatre* had a little run here and *Reunion* had a little run here, and a couple of other ones. But *Buffalo* was a big success. That was a long time ago, six years ago.

HARRIOTT: And it's on right now.

MAMET: That's a different production. The production right now is with Al Pacino. That's a Broadway production.

HARRIOTT: Do you notice any difference in the way your plays are received here, and is it easier to do something at the National Theatre than at a commercial theater at home?

MAMET: Well, it's easier because I have a very good relationship with them, for which I'm very, very grateful. They view the theater over here, at least in my personal experience, as art instead of entertainment, so that's kind of nice. That's kind of what I think, so it makes *me* comfy. And they seem to like my stuff, which is nice.

HARRIOTT: Do they view it as art rather than entertainment because theater here is treated as a cultural institution and not as a business enterprise?

MAMET: Well, it's treated as a business enterprise over here, too. It's just a tradition that they have about doing the theater as art. They inherit the tradition of Shakespeare and Congreve and Sheridan, all of these turkeys, over here. Over there we inherit the tradition of George M. Cohan. Today's New York theater comes out of a completely different tradition.

HARRIOTT: Out of the tradition of vaudeville?

MAMET: It comes out of the tradition of popular entertainment, right? It doesn't come out of the tradition of dramatic art.

HARRIOTT: And it doesn't come out of the tradition of language, as it does in England.

MAMET: That's right. There's nothing wrong with the tradition of entertainment, it's just different.

HARRIOTT: I wouldn't have thought that *Glengarry Glen Ross* would have been so enthusiastically received here because...

MAMET: I wouldn't either. (Laughs)

HARRIOTT: I thought, the first time I saw it, that it was such an

American play. But I guess it transcends that. It seems to be very understandable to the English audience.

MAMET: Well, I was pleasantly shocked.

HARRIOTT: What was Pinter's connection with the play?

MAMET: He was instrumental in getting it done over here.

HARRIOTT: I thought of your use of profanity when I read an interview of Pinter in *The Paris Review* series *Writers at Work*. He said in it that he thought obscenity was a wonderful, dark, secret language that should be used very sparingly. I don't know if he still feels that way—this was a while ago—but I thought it was interesting that he happened to make a point of saying that in the interview. He's an admirer of your work, and yet you certainly don't use obscenity sparingly.

MAMET: You know, you gotta write what you gotta write. People said to Rouault, "Why do you put those black lines around people's heads?" He said, "I don't know. It drives me nuts, too." As Gypsy Rose Lee said, you know, "You can't tease everybody."

HARRIOTT: It's interesting how that language has become more accepted. In Brendan Gill's review of the first production he saw of *American Buffalo*, he found the language distasteful. In his review of the most recent production he said that the language had started to sound lyrical to him.

MAMET: Yeah. I guess the play improved, huh?

HARRIOTT: (Laughs) O.K. When you have so many misogynistic men in your plays, are you trying to show a certain kind of attitude towards women?

MAMET: I'm not trying to show anything, I'm just writing a play. But if you look around the United States of America you will see that we do have a certain amount of misogynistic men. For example, all of them. So there you are.

HARRIOTT: No exceptions?

MAMET: Oh, sure. A couple of exceptions.

HARRIOTT: You say you just write the play, you write what you have to write. Is one of the things that you don't have to write or haven't had to write, with a couple of exceptions so far, a play with important women's roles?

MAMET: I've written plays with important women's roles.

HARRIOTT: *The Woods* and *Reunion*. But I think of your plays as plays about men.

MAMET: Well, I happen to be a man. Claire Booth Luce wrote a wonderful play about women, which I couldn't write, not being a woman.

HARRIOTT: I'm not asking that as any kind of challenge.

MAMET: See, there's no answer to it. We live in a very litigious society.

84

Everyone thinks that things can be legislated. There are a lot of organizations which want to have groups to help women writers. Well, that's nonsense, as far as I'm concerned, because someone is either a writer or they aren't. And being supported—I speak from experience of having tried to teach playwriting at Yale—being supported by an organization that says, because of some aspect of your physical or psychological or ethnic background we are going to jump you a step up the ladder and support you as an artist, this is an incredibly destructive thing to do. It's not helpful to anybody, because it saddles them with the unfortunate burden of feeling they have to produce, without having instilled them with the fortunate, beneficent guidance of the muses. So what they are, is fucked. You can't have an organization which says, "For women playwrights, to promote women playwrights." You can't promote playwrights. If someone needs to write a play, they'll write the damn play, and if they don't absolutely need to write the play, nothing, including a pat on the back, is going to make writing that play easy enough for them to induce them to sit down and write the play.

HARRIOTT: But can they help them to get the written play produced?

MAMET: Yes, but not because of a law, but because the play's any good. Right? Traditionally, women have not been playwrights. Well, there may be many reasons for this. George Orwell says that women have not been chefs, not because they can't cook as well as men, because obviously both sexes can cook equally well, but because the women couldn't stand—weren't brought up to stand—the strain of dealing with 500 people in a kitchen in a major hotel. Now, perhaps that's going to change, and the woman who wasn't brought up to stand the strain in 1920, obviously a woman may be better suited to standing that strain in 1990. And maybe the same is true of women as playwrights—that they weren't traditionally brought up in the theater, and perhaps now that the times are changing and they *are* brought up in the theater, we'll have better women playwrights and more women playwrights, just as a matter of course. But legislating it into existence ain't gonna help. We're just going to have more bad plays.

HARRIOTT: Do you think that kind of legislating goes on with black playwrights too, or do you think that's a whole different question?

MAMET: I do think it's a whole different question. I don't know why I think that, but I do think that.

HARRIOTT: In *Edmond* were you trying to get the audience to identify with Edmond?

MAMET: I'm never trying to get the audience to identify with anything. I'm not trying to show anybody anything, I'm not trying to convince anybody of anything. I'm just writing the play. That's all I'm doing. The play has rules of its own. I'm trying to get the play right. You paint a picture, you try to get the picture right. Any attempt to do anything beyond that is not drama, it's not art. It's advertising. It's trying to use the technique of art to influence the behavior of somebody else. That's what advertising is. It's not art.

HARRIOTT: Or it's agitprop.

MAMET: Sure. That's not art, either. It's like actors will say, "What about doing commercials?" My wife had a great—we teach a lot—she had a great answer. She said, "Do commercials if you want, but you're not an actor any more. What you are is a salesman." Using the technique of acting to induce somebody to buy something is salesmanship, it's not acting.

HARRIOTT: So it's between you and the paper?

MAMET: Exactly.

HARRIOTT: Are you a workaholic?

MAMET: Sometimes yes, sometimes no.

HARRIOTT: That means that when you're working you work very hard?

MAMET: Well, if someone is paying me, for example, to do something by a certain date, I'll work very, very hard to give it to him or to her.

HARRIOTT: I was thinking of all the things that you're involved in, such as running the school, for example.

MAMET: That's just six weeks in summertime. There's a lot of things I'm involved in. I'm having a good time, that's the important thing.

HARRIOTT: I read one time that your favorite writers are Willa Cather and Theodore Dreiser. Is that right?

MAMET: Yeah, they're a couple of them.

HARRIOTT: Is that because their regional background is the same as yours?

MAMET: I like the way they write. They seem to be very American. They seem to have something to say to *me*. They both do a lot of writing in and about Chicago.

HARRIOTT: Dreiser also writes people actually working, which is something that you do.

MAMET: Right.

HARRIOTT: How has being Jewish affected your playwriting, or has it? I don't think I would have asked that question had I not read that short article by John Lahr in the National Theatre program. You're quoted as saying that one of the things that went on in your family was obliteration of distinctions, such as being Jewish.

MAMET: Well, I'm sure it has affected it. I'm not quite sure how—in some way, certainly.

HARRIOTT: Maybe in the speech patterns.

MAMET: The speech patterns, certainly. And also, why do black people become basketball players? Because they're genetically better at basketball than white people? No. It's because of a racial tradition, of models to a certain extent.

HARRIOTT: Are dramatists in the Jewish tradition?

MAMET: Sure. In the United States you go back to comedians more than dramatists, but people involved in the theater—directors, certainly. Racially the tradition of being quick-witted and silver-tongued and rooting and tooting, as it were, was one which was held up to me as a Jewish kid, or which I held up to myself. You grew up watching television all the time—who were the great people on television? Jack Benny, Phil Silvers, Milton Berle, later on Mort Sahl, Nichols and May.

HARRIOTT: What about Lenny Bruce?

MAMET: Lenny Bruce, certainly.

HARRIOTT: Did he do some of the things you do, which is to be funny and shocking, but really a moralist?

MAMET: He was just a comedian.

HARRIOTT: I always thought that he was very serious about exposing the barbarisms under the gentility.

MAMET: That's what made him a *great* comedian, I think. He was just a comedian. He didn't wanna be no moralist.

HARRIOTT: But what you want to be and what comes out is not necessarily the same thing, either.

MAMET: Indeed. Indeed it isn't. So all those people were Jewish, and I'm Jewish, so there you are. I guess perhaps to some extent they were my heroes.

HARRIOTT: Could you talk a little bit about the genesis of a play? Although it seems that you answer most of these questions as though your writing is just instinctive—it's your art, and I'm trying to atomize it too much.

MAMET: Do you cook?

HARRIOTT: Yeah.

MAMET: Did you ever have a special friend over for dinner?

HARRIOTT: Yeah.

MAMET: Do you say to yourself, "What am I going to make them?"

HARRIOTT: Yeah.

MAMET: An idea comes into your head?

HARRIOTT: It's like that?

MAMET: Of course. How could it be any different? You say, "Where do you get your ideas?" You think of them.

David Mamet

HARRIOTT: That's not the same thing.

MAMET: Of course it is.

HARRIOTT: I'm using somebody else's recipes.

MAMET: That's not the point. The point is where do you get the idea? Your question was where does the idea come from for the genesis of the play? Where does the idea come from for the genesis of the meal? You very simply think of it. It comes into your head, who knows why.

HARRIOTT: I guess what I meant was, might the kernel be from a certain line of speech or might it be a certain image...

MAMET: It could be anything, just like the idea for the dinner could be anything. It could be sparked by memory, it could be sparked by something that you read, it could be sparked by an old recollection of something you'd always wanted to cook. It might have an association with a flower that you smelled in the lobby that made you think of.... Who the hell knows why? It's really not important. It's just an idea.

HARRIOTT: Do you have any trouble summoning up these ideas, or are they always there?

MAMET: They're always there, just like they are in you, just like they are in anybody. Everybody's thinking all the time.

HARRIOTT: There *is* such a thing as writer's block.

MAMET: Sure.

HARRIOTT: You haven't struggled with that?

MAMET: Sure. Everybody struggles with it a little bit. The purpose of technique is to get you past your own conscious inhibitions, to free your accessibility to the unconscious mind.

HARRIOTT: When you're writing a play do you read it aloud?

MAMET: I just write it. I just write it down.

HARRIOTT: You just hear it in your inner ear.

MAMET: Mm hmm.

HARRIOTT: Do you think that your career has been a lot easier because you've written your plays expressly for the Goodman Theater?

MAMET: Yeah, I had my own theater company for a number of years, then I worked with the Goodman. I think it's been happier working with people that I know all the time. I don't know if it's been easier or not—probably it has—but it's most certainly been happier.

HARRIOTT: Broadway is a whole other thing because of the enormous financing.

MAMET: Sure. And you have to work with a whole different kind of people.

HARRIOTT: More entrepreneurial?

MAMET: Yeah, that's their business. It's their turf.

HARRIOTT: What was your route to playwriting? You started before you graduated from college.

MAMET: I think I started playwriting actually when I was in my last year at college. I just started writing, that's all. I just sat down and started. People say, you know, if you devote all your leisure time to something, you'll soon become expert at it. It's an old saw. I don't know if I've become expert at it, but I've become good at it. I did devote all my leisure time to it for a number of years.

HARRIOTT: How much time do you devote to it when you're working? Is that something that you do, say, half a day, or isn't it that neat a pattern?

MAMET: I devote some time to it sometimes. It depends on the nature of what I'm working on and the point in its evolution. It depends on a lot of things.

HARRIOTT: You leave more up to the director than a lot of playwrights do, don't you? You're very explicit about how things should sound but you leave the appearance of the play up to the director.

MAMET: Well, one leaves it up to the director anyway. No matter how much stage direction you're going to write, the director and the actors are going to... You know, Tolstoy said, "You can't carry out an order which is incapable of being carried out." It doesn't do any good to give it.

HARRIOTT: Is that why you don't?

MAMET: Well, also because it's not the playwright's job to give stage directions. You're doing something wrong if you're writing a lot of stage directions, because what's happening should be crystal clear from the dialogue. That's the playwright's job – to write dialogue, period. A good play should be able to be done on the radio just like that.

HARRIOTT: I'm thinking, for example, of how Sam Shepard always says what color lighting he wants or exactly what the characters should be wearing.

MAMET: So what? Does it make any difference to the audience? Can it possibly make a difference to the audience? It makes a difference to Sam Shepard. There's nothing wrong with that.

HARRIOTT: I think it could make a difference not to the audience but to the director.

MAMET: Yeah, but the important thing is not the director but the audience, so why write the stage directions which aren't going to help the audience? Authors write to help the audience, to make the dialogue crystal clear, to make the intentions crystal clear.

HARRIOTT: I'm thinking of a production of *A Life in the Theatre* that I saw, and the length of the scene breaks, which you leave up to the director, slowed down the pace.

David Mamet

MAMET: Yeah, they probably couldn't figure out how to switch scenes quick enough, because it's a very difficult play to stage. You see, people are going to take the play, they're going to pay me to do it, they're going to do it however they want. They've bought that right. It's not my responsibility to try to coerce or cajole them into doing it in a way that I think it should be done. I told them the way I think it should be done—I wrote it down. If somebody wants to license that right for an evening or for a week...

HARRIOTT: Oh, you *did* write that down?

MAMET: I wrote the dialogue. That's it. That's the way the play should be done. You know, if something's funny and somebody doesn't understand that from the way it's written, telling them about it is not going to help them. Did you ever have to explain a joke to somebody? They might have understood that it was funny, but they didn't laugh. So there you are.

HARRIOTT: You mentioned radio, which they take seriously in this country. Have you ever thought of having any of your plays done on radio here?

MAMET: Sure. I'm looking into it.

HARRIOTT: Getting back to the critics, have you ever felt totally misunderstood? I thought both Walter Kerr and Frank Rich were writing about *Edmond* as though it were intended to be absolutely realistic.

MAMET: Well, there are only a couple of good critics in the country that I know of, that is to say people who feel a responsibility as to the idea of theater. These are excellent men and women I'm talking about.

HARRIOTT: Who are they?

MAMET: There's Roger Downey in Seattle, there's Michael Feingold on *The Village Voice*, there's Richard Christiansen and Glenna Syse on *The Chicago Tribune* and *The Chicago Sun-Times*, and there are undoubtedly a couple more. There's a wonderful woman I read—I've forgotten her name—on some small paper called *The Alternate* or *The Advocate*, some *Nation* type of paper. There's Robert Brustein. There's maybe ten people throughout the country. There are probably more, but maybe ten I could name, who are excellent men and women. On the other hand, it's a debased profession. It's a profession of second-raters.

HARRIOTT: Why do you say that?

MAMET: Well, look at the people who it attracts. It attracts people who are failed at something.

HARRIOTT: Do you mean that drama criticism or criticism in general attracts the failed writer?

MAMET: Drama criticism is the only criticism I'm conversant with. It tends to attract the failed writer and the failed something—the failed teacher. As police work might attract people who have a great interest in order and in peace, it might also attract people who have a desire to exercise force over their fellow citizens. Just so with drama critics. Though it might attract people who are dedicated to the idea of purity in art, it might also attract people, as it does, who are dedicated to the idea of exercising censure over their betters. And those are most of the people who are drawn to and continue in theatrical criticism. Because it draws to it a lot of unhappy people. These people, given a certain amount of currency and, as they might feel because of that currency a certain amount of power, tend to become worse as the years go on. Because they *are* failed, because they are envious, because they are people who can't acknowledge the truth in themselves, the bad ones become more vituperative. For these reasons, and also because anyone who's not good at what they do, becomes angry at themselves over a period of time, *especially* when they're successful at it. So there you are.

HARRIOTT: *Especially* when they're successful at it?

MAMET: Of course. That's why many doctors are dope addicts. Right? It's a huge problem. That's because people do not have the power to alleviate sickness, to instill health, to save someone from pain. These people are very, very successful at their jobs, but they still don't have that power. Eventually their self-loathing gets manifested in some outward form. They seek to destroy themselves. That happens to movie stars. A lot. People who aren't happy being an actor are going to be incredibly unhappy being a movie star.

HARRIOTT: Are playwrights a happy profession?

MAMET: I don't know. Well, maybe I do know. Most of the playwrights I know, perhaps all of the playwrights I know, seem to be happy people.

HARRIOTT: In spite of the obstacles.

MAMET: Well, you know, everything has its price.

HARRIOTT: Just to turn things around a little bit, is there anything that especially interests you that you wish interviewers would ask you about, instead of the same old questions? You must also feel extremely interviewed.

MAMET: Well, it's my choice. One can always say no. I wish people wouldn't ask me questions to which there is no answer.

HARRIOTT: How do they know, when they're asking you?

MAMET: Well, one has to think a little bit, you know, as a human being.

HARRIOTT: Questions to which there's no answer, such as my question, "How do your plays start?"

MAMET: Yeah.

HARRIOTT: But, you see, some writers *do* have answers to that question.

MAMET: If you look at a painting by Mondrian and say, "What the hell is that?" and it says, "Still Life with Oranges," for someone untutored in art, such as myself, that's obviously going to increase my enjoyment a little bit, because I'm going to feel a little bit less lost. On the other hand, if I want to become an art critic, I would probably say to myself, "You know, Dave, you're really going to have to learn to look at these paintings without looking at the title." Right? There you have it.

HARRIOTT: Yeah, except that if the artist has chosen to give the painting a title, then he wants the viewer to consider that too, and that becomes part of his intention.

MAMET: That's an ancillary endeavor. It has nothing to do with the painting. It has something to do with what the artist is saying about the painting.

HARRIOTT: So that the analogy with the play...

MAMET: Is that the play stands by itself. Questions about the play perhaps might have a greater validity than questions about, in effect, "Tell me the secret name of the play that you've been withholding from me." The artist hasn't been withholding anything from the audience, one would hope, or certainly he or she doesn't wish to. The point is, given the form, to share everything with the audience, to let the stringency of the form conduce to greater communication between the audience and the playwright, not to leave something out which has to be told on the sly.

HARRIOTT: What do you mean when you say "stringency of the form"?

MAMET: The strictness of the dramatic form should conduce to a greater level of communication between the playwright and the audience, just like the stringency of the sonnet form should conduce to a greater communication between the writer and the reader. It causes the writer to be very precise.

HARRIOTT: So in a way you think that form is more conducive to making a play communicate itself than a novel, because the novel's form is not as strict as a play's or a sonnet's?

MAMET: It has different rules. The rules of drama are so strict that if both parties—the critic and the author—understand those rules, *that* should be the basis and the vocabulary for discussion, rather than for the critic or the audience to place themselves in the position of, in effect, a know-nothing, in the historical sense of the term, and saying, "Golly, I don't know. Let's both start from square one and talk about this," as if you had no experience of art and no background in esthetic reasoning, and "Let's speak about it with very, very imprecise terms."

HARRIOTT: In very impressionistic and subjective terms?

MAMET: Yeah. Most critics are wasting their time and the time of their own readership.

HARRIOTT: When you talk about strict rules, you mean very specific things, like Aristotelian unities.

MAMET: Of course.

HARRIOTT: What else do you mean?

MAMET: Well, that's basically it. That's what I teach in my class in the summertime. It's basically a class in theatrical esthetics. And that's it. One should understand the theory of true action as put forth by Aristotle and also put forth by Stanislavsky. The understanding of that is the essential understanding of drama. It is that which cannot be taken from the drama. There are, additionally, a lot of tricks, but what they are is tricks, as opposed to technique.

HARRIOTT: The theory of conflict, climax, and denouement doesn't apply in a lot of modern plays, does it?

MAMET: Well, it happens in modern plays. The whole Aristotelian theory, more importantly than based on *Oedipus*, is really based on the theory of human perception, that that's how we perceive a play. Therefore, *as* that's how we perceive a play, it would be nice if the play were structured in a way which were congruent to that perception. Because we're going to perceive it that way anyway. You understand, that's how most non-dramas of the sixties and seventies succeeded. The curtain goes up, 18 things happen, and in our mind we invent a connection between those things. And because they happen over a set period of time that we've been told is the theatrical experience, in our mind we search for and will supply an entanglement, a climax, a denouement, and a coda. We will supply those things whether or not they exist, because that's the way we perceive. So Aristotle is saying and Stanislavsky is saying, "As that's the way we perceive, why don't we write according to that order?"

HARRIOTT: Do you mean that's the order in which we perceive, having become accustomed to thinking that that's what we should expect, or because that's human perception?

MAMET: Of course it is. We connect things which we are told fall into the same frame, whether or not they are connected, even if they are completely random.

HARRIOTT: Yes, I understand that we look for a coherence, but I guess I don't understand that we necessarily look for a climax.

MAMET: That may be learned. As you say, that may be the learned aspect of our perception. Human beings are very suggestible. If we are told something is a dramatic event, we see it as a dramatic event. Whether or not it *is* a dramatic event, which is to say, whether or not it is the quest of a protagonist for a single goal, we perceive it as such if we're told it's a dramatic event.

HARRIOTT: Is the quest of a protagonist for a single goal what plays are really about?

MAMET: Sure.

HARRIOTT: A protagonist.

MAMET: Yes.

HARRIOTT: Who's the single protagonist in *Glengarry Glen Ross?*

MAMET: Well, *Glengarry Glen Ross*, in terms of traditional theater, is rather a new development. It gets down to the gang drama or the gang comedy, which we saw a lot of in the thirties. It's really a twentieth-century American invention, if you look at plays like *Men in White* or *Detective Story* or *The Front Page* or *The Women*. It's a play about a group of people who are laboring in a given set of circumstances that affects them all, and it's a play about how that circumstance affects them all in their interactions with each other. And what happens in these plays is that the protagonist is split into a number of different aspects, just as it happens in a dream. The protagonist is not now one protagonist, but a bunch of different aspects in search of the same goal.

HARRIOTT: Is Williamson [in *Glengarry*] the antagonist?

MAMET: I don't know who the antagonist is. I think perhaps it's him. Scene by scene, they become the antagonist to each other, as you see in the first act.

HARRIOTT: Yes. Except that from the audience's point of view, they're all sympathetic except Williamson.

MAMET: To take a psychoanalytic point of view for a second, this would help. I don't know if he's the antagonist, but he's definitely the superego. If you say that this is a play about a personality which has been split into various forms, Williamson stands for the superego. He stands for the character the protagonist has elected for itself to control its own actions, and therefore instill in itself the possibility of shame, guilt, remorse, rather than living in a world where one's actions are controlled by others.

HARRIOTT: Is there a character who's an id, then?

MAMET: Well, sure. Both Roma and. . . . They all stand for an aspect of the id at different times, when they're involved in the unfettered pursuit of pleasure, which is to a certain extent what they're all searching for, in this case the "leads" or the big sale.

HARRIOTT: Have you ever written theoretical articles?

MAMET: Millions of them.

HARRIOTT: Where have they been published?

MAMET: Oh, all over. *Dramatists Guild Quarterly*, *Horizon* magazine, newspapers in Chicago, *Oui* magazine, *Life* magazine. I wrote a wonderful article for *Life*. They hired me to write it, but it didn't run. It's about the movie *Iceman.* They didn't like the movie, so they didn't run the article. [Looks around room] I'm just looking around to see who's here. This place is the Polo Lounge of Europe, where all the American film people stay.

HARRIOTT: While I was waiting for you, I was marvelling at the contrast between this hotel and the one where I'm staying, which is typically English shabby-genteel.

MAMET: Right. That's why the film people stay here, because the English idea of gentility and luxury is, to Hollywood taste, a little bit strange.

HARRIOTT: Are you just vacationing in London, or are you here because of the play?

MAMET: I'm here to take a little vacation, look at the play, visit some people from France—Lindsay's going over to France tomorrow to talk some business, and they were over here talking some business with us—and that's about it.

HARRIOTT: What happens when you go back to the States?

MAMET: I've got to go to Las Vegas to write an article for *Esquire* magazine at the end of the month. I've got a few plays to finish up. I've got a translation that I have to finish up with Pierre LaVille, and I've got to work on my movie with Elaine May, and that's about it.

HARRIOTT: What's the movie about?

MAMET: We wrote a movie about a movie company that comes to a small town in Vermont, and about what happens.

HARRIOTT: Did you know her when she was in the Second City?

MAMET: No. She left the Second City before I was working there.

HARRIOTT: It's interesting that you got together now.

MAMET: I don't know if she ever was a member of the Second City. I think she was just a member of the Compass Players. She and Mike [Nichols] were members of the Compass Players. They were closely aligned with everybody at the Second City.

HARRIOTT: Were the Compass Players improvisatory too?

MAMET: The Compass Players were an improvisatory group that had also Shelly Berman in it, and that gave birth to the Playwrights Company, which did plays, and also to Second City, and everybody was very, very closely aligned to the same group. It centered around those guys—Del Close, Alan Arkin, Paul Sills, Bernie Sahlins, et cetera, but I don't know if Elaine and Mike were ever really part of Second City. I don't think so.

HARRIOTT: Is your article for *Esquire* magazine going to be on the theater?

MAMET: No, it's on a soldier of fortune show at the Sahara Hotel in Las Vegas.

HARRIOTT: So this is really a journalistic assignment. Why are you going to do it—just for fun?

MAMET: I do it a lot. It's one of the things I do. I review books for *The Chicago Tribune*, I write journalism, I write essays.

HARRIOTT: You must be awfully well-organized.

MAMET: I don't think I'm as well-organized so much as I like writing, and I'm really driven to work, and to make a living, and to work and produce.

HARRIOTT: You also seem to be a very responsible parent.

MAMET: I hope so. Do you have kids?

HARRIOTT: Yeah.

MAMET: There you are. It's the most important thing, isn't it?

HARRIOTT: Is that connected to your feeling about continuity that John Lahr quoted? I can't remember exactly how you worded it, but the idea was that you thought continuity was the most important value—which is sort of interesting, coming from an American.

MAMET: Well, I think it's important to have a happy kid. . . . John Lahr is an example of an excellent critic. An excellent writer, who happens to also write criticism.

HARRIOTT: Yes. He does have a bit of a political axe to grind sometimes.

MAMET: Nobody's pluperfect, you know. I think it's a shame Benedict Nightingale isn't going to work for the *Times* anymore. I kind of liked him. I think Mel Gussow is a good critic. I think that he should have been given the honcho spot a long time ago. They exist. Bill Collins on *The Philadelphia Inquirer*. There are a lot of people who really care. There are a lot of people who just don't care.

HARRIOTT: Do you think Frank Rich is a good critic?

MAMET: Frank Rich is a terrible critic. He's an unfortunate blot on the American theater and he should, as he eventually will do and I hope it will be soon, retire to lord it over unfortunate undergraduates at some college. He's a boy, he's an untutored boy who doesn't realize there's anything higher than his own perceptions. As Tolstoy said, "Mediocre men must of necessity have a mediocre idea of what constitutes greatness," and he was speaking of Mr. Rich when he wrote it.

HARRIOTT: Do you do a lot of reading?

MAMET: Sure. (Pause.)

HARRIOTT: Well, I hope that I didn't ask you a lot of questions that were pointless.

MAMET: Not at all. You asked what you wanted to know and I answered them as best as I could. I'm very glad that I had the opportunity to make some slight amend for my rampant incommunicado over the last year. It was very, very good of you to keep your good humor, and I'm sorry that I disappointed you so many times in the past, and I hope I've been of some help today.

HARRIOTT: You have been, and I'm grateful to you, especially since I know that everybody's sort of *after* you these days.

MAMET: My pleasure. It's always a pleasure to talk to somebody who's serious.

London
August 1984

Charles Fuller:
The Quest for Justice

The Quest for Justice

CHARLES FULLER is almost alone among contemporary American playwrights in focusing attention on social issues. The general tone of contemporary American drama and fiction has been narrowly introspective — the playwright holding the mirror up to himself instead of to society. But Fuller, in the tradition of black playwrights, takes the public role of the theater seriously. From the time of the Harlem Renaissance in the 1920s, black theater's first flourishing period, black writers have emphasized the theater's importance to the black struggle. Alain Locke, one of the principal theoreticians of the Harlem Renaissance, explained that blacks had to come to grips with the theater because "it was in this sphere that the image of the Negro has been most vilified."[1]

The American theater has been a source and a reinforcement of black stereotypes. The earliest image of the stage Negro derived from the minstrel show, a form appropriated by white players from the entertainments put on by slaves for their plantation masters. In 1828 a white man, Thomas Dartmouth ("Daddy") Rice, blackened his face and made a dance called the "Jim Crow" famous, and for the next hundred years white men in blackface caricatured black speech, black movement, and black gestures.[2] The figure with the rolling eyes, the ready grin, and the shuffling gait became an enduring icon in the gallery of stereotypes.

Other stereotypes were ingrained via the stage. The submissive Uncle Tom was transferred from Harriet Beecher Stowe's novel Uncle Tom's Cabin to the stage in 1852 and remained there for 80 years, with a production of the play regularly performed somewhere in the United States until 1932.[3] The stage progenitor for Uncle Tom's opposite self, the Brute, who hated white men and lusted after their women, was the rapist in Thomas Dixon's 1906 novel and play The Clansman, and its subsequent film adaptation, The Birth of a Nation. Another stereotype was the Exotic Primitive who appeared in plays from Eugene O'Neill's The Emperor Jones to Oscar Hammerstein's Carmen Jones, and whose life of unrestrained impulse, signified by jazz, sex, partying, and extravagant clothes, was equally attractive and reprehensible to Puritan America. Still another was the Noble Savage, whose characteristics critic Stark Young, America's greatest drama critic in the thirties and forties, described in patronizing fashion in his review of Marc Connelly's popular Broadway play The Green Pastures:

> We can thank Mr. Connelly for what [he] has done about the Negro. . . . It is high time we heard more of their fancy, humor and patience; their devotion, easy temper and rich sensuous gifts, their easy and imaginative love of life and their simple, natural goodness.[4]

Charles Fuller

A consistently stated objective in black critical writing about the theater has been to correct the distorted images of blacks and, in a world defined by whites, to find and assert a distinctive identity. Like Joyce's Stephen Dedalus, the black playwright has sought to forge the uncreated conscience of his race. This sense of mission has provided the opportunity to avoid the kind of trivialism that has diminished the contemporary white theater, but it has sometimes led to the sacrifice of art for polemic. In Fuller's case, a largeness of vision raises his drama above the level of political tract. At the same time that he writes about immediate social problems, he is concerned with universal themes: good and evil, the tension between social causation and individual responsibility, the role of the just man.

Fuller is a careful writer, and that is both his virtue and his limitation. He maps out his structure and language with precision and control. There is no sloppiness, but there is no transport either. One longs for excess or even a false move. There isn't a word out of place, but neither are there the imaginative leaps that might make his plays spring to more intense life. He has succeeded, however, in creating heroic protagonists. They have not withdrawn, like their alienated white counterparts, into nihilism or narcissistic despair. Even though his plays are about the anguish of racism in American life, they are hopeful. The hope is his heroes' belief in the possibility of making a difference.

Fuller is a product both of the radical activism of the Black Theater Movement of the 1960s and of the more moderate vision of the Negro Ensemble Company. The Movement demanded black plays in black theaters in black communities, but Douglas Turner Ward, the actor and director who founded the Negro Ensemble Company in 1967, argued that until the ghettoes were rebuilt, their theaters would be islands. He advocated establishing a theater Off Broadway that would emphasize black themes, "but also [be] resilient enough to incorporate world drama," that would address blacks as its "primary audience," but not to the exclusion of white audiences.[5] Although the Negro Ensemble Company was attacked at the start by black critics, particularly for its practice of including white playwrights in its repertory and white employees on its administrative and technical staff, Ward's approach has enabled the company to survive in a white-dominated society without abandoning its essential goals. Since its inception it has presented the works of a sizable number of talented black playwrights, the most prominent, at present, being Fuller.

Fuller was born in Philadelphia in 1939 and educated at Roman Catholic High School and Villanova Univeristy. His first professionally produced play was *The Perfect Party*, staged at the McCarter Theater in Princeton, New Jersey, in 1968, and at the Gate Theater in New York the following year. In 1970, supported by grants, Fuller gave up his job as a housing inspector in Philadelphia to write full-time, and his plays began to be produced at black theaters in New York. He first came to critical attention when the Negro Ensemble Company produced his work, beginning in 1974 with *In the Deepest Part of Sleep*, a domestic drama that received respectable if unexcited reviews. Fuller's next three plays, all presented at N.E.C., are larger in scope. The context of each is an aspect of racism: the institutionalized racism of the army in *The Brownsville Raid* (1976), the pathology of ghetto life in *Zooman and the Sign* (1980), and racism internalized as self-hatred in *A Soldier's Play* (1981).* *A Soldier's Play* was especially successful. It ran in New York for over a year, and Fuller became the second black playwright (the first was Charles Gordone in 1970) to win the Pulitzer Prize. Warner Bros. made it into a movie, *A Soldier's Story*, for which Fuller wrote the screenplay. He received a 1984 Academy Award nomination for it.

Like his predecessors, Fuller is concerned with correcting "the compendium of stereotypes," but rather than counter them with stereotypes of whites, as a number of black playwrights have done, he attempts to create new images of black men.[6] "Niggahs can't be heroes," says Zooman, the street kid in *Zooman and the Sign*, and that is the principal stereotype that Fuller refutes.[7] Each of his plays is about a hero with a quest for justice. It is an almost hopeless quest for a black man in a white society, but his protagonists are heroes precisely because of their dogged refusal to be deflected from their goals.

Sergeant-Major Mingo Saunders, a 50-year-old career soldier and Medal of Honor winner, is the hero of *The Brownsville Raid*. The town of Brownsville, Texas, has been shot up in a night raid, and two men have been killed. The black company is accused by the people of Brownsville of having done this in retaliation for the incidents of racial discrimination they suffered on their arrival from the North two weeks before. The company's white captain orders Mingo to find the guilty soldiers and to turn them in. When none are uncovered, the army sends a major, then a general, to investigate the matter further. Whether convinced that a conspiracy of silence is protecting the guilty, or simply determined to find a scapegoat to satisfy public opinion, the figures of command—all the way up to the president of the United States—demand punishment for the shooting.

The play is based on a historically documented incident that took place in 1906 and became a national issue, ultimately involving President Theodore Roosevelt. By coincidence, 1906 was the same year that the

---

Fuller gave me the scripts of these three plays, advising me that his earlier plays were not worthy of study.

Dreyfus affair was settled in France. But the Brownsville soldiers had no Zola to cry *j'accuse!,* and the case ended with the dishonorable discharge of the entire company. In Fuller's dramatization, Mingo's initial quest is to find out who is responsible for the raid, and he accrues his information with the singleminded passion typical of Fuller's heroes. It is not evidence that the army is after, however. It wants a culprit, and it will hold everyone in the black regiment responsible until one is found.

In an effective dramaturgical twist, Fuller introduces the figure of Private Holliman, a black soldier who, on the night of the raid, is seen by another soldier—and by the audience—sneaking into the barracks long after "lights out." Holliman is a disreputable gambler and loan shark to whom all the men are in debt, and whose shabby alibi, true or false, for being out of the barracks on the night of the raid, is that he is having an affair with the wife of the most uxorious of his fellow soldiers. His presence in the play shifts the focus from a straightforward illustration of white racism to the more complex matter of what constitutes justice.

Mingo's 26-year career is at stake. He could save it, and the careers of his men, by reporting Holliman's suspicious movements. The dilemma is whether it would be worse to sacrifice the whole company for one morally questionable soldier, or to report a rumor that would be seized on by the army as proof of Holliman's guilt. The men understandably want to name him in order to save the others. But Mingo's passionate insistence on justice means justice for Holliman as well. To turn him in would be to produce a scapegoat, an act that would echo the racism of the white power structure. The only honor left to Mingo now is to refuse collusion with the army in its betrayal of justice. He persuades his men to remain silent; the result is blanket discharge and disgrace. At the end of the play, Mingo is left with the integrity of his person and the wreckage of his career.

The considerable impact of *The Brownsville Raid* comes from Fuller's presentation of large, abstract issues in concrete, human instances. What dilutes it is language and characterization that are no more than adequate to illustrate the point he is making. The dialogue in the barracks scenes, which are the heart of the play, has a vitality and humor lacking in the rest, but the characters are not differentiated by the way they talk: we come to know them as we accumulate information about them. When Holliman says that he paid one of the soldiers, Private Johnson, to help him switch guns, it doesn't seem in character for Johnson. But then it doesn't *not* seem in character either, because he is never fully developed by the playwright. None of the supporting roles are. Holliman's, the most distinctive, comes from the requirements of the play's argument. His distinguishing characteristic of mendacity is used to create the moral dilemma.

Although Fuller avoids the morality play approach with its simplistic equations of black as good, white as bad, three of the white officials—the mayor of Brownsville, the major, and the general—are little more than exemplars of white supremacist attitudes. Fuller's stage instructions that the same white actor play all three roles suggest that their one-dimensional quality is deliberate. But when that quality is used for Theodore Roosevelt, making him into a cardboard figure, it weakens the historical and dramatic seriousness of his part in the Brownsville matter. By succumbing to stereotype here, Fuller departs from the moral complexity that he achieves in the rest.

The scenes between Mingo and his wife, Dolly, suffer from being underwritten too. The army's betrayal shakes Dolly's faith that in marrying a career soldier she has found protection from the fear with which she, as a black woman, has always lived. This touches on a profound and recurring theme in black life: how the manhood of a black man is defined, controlled, and destroyed by white society. Fuller is one of the few playwrights to remind us of the impact of public life on private lives. But because he fails to develop the marital relationship beyond the bare bones needed for the plot, he states rather than illuminates his argument.

If these are the weaknesses of the writing, the strengths are that it never resorts to heroics or pieties. Occasionally its understatedness increases the poignancy, as at the end of the play when the captain strips each black soldier of his insignia and rifle. This action is accompanied by the orderly's flat, documentary-style recital of the manner in which the man's life is to be ruined by the dishonorable discharge. His uninflected litany is more painful than any virtuoso language would be: it underscores the baldness of the indignity.

The hero of *Zooman and the Sign* is Reuben Tate, a bus driver whose twelve-year-old daughter has been killed accidentally by a teenager named Zooman. None of the neighbors, most of whom witnessed the crime, will come forward to identify him for the police. Zooman points out, "If a black kills a black, and they don't catch you right away, they liable to forget about it" (ZS 2:16). The indifference of the police to black victims results in and is compounded by the unwillingness of the black community to report black crimes. Reuben, outraged by their silence, erects a sign on his front porch that reads, "The killers of our daughter Jinny are free because our neighbors will not identify them" (ZS 1:26). The neighbors' response is to accuse Reuben of giving the black community a bad name and to threaten him with violence of their own. Fuller makes you feel the powerlessness of the wronged who find that they have no recourse. In the old days, Reuben would have taken familial revenge on the murderer of his daughter. But he

105

rejects hunting Zooman down as his uncle urges; he wants to progress from the violent and useless status quo. When his wife, frantic, mocks him for trying to be "like Martin Luther King," Reuben answers simply, "If somebody comes forward, maybe boys won't run through here no more" (ZS 2: 27). That becomes his quest. Eventually the sign brings an offer of help from the police, and then a few shops in the community add signs of their own.

Fuller's understated writing is used to advantage in Zooman's soliloquies. The casual way that Zooman announces, "I just killed someone—a little girl, I think," is a reminder of the apparent senselessness of so much urban violence (ZS 1:26). The details of his existence—homelessness in a neighborhood where junkies proliferate like blight, sporadic contact with a sporadic family ("I got people everywhere," Zooman comments euphemistically), indifferent or hostile teachers, arrest and detention on a false charge of rape—are made more harrowing because of Zooman's almost affectless recounting of them (ZS 1:18). We feel the grief of the boy under the bravado of the hoodlum. At the end of the play, after Reuben's uncle shoots Zooman accidentally, a second sign is seen rising on the Tates' porch. It reads, "Here, Lester Johnson was killed. He will be missed by family and friends. He was known as Zooman" (ZS 2:32). In death, he is treated as a human being for the first time. Without writing a heavy-handed apologia, Fuller shows how the environment has shaped Zooman, and it is his achievement that we come to feel nearly as much pity for the killer as for his victim.

There are suggestions here of Fuller's ability to write richer roles. The character of Ash Boswell, a family relative, is arresting because her speech is expressively comic. Fuller uses it to advance his thesis too, but here the language is complementary rather than subservient to it. For example, immediately after Reuben's impassioned outburst against the neighbors, Ash says, "I blame a lot of this on them food stamps, Honey." It's a funny line, but its function is not simply to amuse. It leads into Fuller's concern about individual responsibility:

> *Ash:* That's right! When the "Negro" was hungrier we treated each other better. Nowadays everybody's got their bellies full and we sit up belchin', watchin' those damn soap operas and game shows all day—hot dog in one hand, the phone in the other, a beer or a Pepsi on the floor beside us—the baby crawlin' around dirty, the whole house filthy, and Honey don't give a damn about nobody! You hear me? *(Slight pause)* When we knew we might have to borrow a cup of flour—or a pair of pants—or a white shirt from the people across the street, we were a lot more concerned about them, and a lot more conscientious about ourselves (ZS 1:19, 20).

Generally, however, the characters do not come to vivid life because their scenes lack emotional depth. When Fuller places the marital quarrel between Reuben and Rachel alongside their quarrel over the community's responsibilities, he fails to achieve the dramatic potential of that juxtaposition. The couple's passionate and problematic relationship is more discussed than felt. It's as though Fuller is so intent on making the drama's moral statements that he doesn't write one more word than is necessary for that purpose.

Like *The Brownsville Raid*, *A Soldier's Play* is set in an army barracks in the South. The situation is reversed this time, with suspicion cast on the white town for the murder of a black soldier. What remains the same is that the army is still segregated—the time is World War II—and justice is still directed by whites.

Technical Sergeant Vernon Waters, a black noncommissioned officer, has been murdered just outside the army camp, and Captain Richard Davenport, a black lawyer, is brought in to investigate the case. He is opposed from the outset by the unit's white commissioned officer, Captain Charles Taylor, who is convinced that by sending a black man to conduct the investigation the army is making sure that no white man will be charged. "Whites down here don't see their duty—or justice. They'll see you!" he tells Davenport. "And once they do, the law—due process—it all goes. And what is the point of continuing an investigation that can't possibly get at the truth?"[9] The unified goal of the two men makes for a more interesting conflict between them than if the white captain were simply trying to obstruct justice.

In the sober, determined way of Fuller's heroes, Davenport keeps on until he solves the murder. His investigation establishes the structure of a trial, with a trial's reliable suspense. But the play's real subject is self-hatred, dramatized in the relationship between Waters and one of his men. Although Davenport is the hero of the play, Waters is at the center of it.

Fuller has based *A Soldier's Play* on Melville's *Billy Budd*. Private C.J. Memphis, an uneducated young black soldier, is the Billy Budd figure, and Waters, a martinet loathed by all the men except for the angelic C.J., is modeled after Claggart. Although Waters' hatred of C.J., like Claggart's of Billy, is the hatred that evil feels for innocent goodness, his evil is not what Melville called the "natural depravity" of Claggart. It is caused by his having internalized all the values of white society, including its prejudice against blacks. Fuller shows how this result of racism can be the most insidious, damaging, and tragic of all.

Waters, we come to see in flashbacks, is a career soldier who has struggled against impossible obstacles in the white man's institution of the army. He explains that he became a soldier because it was "the closest I figured the white man would let me get to any kind of authority" (*SP* 1:22). He has no patience with any black who points out that there has not been equal opportunity. "Not havin' ain't no excuse for not gettin'," he says, and is confident that by sending his children to a white college to learn the white man's language and ways, he is insuring their advance in white society (*SP* 1:22).

Waters does not despise blacks like C.J. at a cold and grand distance. He is aware of C.J.'s Southern country-black behavior with every nerve in his body and through introjected white eyes. C.J., an easygoing, superstitious, guitar-picking, blues-singing, spontaneous, sensual black man, embodies the stereotypes that Waters hates: they make a mockery of his goal to show the white man that blacks are just like them. In ironically twisted praise of racism, Waters tells C.J., "Them Nazis ain't all crazy—a whole lot of people just can't fit into where things seem to be going—like you, C.J. The black race can't afford you no more" (*SP* 2:13). It is too dangerous to hate the oppressor, and so his hatred is directed at the oppressed.

Open conflict between Waters and C.J. begins after Waters answers the men's complaints about his obsessive discipline by telling them about the rigors of warfare. "Don't look like to me we could do too much to those Nazis wit' paint brushes, Sarge," is C.J.'s humorous response, and it reminds everyone that these soldiers only get clean-up detail, an echo of their traditional civilian roles (*SP* 1:31). Waters is furious to be made an occasion for laughter by this "ignorant, low-class geechy," talking about matters outside his province (*SP* 1:31).

Like Claggart in *Billy Budd*, Waters uses a trumped-up accusation against C.J., and like Billy, C.J. strikes his adversary in frustration, an act of military insubordination that puts him behind bars. But while Billy's momentary resort to violence is convincing, C.J.'s isn't, because Fuller's characterization of him has not prepared us for so strong an outburst. In *Billy Budd*, too, there is the inexorability of Greek tragedy that leads to the dramatic climax of Billy's execution. In *A Soldier's Play*, the events of C.J.'s provocation by Waters and his subsequent arrest and suicide do not have that awful inevitability: they seem like a playwright's invention for the sake of plot. The effect of C.J.'s suicide, which is the beginning of Waters' spiritual death to be followed by his actual death, is dulled by reducing it to a few expository sentences. "C.J. he hung hisself, Sir," one of the men explains to Davenport. "Suicide—he jes' couldn't stand it. M.P.'s found him hung from the bars" (*SP* 2:15).

A variation of internecine racial conflict is the murder of Waters, discovered by Davenport to have been committed not by the suspected white officers or townspeople or Ku Klux Klan, but by one of Waters' black soldiers, and witnessed and concealed by another. It is retribution for C.J.'s death, but it is also displaced rage. Just before Pfc. Peterson kills Waters he says to his watching buddy, "If this was a German would you kill it? If it was Hitler – or that fuckin' Tojo? Would you kill him?" (*SP* 2:35). The black soldiers have not up to this point been allowed to fight the Germans or Japanese. It is the wartime version of the frustration at being powerless to fight the real enemy, and so they fight each other.

On the night of his murder, Waters, extremely drunk, dances and carries on, in deliberately exaggerated stereotype, in front of the white officers, both to debase himself and as his ultimate insult to them. He has finally acknowledged the futility of his attempts to live according to white codes. Just before Peterson kills him, Waters, raving in drunkenness and guilt over C.J.'s suicide, tells him, "You got to be like them! And I was! I was – but the rules are fixed . . . it doesn't make any difference. They still hate you!" (*SP* 2:36). Waters' tragedy is that he tried to reinvent himself as a white. His dream was acceptance by white society, but to his would-be colleagues in the army, he was not a heroic soldier decorated in France during World War I: he was just another black man who, in the end, forgot his place.

Once again, as in *Zooman and the Sign*, Fuller makes us feel compassion for the "villain." When Waters explains the guiding principle of his life to his aide, he illustrates it with a powerful, horrifying tale:

> We were in France during the First War, Wilkie. We had won decorations, but the white boys had told all the French gals we had tails. And they found this ignorant colored soldier. Paid him to tie a tail to his ass and parade around naked making monkey sounds. *(Shakes his head)*. They sat him on a big, round table in the Cafe Napoleon, put a reed in his hand, a crown on his head, a blanket on his shoulders and made him eat bananas in front of them Frenchies. And ohhh, the white boys danced that night – passed out leaflets with that boy's picture on them – called him "Moonshine, King of the Monkeys." And when we slit his throat, you know that fool asked us, what he had done wrong? *(Pause)*. My Daddy told me, we got to turn our backs to his kind, Wilkie. Close our ranks to the chitlins, the collard greens – the cornbread style. . . . I don't intend to have our race cheated out of its place of honor and respect in *this* war because of fools like C.J.! [*SP* 2:29].

Learning the futility and destructiveness of this principle has been Waters' terrible epiphany. "Look what it's done to me! . . . I hate myself!" he shouts drunkenly and brokenheartedly at the white officers. "Don't blame us, boy!" one of them protests, "God made you black, not me!" (*SP* 1:43).

109

Waters is Fuller's best creation thus far, but even here the characterization is pared down to those attributes needed to illustrate the cause, process, and results of self-hatred. Because the phenomenon is complex, Waters is more complex than the others. Yet he is portrayed more as the embodiment of a tragic problem than as an individualized tragic character. While it is true that in *Billy Budd* only the essence of Claggart is revealed, Melville was writing a parable in which Billy stood for absolute good, Claggart for absolute evil. *A Soldier's Play* is a realistic drama, and consequently we expect its characters to be more than personifications. The play is moving, but a fully realized portrait of Sergeant Waters might have made it shattering.

Davenport's chief quality is that he is resolute. His quiet heroism has a subtlety and dimension that traditional "macho" heroism does not. Like Mingo and Reuben, he is convincing as a decent man, ennobled by his moral stand. But Fuller does not penetrate to the interior. Again, one wonders if he would flesh out his characters more if he were not so anxious to demonstrate a point. There are moments when Davenport's understated manner is dramatically effective, as in his summation at the end of the play. In the ironic, pseudo-documentary style of *The Brownsville Raid*, he ties up the threads after the death of C.J.: "A style of guitar-pickin' and a dance called the 'C.J.' caught on for a while in Tynin saloons during 1945." And of Waters:

> In Northern New Jersey, through a military foul-up, Sergeant Waters' family was informed that he had been killed in action. The Sergeant was, therefore, thought and unofficially rumored to have been the first colored casualty of the war from that country and under the circumstances was declared a hero. Nothing could be done officially, but his picture was hung on a "Wall-of-honor" in the Dorie Miller VFW Post #978.

And of the rest of the company:

> The men of the 221st Chemical Smoke Generating Company? The entire outfit, officers and enlisted men were wiped out in the Ruhr Valley during a German advance [SP 2:38].

The tension here between the plain speech and its shocking content is powerful. But it is the expression of Davenport, the public figure; we have not come to know the private man.

Having noted Fuller's drawbacks, it is important to emphasize his achievements. He is concerned with morality, but he never preaches. He shows how social life reverberates in private life but, by emphasizing the human drama, avoids a sociological approach. He conveys the horrors and indignities of black life in America without sensationalism or self-righteousness. Nor does he make society the whipping boy: Fuller's strongest theme is the need for personal responsibility.

These are thoughtful, intelligent plays, elevated by moral concerns. If Fuller's emphasis on their construction inhibits their intensity, it is an emphasis at the service not of a "well-made play," but of ideas, and the ideas are informed by the playwright's passion. Fuller's gifts have deepened over the course of the three plays discussed here. When he learns to bring an emotional power to his language that matches the moral power of his themes, his drama will have achieved the potential of his vision.

Interview with Charles Fuller

*Charles Fuller, at over six feet tall, a commanding presence, is expansive, in-
finitely talkative, and likable. The interview with him took place in May, 1982,
in the midtown New York office of one of his friends. It was five in the afternoon
and Fuller had just finished a two-hour interview with a reporter from the* Village
Voice. *Early that day he had appeared on the* Today Show. *These were just two
in a multiplicity of events amid the flurry of media attention that followed his winning the Pulitzer Prize for* A Soldier's Play *two months earlier, and Fuller's
response was a combination of amusement, good nature, and fatigue. He was eager
to get the interviews over with so that he could begin writing the movie version
of his play that was to become* A Soldier's Story.

ESTHER HARRIOTT: Where do you get the ideas for your plays? History
must be one source.

CHARLES FULLER: Everything I touch, really everything. I can't really
point at one thing. I do a lot of reading in history. I read novels. I read all
sorts of interesting pieces. For example, right now I'm reading *True Confes-
sions* from 1917 (I think) through 1979, just to see how the magazine has
changed, how our tastes have changed.

HARRIOTT: Do you have certain obligations as a black playwright? Is
there pressure put on you to be a spokesman?

FULLER: No. There never has been any pressure put on me to be a
spokesman for anybody. No one has ever come to me and said to me, "Do
this. Why don't you consider this or why don't you try looking at this or
why aren't you looking at that?" I have been very fortunate in not ever having to deal with that.

HARRIOTT: So that when you write you're not trying to do anything in
your writing other than to write what's inside of you?

FULLER: I'm trying to capture my experience. I'm translating the kind
of contact that I've made with people, most of them black. But how I would
write anything that is presumptuous enough to masquerade as being something that speaks for black people is beyond me. I'm just not that sort of
person.

HARRIOTT: What about addressing the audience? I guess that's what my question was getting at. Are you trying to make your audience change in any way?

FULLER: Oh, of course. There are lots of things that have to change. How people see black people must change. That we are two-dimensional, length-and-width type people that have no depth is simply not true. And I think it's important to display that sense of having more to us than simply the stuff of protest or of being victimized. There's much more to us than that. I'm simply expressing what is real, not what people like to think we are. So far we've been the victims of a compendium of stereotypes about ourselves. The very idea that black people are complex psychological beings is simply not dealt with.

HARRIOTT: Don't you think that anybody has dealt with that at all? Ralph Ellison, for example?

FULLER: Yes. But part of the problem with the novel is that it takes a long time to be read by lots of people. The one advantage of working in the theater is that I know I'm going to get an instant response.

HARRIOTT: On the other hand, if someone writes poetry or fiction, he can count on more people reading him than a playwright can count on people seeing him. And if a play isn't produced, nobody at all is going to know what you've written.

FULLER: Well, that's never happened. I also don't believe in an age of this great visual explosion that we have, that a whole lot of people take the time to go to a bookstore to find a book. The number of black publications produced every year will certainly attest to that fact. People are not reading a whole lot of black material. But if there's a play that you can come to, sit for two hours, and be moved in some way, and get up and tell your friends, that's a lot easier than spending a week with a book. And then a writer isn't quite sure, after you've read it, what you've got out of it. I'm fairly certain when an audience walks out whether they like or dislike what I've done. I don't want to wait six months, having written for six years.

HARRIOTT: Do you think, speaking of the visual explosion, that television and movies have hurt the theater?

FULLER: They might have, but it hasn't been my experience. I think there's a place for all of it. We tend to be very drastic in the way we see things. We say television or the movies are hurting the theater and putting it out of business. The money that the long-running shows have made seems to me to belie the fact that television has cut across a lot of it. Certainly it has taken some money out of the box offices. But there's room enough for everybody.

HARRIOTT: You sound optimistic. I keep hearing that the theater is in crisis.

Charles Fuller

FULLER: Well, that's for people who want to look at the things that used to be. The past is in crisis. The idea that old ways of perceiving the world are still viable in a changed era is in crisis. But that's always been in crisis throughout our history. I was recently reading an article about the theater being in crisis, and ten years before that there was an article about the theater being in crisis. People really don't know what to say about theater, quite frankly. I don't think they've known since Euripides and Sophocles. It's come under fire for ages, constantly under fire.

HARRIOTT: Then you think it's going to last.

FULLER: Sure. Crises are things that involve life and death situations. Someone's life is in danger. That's a crisis to me. Anything in the nature of human affairs that can be taken care of tomorrow or in 24 hours or in 48 hours or next month or next year is certainly not in crisis. That's nonsense. If there's a crisis, there was one last year. If there was one last year, then there was one the year before that.

HARRIOTT: Are you very disciplined?

FULLER: Yes. When it's time to work, I work. When it's time to do something else, I do that. I never let anything confuse me when I know it's a serious time.

HARRIOTT: When you're working, do you work all day?

FULLER: Yes, I work straight through. When I'm not working, I may be doing anything, anywhere. For me, working is really an isolated kind of thing. It's a very steady, long process. Not that it's long in terms of days, but all day every day until the work is finished. It's like the army. When I was in the army, they trained you for six months, but they trained you every day. You got one day off. And you went to school eight hours a day, six days a week. You can't help but learn or get done what it is you set out to do. And that method seems very practical. It works.

HARRIOTT: But your plays get written fairly quickly, don't they?

FULLER: Yes. That's why I like them. They don't take long to do.

HARRIOTT: Have you been drawn to any other forms of writing?

FULLER: I write short stories and essays.

HARRIOTT: You mentioned isolation. The collaboration with people in the theater must be pleasant after being isolated at your desk.

FULLER: It's pleasant for the length of time it takes. It's a kind of closeness that you've got with people for a short period of time. It doesn't mean that you have to do this all year long. I tend to write plays, get them produced, then get out of it for a while. Theater and all the things that attend it are very, very exhausting—the opening, reviews, and all that stuff that goes along with it. So I try to do one a year if I can. And if I can't, I'll do something else. I couldn't do two plays a year. I'd go nuts.

HARRIOTT: Have you been writing one play a year?

FULLER: Just about. But I don't think I'll do it next year.

HARRIOTT: How will you approach your script to make it into a screen play?

FULLER: What I do is make notes about what I am looking at, and what are some of the things that are going to make sense in terms of this play being translated into pictures. Just pictures, flat, two-dimensional pictures. What do you do to make that happen, as opposed to making it three-dimensional, with depth, and with people moving about, who may trip one night and not trip another? What do you do with something that's always going to be the same every time you look at it?

HARRIOTT: I read your penciled questions on your script, and one of them that I really liked was "Would I like Davenport?" Do you remember that?

FULLER: Yes.

HARRIOTT: Why would you explore his character more for a movie than for a play?

FULLER: There's more room to do it in. He's the protagonist of the piece. Now when we talk about doing a movie, he's going to be much more real than when we watched him on the stage. And that's the person they're going to put all the money in. And the characters have to be explored more in the film because when their faces are on the screen they're about 40 feet wide and 20 feet high. The concerns that I had with the play are not the concerns that I'll have with the movie. I know the story is going to be the same, but how do you make sure that the people in the seats stay in the seats? That's what I'm basically saying, whatever I'm doing.

HARRIOTT: You do that very well in the theater. The tension and mood shifts seem to be just right. In movies, though, there's so much less language.

FULLER: Yes, I know. So, there's that to be considered, too. How do you display this intention without two hundred words, without unnecessary babble, the babble of the theater?

HARRIOTT: Before you write a play do you write out questions, too?

FULLER: Yes, generally about the people. Where do they come from? Where were they born? What can I know about them? Is there anything you need to know about them before the play? Is there anything you need to know about them after the play? Those kinds of questions I ask myself all the time. And then I sit in the audience and watch the play take place.

HARRIOTT: Do you approach it from characters or theme?

FULLER: I think it's all one and the same. I approach it from the seats, not from on the stage. So I'm guaranteed that what you're watching is what I am watching. And if I like it, I'm praying to God that you do.

HARRIOTT: I didn't mean that, exactly. I meant, do you create a lot of characters first, and then see what happens? I think Shaw said that he created characters and then let them rip.

FULLER: No, the characters aren't really separate from the action. I don't see them outside of the story and I don't see the story outside of them. It's all of a piece, a single piece of music. I like to compare this with music.

HARRIOTT: In what way?

FULLER: Like, for example, if you go to a concert, you go to hear a piece of music and you don't ask yourself if you want to hear more of that piece of music. You don't say, "My goodness, I wish there was another riff." It begins with an explosion of some sort, and it ends with whatever the musician or composer feels it should end with. For me a play is like that. In *Zooman [and the Sign]*, for example, I was trying to make a play in which there were no stops. And I wasn't that successful.

HARRIOTT: What is a play in which there are no stops?

FULLER: A play with no blackouts, but where time changes take place. Rather than blacking out the lights and shifting from Sergeant Waters back to the barracks. I really wanted to do that in one motion, so that you were part of the past and the present at the same time. You didn't even feel it.

HARRIOTT: And in that way it's like music?

FULLER: Yes. In jazz you don't have stops. In the music of the fifties you don't. I come out of the fifties. The music keeps going, the rhythm section keeps going, the piano keeps playing, the bass player keeps going, and someone stops playing and someone else plays. The actors are like that. They come forward, they play an instrument. Then something else happens. It's like listening to "'Round Midnight" with Thelonious Monk, and Miles, and all of them playing at once, to begin the piece. And each one of them settling into their own improvisation until the piece is discovered, until finally you've heard all the music, and it's over. And you go away having felt the entire piece of music. You might remember one solo better than another, but the whole piece of music is what has stirred you. It is the whole piece of music, "'Round Midnight," that you care about. And I think plays ought to function in that way. For me they do. If it's not as fluid as I want it to be, then I'm not happy with it. *Zooman* is not as fluid as I want it to be. *A Soldier's Play* comes closer. It's going back and forth in time without any problems with it.

HARRIOTT: In what way is *Zooman* not fluid?

FULLER: [The character of] Zooman was too isolated out here, and not a part of the whole thing that was going on. Only at the end.

HARRIOTT: But he always has a connection with Victor.

FULLER: Yes, there is a visual connection with Victor. And an age connection. But I still felt he was too far away from the family to be effective at the end of the play. What I tried to do this time was to take a character as extreme, as interesting as Zooman and make him integral, connected.

HARRIOTT: Are there a lot of rewrites?

FULLER: We didn't rewrite any of it with this play. *Zooman* we rewrote. But with this one, we knew we had something that was exciting when we started. And we went right ahead and did it, you know, with all the gusto we could bring to it. It went so smoothly because the director and I didn't have to deal with all that during rehearsal. The actors were much more confident than they are when you're fooling with the script. And tinkering with it doesn't help the actors that much anyway. They like to get into what they're doing.

HARRIOTT: I thought that was just part of it, always.

FULLER: No, that is not always part of it. It doesn't have to be.

HARRIOTT: Is this something that you discuss with Douglas Turner Ward [artistic director of the Negro Ensemble Company] beforehand?

FULLER: No, we just normally work things out that way. We tend to agree about the script and where it's going.

HARRIOTT: You're going to have a lot less of that freedom with the movie, aren't you?

FULLER: Sure. That doesn't bother me.

HARRIOTT: It doesn't? Funny that it shouldn't bother you.

FULLER: Well, lots of things bother me, but these things one can do very little about. The movie is the director's medium. It's foolish for a writer to think that he's going to go to Hollywood and change the way that it has functioned for the last half century.

HARRIOTT: Writers have been treated very badly in Hollywood.

FULLER: Yes. I think that you can be treated better. But no one told any writer he can direct a motion picture better than a motion picture director can.

HARRIOTT: It's just that in the theater the playwright is very important. In the movies you hardly even know who the screenwriter is. In the theater, it's *your* play.

FULLER: But if you are willing to go into that world and stay there, then you have to suffer those consequences. I have no interest in spending the rest of my life writing movies. Every now and then it might be nice to do that, but going to Hollywood and making a career out of writing movies

117

doesn't interest me at all. I want to write them certainly, but I'm not going to lose any sleep over it. Rest assured. I'm 43 years old, and I know I will never be as good at anything else as I am as a writer. There's not enough time. If I began now, there's not enough time to get as good at being a doctor, for example, as I am as a writer. The older I get the less likely it is that I'm going to have the dexterity necessary to handle an operation. But by reading I can always improve my mind and get better at being a writer. So, I don't concern myself with getting good at being a director or getting good at being this or that. What I'm concerned about is trying to produce the best literary material America has ever seen.

HARRIOTT: That's pretty ambitious.

FULLER: Yes, it is. But it's what I'm trying to do. And I think that is an ennobling desire. And I don't think there's anything wrong with it. And I'm not interested in being these other things.

HARRIOTT: I wonder what will happen to you. You've just won a Pulitzer Prize and sold film rights and are going to Hollywood. The world is running to you, right? I wonder if that could be very seductive and distracting?

FULLER: Not really. I have a lovely home, two sons that I'm in love with, a wife I love very much, a lifestyle that isn't confusing. It doesn't need all of this. It's nice and very wonderful, but it's not something I'd like to pursue as a life's work. I have more important things to do. I mean, this morning it was so interesting, you know, I was on the Today Show. I thought, "God forbid that my life would depend on having to be on these things every morning." Everyone asks, how can you turn it off? How can you *not?* Remain who you are. After all, it's *that* that I'm concerned about the most, not television, movies. I know that if I write plays there's a reasonable chance that two out of three will get done. That's not a bad average. I won't hassle that. I'm always challenged by the things that I'm doing anyway. So I'm not terribly worried about losing my interest in things.

HARRIOTT: Did you get discouraged during the period when you didn't think your plays were good?

FULLER: No. I knew I was doing something different, and that people just didn't like it. It didn't bother me terribly. I was trying to do something enormous. I'm dissatisfied because I wasn't able to do what I set out to do. And it is just discouraging not to make any money. But so what? I keep wondering sometimes if the myth about American writers is of their own making or the public's.

HARRIOTT: Which myth?

FULLER: The myth about being so discouraged and hurt and beaten when your work doesn't succeed. Of course there's pain and problems, but you keep on working. If that stops you, then...

HARRIOTT: Then you're not really a writer?

FULLER: It's not painful enough to dwell on for any great length of time. I think it's something in the myth we have about writers, that we want them to be more feeling, more compassionate, more everything than we really are. And the truth of the matter is, we simply do something well that very few people can do—put human beings up on the stage. It's a difficult job to do. I don't perceive it as being anything other than that. Suffering is not an unusual human characteristic. You know what I mean? The specialness of writing is simply that not a whole lot of people do it. It's a small category in human affairs. A lot has been written, but not a whole lot of people wrote it. Certainly the things that have been remembered have been written by a very few people.

HARRIOTT: It sounds as though you constitutionally can't be anything but a writer.

FULLER: I don't want to be anything but a writer.

HARRIOTT: I read that you started off wanting to do something in music.

FULLER: In the fifties we were all caught up in the new wave of jazz—modern jazz, bebop really—Charlie Parker and Dizzy Gillespie. It was something that suggested a most extraordinary future. The music was new, was very exciting. And I wanted to play it. I heard Thelonious Monk one afternoon at my aunt's house and I thought, "My God, where have I been? I haven't heard this before." What he did with the music was so extraordinary. Quite naturally, I wanted to duplicate that. But somewhere along the line, you know, I watched Charlie Parker die of an overdose. It just did not seem like a practical application of one's talents. So many musicians were dying and they suffered so. They had to go through so much about the rights to their music, their jobs. I really didn't want that. And I decided that writing would be a much more realistic endeavor, principally because the foundation of Western civilization was in books. Anything you wanted to know about the proof of Western civilization's power is in the books that Western civilization has written about itself. Such power in words—to be able, with words, to change how people function, how they think. The foundation of our belief in ourselves is the ability to communicate with words and ideas.

HARRIOTT: Reuben [in *Zooman*] has your faith in language, doesn't he?

FULLER: Yes, he understands the value of it. This is what words can do. You can change the whole world, really. If you consider, and I always consider it, and this may be very corny-sounding, but the Declaration of Independence and the Constitution are a group of words that I act on consistently. Once read, you cannot ignore it. Impossible. The words did that.

119

HARRIOTT: Whose words do you like? Who are some of the writers you like?

FULLER: Ellison, Ralph Ellison I like. Albert Murray, a contemporary writer. And classical writers who capture human themes, things that have bothered us for centuries. All the great writers do that. I mean, I can't think of any writer of great worth who hasn't dealt with very fundamental human problems always, always, always. You know the business of nuclear waste materials will go away, but the problem of getting along with one another, the person you love, will never dissipate. There are certain problems that are monumental, because technology has led you that far. The problem of nuclear war is a problem that the people of the fifteenth century didn't have. They still had the problem of dealing with each other. That never disappeared. And when this problem, if we can survive it, disappears, we'll still have the problem of our relationships with one another.

HARRIOTT: I don't even want to ask this question in view of what you've been saying.

FULLER: Go ahead and ask it.

HARRIOTT: Every other black artist I've talked to has been bitter, and it would seem to me that that's unavoidable. But that doesn't seem to be what you're saying.

FULLER: Well, being bitter would imply that I'm not getting something that I should be getting, or that I feel inadequate somehow. In the reality that I'm faced with there is nothing about me that is not in any way adequate to anything that I have to face. So I'm not afraid of anyone.

HARRIOTT: I mean a collective bitterness.

FULLER: About what?

HARRIOTT: About "the madness of race in America," to use your phrase in *A Soldier's Play*.

FULLER: Yes, that's part and parcel of the United States. Anyone who wakes up in the morning and doesn't think that racism exists in the United States is crazy. But I don't have time to spend the rest of my life being angry about it. What will serve me, and benefit, certainly, my people more, it seems to me, is actively functioning in a way that everything I do and produce implies that all the nonsense of racism—certainly the stereotyping of racism—is not true. My argument is on the stage. I don't have to be angry. O.K.? I get it all out right up there. There's no reason to carry this down from the stage and into the seats. And it does not mean that I am not enraged at injustice or prejudice or bigotry. It simply means that I cannot be enraged all the time. To spend one's life being angry, and in the process doing nothing to change it, is to me ridiculous. I could be mad all day long, and if I'm not doing a damn thing, what difference does it make?

HARRIOTT: It could also be very destructive to the art. Not the anger itself, but if it becomes an axe to grind.

FULLER: I think it can strangle you to death. But I'm certain that every now and then it's important to let people know that things have not been forgotten. Certainly *A Soldier's Play* lets you know that, yes, we lived in a country at one time when the whole army was segregated. But let's not think that oppressing means that the people who are oppressed are not human. O.K.? That is to believe what white people have believed about us. I don't believe that, I'm the human being here. I don't need you to tell me that I'm alive or that I'm human or that I have feelings. But to be angry at the fact that you said that I don't have feelings certainly doesn't mean that I stop feeling, or that I believe you, or care what you say. That's still believing that white people decide for you who you are, or what your impulse is going to be in the future. That's nonsense, and insulting to begin with. I mean, what makes anyone think I cannot do with language all the things they can? And I'm perfectly calm and contented doing it. It's ludicrous.

So many sad, angry people spend so much time arguing this question, and they don't get their work done. They get angry about not being received the way white writers have been received, about not getting the kind of support that white writers have gotten, never understanding that our function in this society has been, since we've been in it, to change how people see things. To go on changing, to go on making America a better place to live in, because the landscape is broad enough for everybody to be on it. If you were to see a black man standing there, you would say, yes, that's the American experience too. That the American experience is not just a white experience. It's black experience and Indian experience, Puerto Rican experience. For anyone to believe that anyone can, by simply telling you that you're no good, make you no good, that's nonsense. My argument is with the people who really believe that only white people have done things that are artistically sensible. That very fact that we create the things that we create simply proves that that's not true. Why should I argue with them all my life? That's nonsense.

It is important that we do things that seem to me to be beneficial to our people, and by doing so, benefit the larger landscape of America. It seems to me that making people more human in their presentation on stage is one way of doing that, rather than making them so two-dimensional that all they do is confront each other in violent terms. That doesn't speak to anything, doesn't move us anywhere. You learn nothing about you, and I learn nothing about me. Finally, I must make it somehow sensible for my sons to live in the twenty-first century. I believe that if I don't do something about that, I've failed.

121

HARRIOTT: That's the "finally"?

FULLER: To make it possible that they have no doubts about living in the twenty-first century. That whatever the future is, they will be a part of it, guaranteed. After all, I don't have a future unless they do. And I think that part of this is creating a legacy for them, to make it possible for them to function. Because we are so involved in ourselves that we don't have time to think about the next generation. It is important for me when I am 60 to live in a world where people who have hold of it are sensible. I don't want to live out my life on the edge of fear.

HARRIOTT: Are you really that optimistic about changing things?

FULLER: Yes, because I believe it's not on anybody else. It's on me. Like, I don't look to anyone else to solve a problem on my block, for example. I'm not going to wait for somebody else to get around to doing it.

HARRIOTT: So, by taking charge...

FULLER: By taking some step, I'm sure that, at least as far as I am concerned, something is being done about it.

HARRIOTT: It seems to me that you have a strong sense of self.

FULLER: Yes, well, my parents were marvelous people. My mother is still alive...

HARRIOTT: Your father died last summer?

FULLER: Yes. They were marvelous people who gave us our strong sense of who we were, that given the right amount of interest and studying, we could accomplish anything we set out to do. Anything. I don't want to be president, I'd probably be shot down, but I certainly wanted to be a writer. Within the kinds of attitudes that I had at the time, it's reasonable that I became a writer.

HARRIOTT: What will you do after the screenplay of A *Soldier's Play* is finished?

FULLER: Well, several things. I would like to do a piece for television. A larger piece, something that has the potential of reaching millions of people. I'm not in this to do it for the smallest number. I think it's important to try and reach as many people as you can. And television is a way of doing that. Not that I want to work in television the rest of my life. You see what I'm saying? We're so accustomed, it seems to me, to put people in categories. It's "Oh, he's going to work in television, my God, we're going to lose him on the stage." That's not it at all.

HARRIOTT: That's America. In England, theater people work in television and film and radio, don't they?

FULLER: Yes, Americans are so accustomed to specialization, you know, that they believe it about everything, everything. There's a man that turns the knob and there's a guy that pushes the door. There's no reason to believe that you can't do a variety of things in television and movies and plays. I'll always come back to the stage, though, because I like it so much. I'll do more of that than I'll do of anything else.

HARRIOTT: Your kind of drama, which is largely realistic, would work very well on television.

FULLER: Yes, I think so. I'd like to try some other things, though. I don't think I would like to stay doing realistic drama for the rest of my life. Only because I think as an artist I'll grow. If you watch the work of Picasso from the time he was a young man till the time that he got old, there's an enormous change there.

HARRIOTT: His range is probably broader than any other artist's.

FULLER: Sure, but I think there's room for that kind of range in writing. You know, I don't see it as a problem. It's just a new adventure, something new to try. The human mind can do just about anything. I think anything is possible. Certainly I can continue to store information in it. And I can take all that's been stored in 43 years, including all the books, and all the people, and all the stuff I've read, and the myriad number of things I've come in contact with. It could certainly take 40 more years or 20 more years.

I don't know enough. There's so much I don't know. I feel inadequate a lot of times because there's so much to know. Each play is always trying to do something else that I haven't done before. A story that hasn't been seen before, a way of looking at this that hasn't been done before. Like I wanted to look at American literature with a service play, so I took Melville, because no one had done that. After all, *A Soldier's Play* is based loosely on this particular idea that I saw in *Billy Budd*, that Melville obviously saw in, perhaps, Iago, Othello and that whole thing. And then Shakespeare probably saw it somewhere else.

HARRIOTT: The one thing that you do, I think—this is not to be construed to say that you're better than Shakespeare and Melville [laughs]—one thing that you do that they don't do with Iago or Claggart, is give an indication as to how their evil was motivated.

FULLER: Oh yes, but that's only because they're pre-Freudian people. They don't have the language of psychology to do the things that I have done.

HARRIOTT: I've always thought Shakespeare was very Freudian without being post-Freud.

FULLER: I think Melville was, too. Indeed, the marvelous nature of *Hamlet* is the groping, the attempt to explain the very psychological situation without the language.

HARRIOTT: But I don't think that happens with Iago. He's simply evil personified and he hates Othello because Othello is good, as much as for any other reason.

FULLER: But I also don't think that Shakespeare could deal with it in any other way. There wasn't any language to say that there was more to this evil man than just evil. The religion of the time, the attitude of people at the time, the concept of evil at the time did not permit for variations.

HARRIOTT: But Sergeant Waters isn't really a Freudian character. The explanation of Waters is much more what's been done to him socially than individually. His self-hate is a cultural phenomenon, isn't it?

FULLER: Yes. That's a kind of madness that I haven't seen explained very well. There's also the craziness in *A Soldier's Play* of believing that technology is racial.

HARRIOTT: Are power and success equated with technology in the play?

FULLER: You see, Waters implies that we need the technology, or we need to be like white people in order to do the things we want to do. He's equating technical achievement with race. And that's a mistake. It's been a mistake for centuries. But people do it.

HARRIOTT: But he's also just saying, "Copy the people who are in power."

FULLER: Yes, he's making all those achievements racial achievements. And what does he really mean by the white man's language? English? He's speaking it. It's a *way* of speaking it that he's describing in racial terms. It's as if the achievements of a society are racial achievements. They simply are not. Toasters don't have colors, and that they pop up isn't racial at all. That your stove goes on and off has nothing to do with race. And that you can learn to fix the stove has nothing to do with race. The things that are racial are more human, much more difficult to define.

HARRIOTT: Why do they get so uncomfortable in the play when C.J. starts saying, "It's not American eagle, it's crow"? Is that because he's going to bring up a primitive superstition?

FULLER: No, that's because in any group the person who comes up with all that backwater stuff embarrasses you. And every ethnic and racial group has it. It's not something that's just black. It's the Italian family whose grandfather comes in from the old country and starts raving. And they're shaking. "Yes, Papa, but we're in New York now. We're not in Italy."

HARRIOTT: When you talk about every ethnic group, I can really identify with that. Growing up as a Jew in a small town that was 99.9 percent WASP, I was very aware of a lot of those feelings. Jews are always aware of being hated—I mean historically—and that hatred can turn inward and become self-hate.

FULLER: Yes. In any ethnic group that has been oppressed, the worst person is the one who betrays the group's image of itself, not the one who oppresses you. That's why internecine conflict is so incredibly violent. It's easy to hit the person who looks like you. "Why are you doing it? You shame us all." That one person takes on the quality of all the people. That's why Waters gets so angry with this boy. He believes that everybody is affected by what this one boy does.

HARRIOTT: Why does he love him so much in the beginning?

FULLER: Music, music. The blues. But that's Waters' deviousness, too. He is, after all, waiting, as Claggart waited for Billy Budd.

HARRIOTT: Have you written any plays with big parts in them for women?

FULLER: Yes. Some early pieces. I want to get back to that eventually. Right now my focus is somewhere else. I'll do it eventually. No pressure to do it. No pressure at all.

New York City
May 1982

Marsha Norman:
Getting Out

Getting Out

MARSHA NORMAN called her first play *Getting Out,* and that could be the subtitle of each of her plays since. She writes about people who are on the point of cutting ties—to the past, to the present, or even to the future, to their families or friends, or to their former selves. "Getting out," with its implied corollary of "starting over," suggests the typically American faith in the possibility of remaking one's life, or even one's person. It is not the Gatsby-esque notion of creating an ideal conception of oneself that drives Norman's characters, however; their immediate goal, their passion, is to escape from the situations in which they feel trapped.

In *Getting Out* (1977), Arlene, having just been released from prison, is determined to free herself from the prison of her former self. Jessie, in *'Night, Mother* (1983), is equally determined to free herself, through suicide, from a life that feels like a life sentence. In *The Laundromat* (1978), Alberta takes the first step towards emancipation by washing her deceased husband's clothes that she had been preserving like objects in a shrine, while her laundromat companion, Deedee, begins to consider the possibility of leaving her oppressive marriage. And in *Traveler in the Dark* (1984), the action revolves around Sam's decision to divorce his wife and quit his profession.

Each struggle becomes the occasion for an encounter between a parent and child that has the special pain of familial confrontation, with its recriminations, anatomizings, and remorseless memories. There is no statute of limitations in family quarrels, and old grievances have the immediacy of fresh wounds. Arlene's failed reunion with her mother reveals the pathology of their family life that shaped the young "Arlie" who went to prison, and makes clear to the mature Arlene that, if she is to change her life, she must give up any expectation of maternal acceptance. Both *Third and Oak: The Laundromat* and its companion play, *Third and Oak: The Pool Hall,* consist of an extended argument between a parent-figure and child, the first between two women who meet in a laundromat, the second between a pool hall owner and the son of his now dead best friend. *'Night, Mother* is a battle between mother and daughter, with the daughter's life at stake, and in *Traveler in the Dark* the antagonism of the son towards his father threatens to be duplicated in the next generation by his own son.

Norman was born in Louisville in 1947, the oldest of the four children of Billie and Bertha Williams, and raised according to her parents' strict fundamentalist beliefs. This may have had something to do with the subject of her first published work, an essay written when she was in junior high school. Called "Why Do Good Men Suffer?"—the question is still implicit in Norman's writing—the essay won first prize in a Louisville literary contest.

She attended Agnes Scott College in Decatur, Georgia, and after graduating in 1969, returned to Louisville, where she married her high school English teacher, Michael Norman, earned her M.A. at the University of Louisville, and worked as a volunteer teacher of disturbed children at the state hospital. One of these children became the model for Arlie in *Getting Out*. In 1973, Norman was hired by a school for gifted children and began writing for the *Louisville Times*, eventually creating a children's supplement, "The Jelly Bean Journal." At the same time, she was writing her first play—a book for a musical about American inventors, designed for adolescents. She sent the manuscript to Jon Jory, artistic director of the Actors Theatre of Louisville, who was impressed by her talent but suggested that she try another subject. The result was *Getting Out*, written when Norman was 29.

Jory staged it at the 1977 Festival of New Plays, and it was an enormous success. Co-winner of the festival's playwriting award, it went on in 1978 to productions at the Mark Taper Forum in Los Angeles and in the Phoenix Theatre's Off Broadway Festival in New York. In 1979 it was revived Off Broadway at the Theatre de Lys, where it ran for eight months and received considerable critical recognition, including awards for new playwrights given by the Outer Critics Circle and *Newsday*.

Norman also won a National Endowment for the Arts playwright-in-residence grant, which she used in 1978 and 1979 at the Actors Theatre, writing the successful *Third and Oak* double bill, and her first critical and audience failure, *Circus Valentine*. Her next play, *The Hold-up*, was given a workshop production at Actors Theatre in 1980 and a full production at the Actors Conservatory Theatre in San Francisco in 1983.

In 1978, Norman, whose first marriage had ended in divorce in 1974, married Dann Byck, Jr., a prominent Louisville businessman and a founder of Actors Theatre. In 1981 they moved to New York, where Norman wrote 'Night, Mother'. Its premiere was at the American Repertory Theatre in Boston in January 1983, and in March of that year, Byck produced it on Broadway. The play created a great sensation, and Norman won the 1983 Pulitzer Prize for drama. Her next play, *Traveler in the Dark*, premiered at ART as well, in February 1984, but the generally poor reviews precluded a Broadway venture. It was, however, presented at the Mark Taper Forum in 1985.

Norman is still a young playwright who has not yet produced a substantial body of work. But two of her plays, *Getting Out* and 'Night, Mother', are the writings of an accomplished dramatist, and 'Night, Mother' stands on its own as a significant achievement in the American theater.

Getting Out takes place during the first 24 hours after Arlene Holsclaw's release from prison, where she has served eight years for the murder of a cab driver, committed while she was escaping from an earlier prison sentence for forgery and prostitution. Arlene's struggle to liberate herself from her former anti-social and self-destructive patterns is dramatized by making her younger self, Arlie, another character in the play. As Arlene faces the present in the Louisville apartment that is her new home, Arlie re-enacts the past in flashbacks that trace her development from mistreated child to intractable juvenile to unregenerate prisoner.

The change of name from "Arlie" to "Arlene" is significant. It is not just the discarding of the diminutive form used for the child. It symbolizes Arlene's desire to separate from her younger self, and it introduces the catalytic role played by the prison chaplain toward that separation. As the first person in Arlie's life to address her by her full name, the chaplain was also the first to acknowledge her as a full human being. Arlie's life is a history of dehumanization: ignored by her family except for her father who abused her sexually; depersonalized by teachers and counselors; exploited by her lover-pimp; humiliated verbally and sexually by prison guards and fellow inmates; and deprived of the greatest affirmation of her humanity — her baby — by the prison doctors who tried, unsuccessfully, to force abortion on her, then took the newborn baby away.

Like a morality play in its stark focus on the lessons learned by the protagonist as she encounters the successive figures who represent the directions she can take or reject, *Getting Out* dramatizes the confrontations that constitute the beginning of Arlene's moral education. The first of these is with her mother, who makes it unequivocally clear that she has no use for her children. When Arlene asks about her sister Candy, whose apartment she has been given, her mother says, "You got her place so what do you care? I got her outta my house so whatta I care?"[1] Her report to Arlene on each member of the family is an almost comic litany of haplessness and depravity: a son in the detention center, a son-in-law in jail, one daughter a thief, another a prostitute, a third a dope dealer, her own wife-beating husband, a grandson (Arlene's son, Joey) in a foster home because Arlene's sister refused to keep him while Arlene was in prison: "She's the only smart kid I got," says Mother (GO 25). To Arlene's urgent questioning about Joey, her mother responds that she saw him waiting for a bus when she was driving her cab. When Arlene asks, "What'd he say?" her mother replies, "Oh, I didn't stop" (GO 20).

The juxtaposed flashbacks to Arlie show the child's painful relationship with her cold mother: fearfully denying to her that she has been sexually abused by her father (because her father has threatened her with punishment if she tells); defying the school principal who tells Arlie that her mother wants her "put away somewhere" (GO 22); defending her mother

131

against a playmate's charge that she is a whore. They also show Arlie's admiration for her mother's independence ("She drives the cab to buy us stuff, cause we don't take no charity from nobody, cause we got money cause she earned it") and (GO 24) good looks. In a characteristic exchange, when the grown Arlene reminds her mother, "You was pretty," her mother's reply is, "You could look better'n you do. Do something with your hair. I always thought if you looked better you wouldn't have got in so much trouble" (GO 23). There is a touching moment when Arlene, after noting her appearance in the mirror with disapproval, tugs at her hair and asks her mother, who pays no attention, "You still cut hair?" (GO 24).

This hinted request ignored, Arlene makes a more serious one: to be invited for Sunday dinner. Her mother parries it by saying "Sunday . . . is my day to clean house now" (GO 25). It is Arlene's appeal to be allowed back into the family, and it is refused. Having paid her obligatory visit, bearing housewarming gifts of dishtowels, an old teapot (Arlene doesn't drink tea), and an old bedspread, and having completed a perfunctory cleaning up, her mother is ready to wash her hands of Arlene. It is consistent with her past treatment of her daughter, whom she neither visited nor wrote to during the years she was in prison. But her unkindest cut, after Arlene confides her goal of working to earn money so that she can be a mother to Joey, is to say, "He don't even know who you are Arlie." To which Arlene, devastated, can only respond with the correction of her name: "Arlene" (GO 26).

The meeting ends when Arlene's mother discovers the hat belonging to the guard who has driven Arlene back from prison to her home in Kentucky. Refusing to listen to Arlene's explanation, her mother, all moral indignation, scoops up her gift bedspread and leaves. Her last words to Arlene, who has rushed towards her with an inchoate notion of reconciliation, are "Don't you touch me" (GO 30). The encounter leaves Arlene hurt and stunned. Then her anger takes over, constructively now, not as the fury of the past but as an aid to recovery and to facing up to the uselessness of hoping for a rapprochement with her mother. For Norman's characters, the most important first lesson is to see things as they are.

Arlene's next encounter is with Bennie, the guard, who, on the pretext of coming to Kentucky for a fishing vacation, has offered to help Arlene settle in. In fact, he has retired from the prison, and is sexually interested in her. Bennie is portrayed as a man whose decent instincts have been corrupted by his role in the prison, and his relationship with Arlene in that environment distorts the relationship now. He is well-meaning and menacing by turns, on the one hand encouraging Arlene's progress, on the other, by his very presence with its reminders of where she has been, and by his paternalism, tempting her regression. His ambivalent attraction to

Arlene is expressed through sexual coercion: when she rejects his overtures, he proceeds to force himself on her. She has been a match for any man in the past—flashbacks to Arlie show her prodigious physical strength when attacked. But the horror of *this* situation is Bennie's special power over Arlene: he is the prison guard, she the parolee. If she hurts—or kills—him, as she hurt a male inmate and accidentally killed the cab driver, she will be put back in jail. Bitter and resourceful, Arlene uses words this time instead of force and accuses Bennie of being a rapist. Shocked at this perception of his behavior, Bennie backs off, insisting, "I ain't no rapist, Arlie." "And I ain't Arlie," says Arlene, "Arlie coulda killed you" (GO 39). It is her second test, and meeting it with strategy instead of with violence is an important step in Arlene's conversion. Her rejection of the benevolent side of Bennie is important, too. It would be easier to let him take care of her, but it would be a resumption of the relation between prisoner and keeper.

Carl, Arlene's former lover, pimp, and unknowing father of her child, offers another kind of temptation. Recently escaped from prison, he has come after his meal ticket and tries to persuade Arlene to run away to New York with him. In his inept and irresponsible way he cares for her, and she feels a residual tenderness for him. Carl's argument that as a dishwasher (the only kind of job open to Arlene as an ex-convict) she will have no money, no prospects, no life, is convincing, too. She rejects it all the same, even when he switches from fantasies of luxuries for her to fantasies of gifts and trips to New York for her son. But Arlene, who in the past subjected herself to Carl and his customers and took the rap for his forgery, refuses him this time. She sees that he will end up in jail again, and she is fighting not to end up back there with him.

Arlene's final encounter is with Ruby, her new neighbor, a former convict who has adjusted to her new life. Having at first resisted her offers of friendship—and we see in flashbacks that Arlene's wariness is an extension of having had to defend herself against Lesbian advances in prison—Arlene gradually realizes that Ruby is the only one who will not tempt her to revert to what she was before.

It is to Ruby that she expresses her correct view of this new life as another kind of imprisonment, where she lives in a dingy, one-room apartment with bars on the window, and where the only kinds of jobs open to her, besides being exhausting and demeaning, will keep her from earning the money needed to realize her dream of making a home for her son. "What kind of life is that?" she asks bitterly. "It's outside," answers Ruby (GO 59). Arlene is not impressed. "Outside's where you get to do what you want," she says, "not where you gotta do some shit job jus so's you can eat worse than you did in prison" (GO 60). Ruby, with the clear-eyed outlook of

Norman's "good" characters, tells Arlene that this is the way it's going to be, "and the sooner you believe it, the better off you'll be" (GO 60).

Throughout this second act the flashbacks have shown Arlie's progress in prison: her savagely defiant behavior, her hatred of solitary confinement, her initial resistance to a visit from the chaplain and her subsequent growing interest in reading the Bible that he has given her and has inscribed with her full name. In the emotional climax of the play, Arlene breaks down as she tells Ruby the circumstances of her attempted suicide.

The chaplain had used the name Arlie as a metaphor for Arlene's "hateful self," telling her that God would take away that self somehow and replace it with a "meek" self—the kind that inherits the earth (GO 61). Arlie, half crazed with grief over the chaplain's unannounced transfer out of her prison, and her spirit broken from her stay in solitary, reacted to his words literally and tried to stab herself to death. This breakdown was an exorcism for Arlie and was followed by her transformation into a model prisoner, but now Arlene grieves for the loss of her younger self.

At the end of the play, Arlie, calling out to Arlene for the first time, repeats an anecdote from the past that amuses them both and they speak a reminiscing line in unison. It is a tiny but moving reconciliation and suggests that rather than eradicating her earlier self, Arlene will incorporate it. If Arlene is to survive, Arlie's vitality must survive as well. (It's a reversal of the denouement of Peter Shaffer's *Equus*, whose protagonist's cure squelched the passion of his younger self.)

Norman knows how to write for the theater, making a virtue of its limitations. She uses the confined space to emphasize the intensity of Arlene's encounters and her overwhelming sense of being trapped. The play has no sensuous aspects: its structure is as spare as its sets, the action proceeding without deviation to its completion. Complementing the tightness of structure is the economy of language. Every sentence has its purpose: there is nothing random about Norman's writing. When, for example, Ruby says to Arlene, "Hey! You have a good trip? Candy said you was in Arkansas," and Arlene answers, "Alabama," it is not only a snatch of lifelike conversation, but an illustration of her family's indifference (GO 48). All that Candy can remember of her sister's whereabouts is the first letter of the state. (It's a measure of Norman's skill at economic characterization that we are certain, from the little we have heard of Candy and seen of Ruby, that it was Candy's, not Ruby's, error.) With similar economy Bennie's callousness is indicated in his brief reminiscence of an elderly prisoner who threw a rock at him and was shot as punishment. "You shoot him?" asks Arlene. "Nope. Somebody else did," says Bennie, "I forget who" (GO 14).

The humor of the play—and despite its grimness, there is considerable humor—is understated too. At the beginning of their reunion, when her mother observes unsympathetically that Arlene looks tired, Arlene replies with laconic irony, "It was a long drive" (GO 18). Bennie's gift to Arlene of the package of paper towelettes, accompanied by his explanation "...they was in the chicken last night. I thought I might be needin' em, but they give us new towels every day at the motel," is both a joke at Bennie's expense and an insight into the pathetic meanness of the quality of his life (GO 63).

If there is a weakness in the play, it is that we are told about, rather than shown, the change from Arlie to Arlene. We watch Arlie enact moments of the past and we are moved and persuaded by them, but we must take this most significant act—the beginning of her transformation—on faith. The alternating and parallel scenes between the raging Arlie and the carefully controlled Arlene are emotionally and theatrically effective in contrast, but the play would be deepened by the interpenetration of the two selves.

Despite the squalid surroundings, narrow vistas, and insoluble problems that Arlene must contend with, *Getting Out* is not a depressing play. The dramatic tension, the humor, and the playwright's empathy for her protagonist and uncondescending pity for her other characters infuse it with life.

The one-act play *The Laundromat* is like a study drawing for Norman's more fully realized portraits of women. Its companion play, *The Pool Hall*, connects tangentially with it in an extra scene that is used when the plays are done together, but the entertaining dialogue between two black men—a pool hall owner and a disk jockey—is more of an actors' vehicle than a drama. *Laundromat* is the more substantial play, primarily because of the character of Deedee, which is sketched with humor and compassion.

It is an exchange between two women, one old enough to be the other's mother, who meet at three in the morning in an all-night laundromat. Alberta, the older woman, has chosen this out-of-the-way location (she lives in a more affluent part of town) to wash her husband's clothes, but she doesn't reveal to Deedee until quite late in the play that he died earlier that year. Deedee is doing a nocturnal laundry to distract herself from the torment of waiting up for her husband to come home. He claims to be doing a great deal of overtime at the Ford plant, but Deedee knows better. A compulsive talker, she corners the reluctant Alberta in conversation immediately, and in her sad, funny chatter, spills out her life story in no time.

Deedee and Joe live across from the laundromat in an apartment over the Old Mexico Taco Tavern. "That's how Joe picked the apartment," Deedee tells Alberta. "He hates to run out for beer late."[2] This is one of her many little observations that, taken together, give a good picture of her loutish husband. She doesn't say that Joe is an inconsiderate slob; she says that he "thinks hangers are for when you lock your keys in your car" (*L* 6). She doesn't describe his brutal temper, but mentions that when one of his bowling shirts got damaged in his mother-in-law's washing machine, he kicked a chest of drawers, breaking the chest and his toe. Deedee's desired motherhood will have to be postponed, as Joe wants to put the money into a 1964 Chevy for drag racing. Not that he doesn't want children, too. Deedee assures Alberta that he is really looking forward to "winnin' a big race and havin' me and the kids run out on the track and him smilin' and grabbin' up the baby and pourin' beer all over us while the crowd is yellin' and screamin'..." (*L* 13).

Joe's other big interest is the woman with whom Deedee saw him the night before when she dropped into the bowling alley as a surprise. But rather than confront Joe, she fled. This behavior is consistent with the glimpse of Deedee that comes through in her reminiscence about high school—a girl treated as an object, fair game for male advances and insults. Now she plays that role for her husband. Deedee is like the pre–Arlene Arlie, who was a pushover for Carl, and her name—not short for anything else, she tells Alberta—has the same connotations as Arlie's. It is not a full-fledged name and its bearer is not treated as a full-fledged person.

Joe's macho values prevent Deedee from working outside the home and so her only job, kept secret from her husband, is writing names on direct mail pieces. Her excursions are few and pathetic. One of them is to take her laundry to her mother's ("She got matching Maytags"), where the two women sit and watch the soaps on television while they wash and dry their clothes (*L* 6). It is not a cozy mother-and-daughter scene, though. Deedee mentions that her mother takes money from her direct mail earnings to pay for the water that Deedee uses, and that "she don't say two words while I'm there. Ever" (*L* 20). The other diversion Deedee is toying with is a continuation of the flirtation that began one night when the black disc jockey who hangs out at the pool hall next door came into the laundromat.

Alberta's life has been quite different. Her references to a former career as a teacher, trips to Mexico with her husband, her husband's fondness for gardening, and her annual birthday cake for him suggest a happy, comfortable existence. But before Deedee's arrival Alberta has posted two notices on the bulletin board, which we learn are advertisements offering typing services and selling gardening tools that have never been used—her gift to her husband on his last birthday. Alberta finally admits that her husband died of a heart attack on the day before that birthday. There seems to be no strong reason for her to have concealed the death of her husband from Deedee: the secret seems like a dramatic device to produce suspense and then a moment of revelation. Of course, it could be argued that Alberta is an exceedingly reserved woman whose ritual washing of her late husband's clothes is too private an act to discuss with an intrusive stranger. In any case, as the intimacy between the improbable confidantes gradually develops, the insights into Alberta's marriage are less lively and less revealing than Deedee's. Perhaps bad marriages lend themselves better to description. She does express her feelings poignantly in one brief speech: "I found our beachball when I cleaned out the basement. I can't let the air out of it. It's his breath in there" (L 24). The dialogue is written with Norman's usual economy. Deedee talks incessantly as a defense against panic, but there is always a reason for what is said. For example, before Alberta confesses that her husband is dead, she tells Deedee that he is in Akron. Deedee's response is "Akron, he could be sittin' at the bar in some all-night bowling alley polishin' some big blonde's ball" (L 12). It's not just an offensive remark made to the genteel Alberta; it turns out later that Deedee was really talking about having seen her own husband with a blonde, "one of his hands rubbing her hair and the other one rubbing his bowling ball" (L 22).

Alberta, speaking of Deedee's husband, but thinking of her own, points out that "People just can't always be where we want them to be when we want them to be there" (L 16). When Deedee says that she doesn't like that idea, Alberta tells her "You don't have to like it. You just have to know it" (L 16). This is a key statement. Facing the truth, always a high value in a Norman play, is the first step for each of these women in "getting out" of their respective traps.

By the end of the play it seems likely that Alberta will begin to liberate herself from the confines of mourning and get on with a new life, and that perhaps Deedee will learn that being alone is better than being imprisoned in a bad marriage. "Your own face in the mirror," Alberta admonishes her, "is better company than a man who would eat a whole fried egg in one bite" (L 25). Alberta uses this image from one of Deedee's anecdotes about Joe to underscore what Deedee knows already: that he is uncouth, greedy, and insensitive. Deedee even knows that he is "mean and stupid" and that there is no hope for a real marriage with him (L 22).

The ending is ambiguous, as it should be: women with more resources and opportunities than Deedee stay with their own versions of Joe, rather than be alone. This dread of being alone—that is, without a man—that the two women, otherwise so different, share, pervades the play, making *Laundromat* the product of a female sensibility. It is difficult to imagine a dialogue between two men on this subject. It isn't the fear of loneliness that is unique to women, but the degree to which they will make accommodations to hold on to an unworthy man or a dead relationship in order to avoid it.

Laundromat is a small play, but because of Norman's ability to delineate character through pungent and authentic dialogue, it is a humorous and affecting one. And it evokes the kind of spiritually desolate landscape in which a laundromat becomes a symbol for purging and redemption.

Near the beginning of *'Night, Mother*, Jessie Cates announces to her mother that she is going to kill herself. The play-length argument that follows is a nightmare version of the ambivalence of parent-child relationships, accusation alternating with forgiveness, bitterness with affection.

Jessie has many reasons for "getting out." She feels as trapped in the isolated house that she shares with her mother as Arlene felt in solitary confinement. It is a house to which no one comes, not even thieves. As Mama points out, "This is way too far to come for what's out here to steal."[3] It is also a house which Jessie, who returned after her marriage ended, never leaves. She is isolated in her relationships as well. Her father, the only person who loved her or with whom she was comfortable, has died, and her husband, whom she mutely adored, has left her. Her son has moved out and is evolving from a juvenile delinquent into a serious criminal. Jessie's only relationship is with her mother, a benevolent despot who doesn't even clean her own glasses. Jessie's days are circumscribed by household chores; yet she has accepted this role of symbiotic servitude.

Another imprisonment has been her epilepsy. It has limited the jobs she could take, caused people—her former husband included—to be uncomfortable in her presence, and, above all, humiliated her. The repeated indignity of being unconscious, out of control, handled and watched by others may be the cause of Jessie's almost paranoic sensitivity about her privacy. The worst thing about families, according to Jessie, is that they know our secrets. She has never forgiven Dawson and Loretta, her brother and sister-in-law, for opening a package containing her mail order bra with the "little rosebuds" on it, delivered to them by mistake (NM 19). Perhaps she feels that it revealed an incongruous yearning for femininity and sexual attractiveness. Jessie's need for privacy almost suggests that it was the reason, as much as her epilepsy, that she never left the house, never worked for long at an outside job: how would she bear all those additional people looking at her? Her self-consciousness has made her husband's leaving "a relief in a way. I never was what he wanted to see, so it was better when he wasn't looking at me all the time" (NM 41). Another unstated reason that Jessie is going to kill herself is so that no one will ever look at her again.

Like Arlene, Jessie has been imprisoned by others' decisions. But Arlene's powerlessness resulted from a life taken over by institutional authorities, while Jessie's comes from her profound temperamental passivity. Suicide will be her first act of rebellion. If she has not been in charge of her life, she will be in charge of her death. She controls the time, the place, and the method; and, now that she has told her mother of her plan, she controls her mother, too.

Finally, what has driven Jessie to suicide is the absoluteness of her boredom. When she tells her mother that her decision to do this was made at Christmas, her mother asks what happened at Christmas, and Jessie says, "Nothing." Mama asks, "So why Christmas?" "That's it. On the nose," Jessie answers (*NM* 22). And when Mama reminds her of her forthcoming birthday, hoping pathetically that Jessie will be curious about her presents, Jessie predicts not only what they will be, but the familial pleasantries that will accompany them. Her most unrelenting pressure has been the pressure of the humdrum.

Mama fights Jessie with her full arsenal of arguments and strategies, from trivial to profound, from pleas to tantrums. She forbids her to commit suicide on her property, warns her that suicide is a sin, tells her that she will misfire and become a vegetable. She promises to remove any of the possible causes of Jessie's unhappiness—visits from Dawson and Loretta, housework and laundry, newspapers and TV with their bad news. Casting about wildly for something that Jessie might like, her suggestions reflect the narrowness of their lives: she proposes teaching Jessie how to crochet, doing puzzles, putting in a garden, taking a taxi to the A&P, rearranging the furniture. When Jessie says that death is what she wants, "it's dark and quiet," Mama offers a nap, cotton in her ears, keeping the TV off all night (*NM* 16). Jessie speaks in metaphors; Mama is doggedly, maddeningly, and healthily literal. As she frantically tries to make sense of the tragedy that is happening to them—is it because of Jessie's son, her ex-husband, her fits, her confinement to the house? is it Mama herself?—Jessie explains that she is riding a hot, crowded, noisy, bumpy bus and has decided to get off now instead of 50 blocks or 50 years from now, because whenever she gets off, it will be the same place.

Mama is delighted when Jessie asks her to make cocoa and caramel apples, partly to give her mother something to do, partly as a fleeting nostalgia for a kinder time. But when her mother serves the cocoa, Jessie remembers how much she dislikes the taste of milk. "You won't like the apple either," says Mama, and Jessie doesn't contradict her (*NM* 36). She has reached the end of whatever faint desires she ever had.

Mama points out the distortion of the natural cycle of things ("You're supposed to help me die when the time comes"), exhorts Jessie to be braver, urges her to keep trying until things get better (*NM* 48). "I say No!" is Jessie's implacable answer (*NM* 49). "You are my child," Mama cries out, as though to prove that Jessie has no right to leave her, but Jessie's wrenching response is, "I am what became of your child" (NM 50). Grief stricken and furious, Mama contrasts their views of death: "You make me feel like a fool for being alive and you are so wrong. I like it here, and I will stay here until they make me go, until they drag me screaming and I mean screeching into my grave and you're real smart to get away before then because, I mean, honey, you've never heard noise like that in your life" (NM 51). But she realizes the futility of fighting for Jessie's life, acknowledging that "You're gone already, aren't you?... I can't stop you because you're already gone" (NM 51).

The outcome is never in question: Jessie's death is the inevitable conclusion to the drama. What the struggle does accomplish is to make Mama and Jessie look at each other for the first time. In those 90 minutes they come closer in love and hate than they have been in all the preceding years. Jessie asks the questions she has long wanted answers to, learns that her mother never loved her father; that her own husband cheated on her with the daughter of Mama's best friend; that Mama withheld from her that the epilepsy was inherited from her father and began when she was five years old, not, as she had thought, after a fall from a horse when she was married. (One wonders how Jessie could have been oblivious to all those earlier years of seizures, even though Norman, always a careful writer, has her say that she didn't notice most of the fits until she awoke in different clothes.) "That was mine to know, Mama, not yours," Jessie says, reacting to another invasion of her sovereignty and to still another when she blames her mother for unnecessarily shipping her to the hospital in an ambulance, subjecting her to voyeuristic scrutiny (NM 46).

Mama admits that she maneuvered Cecil's proposal to Jessie, and Jessie admits that she wrote Cecil's goodbye letter herself, ashamed that he had just slipped away. She makes a terrible assessment of how she and her son are alike and of how he is cursed by the internalizing of his parents' quarrel forever:

> *Jessie:* I see it on his face. I hear it when he talks. We look out at the world and we see the same thing. Not Fair. And the only difference between us is Ricky's out there trying to get even....
> *Mama:* Ricky isn't through yet. You don't know how he'll turn out!
> *Jessie:* Yes I do and so did Cecil. Ricky is the two of us together for all time in too small a space. And we're tearing each other apart, like always, inside that boy... [NM 40].

Jessie asks what her seizures looked like, listening intently as her mother describes the grotesque symptoms, and her mother marvels at how the new medication has removed those symptoms over the past year. But paradoxically, the remission has strengthened Jessie's resolve to kill herself. If her head had been clear before, she says, she would have done it sooner.

As Jessie finally pulls away, Mama struggles with her physically, but it is to no more avail than the words have been. After a lifetime, and after this night's reprise of a lifetime, Mama must concede that Jessie is a separate person, a difficult concept for a parent to accept. Her final cry to her daughter, after she hears the shot through the locked bedroom door, is "Forgive me! I thought you were mine!" (NM 58).

Just as Jessie and Cecil are internalized in their son's mind, Jessie's parents are internalized in hers. A ruminative, passive dreamer like her father, a fighter like her mother, Jessie manages to arrange for both of them to participate in her death: her father as symbolic instrument of it (she has chosen his gun over Cecil's), her mother as witness.

Jessie succeeds in "getting out," but Mama has been equally trapped. Her life is bounded by television, crocheting, eating junk sweets, and her Saturday night manicure. It is she who captures the tackiness of their surroundings ("We don't have anything anybody'd want, Jessie. I mean, I don't even want what we got, Jessie.") and the boredom of their daily routine, epitomized in her description of doing the laundry: "You put the clothes in. You put the soap in. You turn it on. You wait. Whatever else you find to do you're still mainly waiting. The waiting's the worst part of it" (NM 12, 18). Gregarious by nature, she is not visited by her one close friend, who avoids the house except when Jessie is in the hospital, and she was married to a man who rarely spoke a word to her, but had "quiet little conversations" with Jessie every night (NM 33). Even when he was dying, he had said nothing to his wife. "It was his last chance not to talk to me," Mama says with unintentional humor, "and he took full advantage of it" (NM 36). She feels that Jessie has treated her with similar unspoken contempt. "Nothing I ever did was good enough for you and I want to know why," she declares (NM 37).

A child's suicide is the ultimate punishment of the parent. Although Jessie explains that she is warning her mother beforehand so as to spare her the shock of suddenly hearing the gun shot, in fact she is doubling the punishment: her mother must endure both the suicide and her inability to prevent it. Some of Jessie's remarks to her mother are taunts; others, dropped lightly, will haunt her forever. When Mama's first stunned reaction to the news is to try to call Jessie's brother, as though he could somehow prevent it, Jessie threatens to kill herself as soon as Mama gets off the phone. "Go ahead, call him," she says. "Then call the funeral home. Then," she adds sarcastically, referring to the undeviating Saturday night ritual of giving

Mama a manicure, "call Loretta and see if *she'll* do your nails" (*NM* 15). Throughout the play, in counterpoint to Mama's inventory of protestations, Jessie recites her inventory of the daily chores that Mama will now have to do, implying that Mama can't take of herself without special instructions, and underscoring that she is about to abandon her.

Underneath Jessie's feelings of emptiness is her accumulated rage. She is angry at her prying brother, her condescending sister-in-law, her incorrigible son, her betraying husband. She is angry at her mother for being a silly, interfering, manipulative woman and, especially, for being all that Jessie has and that not being enough. When Jessie says that her decision has nothing to do with her mother, and her mother argues that it has everything to do with her, simply because Jessie is her child, Jessie counters cruelly, "Then what if it does! . . . What if I could take all the rest of it if only I didn't have you here? What if the only way I can get away from you for good is to kill myself? What if it is? I can *still* do it!" (*NM* 47).

Nowhere does Jessie torture her mother more than when she is rehearsing her on what to do when it's all over. She cautions her not to let on to Dawson and Loretta that she knew beforehand. "If they know we talked about it," says Jessie, consciously or unconsciously twisting the knife, "they really won't understand how you let me go" (*NM* 54). Just before the end, when Mama tries to restrain Jessie, saying, "You can't do this . . . I'm scared. I love you," Jessie's only response is "Let go of me, Mama. I've said everything I had to say" (*NM* 56). One of the things she did not say was that she loved her.

Talking about Jessie and Mama this way is like apportioning blame in a family. They are real people. Jessie, in particular, comes off the page. She is both cruel and heartbreaking, and her cruelty does not diminish her, but gives another dimension to her character. Drab in her life, she is powerful in the drama.

Underneath the apparent simplicity of the play is a complex pattern of relationships and emotions, actions and reactions, interplay of past and present. Norman accomplishes this with a purity of writing that leaves out anything that is not essential to the action and that, without ever betraying the integrity of her characters' speech, raises it above their limitations to an expression of the universal language between mother and child.

In *Traveler in the Dark* Norman departs from writing about ordinary people living marginal lives and takes as her protagonist a world-famous surgeon. But Sam is as anxious to quit as Jessie, and he proposes to do so by chucking his marriage and his medical practice and heading to parts unknown—California, maybe, or Africa, he tells his twelve-year-old son Stephen, whom he wants to take with him.

Sam's decision, made with the impulsiveness of a man who has been rigidly rational for too many years, is propelled by his failure to save Mavis, his lifelong friend, office nurse, and, finally, cancer patient, who has died after Sam's unsuccessful operation. It is his panicky response to the second huge loss in his life—his mother's death when he was 12 was the first—and a subconscious way of avoiding a third. If Sam leaves his wife, Glory,now, he can avoid the possibility of having to face her death in the future.

The radical, nihilistic nature of Sam's method of "getting out" comes from his embittered conclusion that there is no efficacy in either works or prayer. When his mother was dying, he tried to keep her from slipping into unconsciousness by repeating the beloved nursery rhymes that they had shared, as a kind of prayer. But he could not save his mother with prayer any more than some 30 years later he could save Mavis with medical science. The only thing he will believe in now, Sam says, is the brevity of love and the obliteration of everything by time. Like Jessie, who said no to hope, Sam is saying no to faith: in God, in love, in medicine, in the power of the mind.

At first Sam appears to represent the clear-eyed facing of the truth that is Norman's highest good. But, in fact, his insistence on factual truth has blinded him to the deeper truth of poetry and religion, the mystery at the center of things that we cannot and, Norman is saying, ought not presume to know. This view of life that values supernatural belief over scientific rationalism and mystery over knowledge seems out of character for the author of such grittily realistic earlier plays. And yet it's not inconsistent with them. The instrument of Arlie's redemption has been the chaplain and his Bible. Jessie is a rationalist like Sam, albeit an untutored one, and it is the spiritual emptiness of her life rather than her specific misfortunes that has led ineluctably to her decision to choose death. The difference is that the earlier plays are, first of all, about people and their relationships with each other, and from that comes an examination of suffering and of possible solutions to the suffering. In *Traveler in the Dark*, the argument—faith versus reason—comes first, and the characters dramatize it. The result is less a drama than a debate.

Another problem is that everything is fraught with symbolism. Sam and Glory have brought Stephen back to their hometown for Mavis's funeral, which will be conducted by Sam's father, a revivalist preacher. The setting is the garden of Sam's childhood home, which becomes the locus of his battle with Glory about the future and with Everett, his father, about the past. Dominating the garden is a wall in which are embedded Sam's old playthings, presided over by a stone Mother Goose. This Garden of Eden, now in disrepair, was created and tended by Sam's mother, whom he likens to Mother Goose and the gingerbread lady—figures of bountiful love, imagination, magic. As Sam begins to clean up the garden (which signifies the values of his childhood, instilled by his mother) Stephen carries out books of nursery rhymes, fairy tales, Bible stories, and Sam's Bible—all of which Sam disapproves, urging Stephen to read, instead, such documents as the chronicle of Donner Pass—that he has discovered in the house.

The visual cues are matched by textual allusions to fairy tales and biblical parables that are contrived and sometimes confusing. Sam was the frog who married the princess, Glory (her name additionally suggesting her spark of the divine), in the mistaken hope that the marriage would turn him into a prince who "... would be handsome, and play tennis and mix martinis, and tell jokes at parties, just like all her other boyfriends. But years later," says Sam, "the prince started to turn, slowly at first, but finally and irreversibly back into the frog he always was."[4] In Sam's interpretation of "The Sleeping Beauty" the thirteenth fairy whom the king neglected to invite to the christening feast is the misfortune in our lives that we cannot control and consequently try to forget. Ignored, the malignant fairy took her revenge on the princess, just as the cancer, overlooked by Sam, took its revenge on Mavis. Glory's interpretation of the story, on the other hand, is that the solution is the prince, the transforming power of love.

The Old Testament story of Abraham and Isaac, besides being a paradigmatic tale of conflict between fathers and sons, is a battleground over which Sam and Everett, each trying to convince Stephen, can expound their views. Sam says that God wanted Abraham to kill Isaac because He was bored; Everett says that God was testing Abraham in preparation for great tasks. An additional significance in the choice of this parable is that Sam who, we learn, was for a time a child preacher, used it as his text on the most triumphant occasion of his preaching career; one month later his mother died.

Sam goes on to explain to Stephen that Job's suffering was the result of a bet that God made with the Devil, and lost. Since then God hasn't been in control, Sam says; He is just another fairy tale king. "If you want to believe," he tells his son, "believe in yourself. In your power, in your mind, in your life. This life. Because that's all there is" (TD I:41).

As for the Donner Pass story, Sam points out that the family had been so anxious to reach their destination that they gradually threw out each of their belongings in order to make the journey lighter, assuming that when they arrived they would figure out how to survive. "It's a pretty standard American idea," he says. "All you need is your brain" (TD II:46). But when they were caught in a blizzard at Donner Pass, devoid of provisions and the means to secure them, they ate each other. Sam seems to be saying here that, having discarded all those values that might have saved him and his family, he is now caught in an emotional blizzard that will destroy them all. Sam's view is far from clear: is it he or the playwright who is saying that his repudiation of religion and his total reliance on reason threaten his family's survival?

The attempt to enrich the play with metaphors, as though to emphasize the play's argument that life is enriched by metaphor, is done with a heavy hand. Equivalences set awkwardly into the text to make a point interfere with the natural flow of Norman's writing. *Traveler in the Dark* is strongest when the dialogue is heightened by the characters' passions rather than by myths and parables. Sam's recollection of his youthful decision to marry Glory (beauty, the senses, divine spark) instead of Mavis (rationality, science), even though part of the thesis of the play and threaded with allusions to the story of the princess and the frog, is not self-consciously freighted with message. The effect makes a more compelling case for the thesis than do schematized interpretations of symbolic tales. For one moment that day, Sam says, he thought back to when he was 16:

> . . .and I had it all to do over again. And I could forget your hair, and forget your mouth and your smell, and love Mavis. Marry her. Someone who believed in hard work, who couldn't wait to be an adult. . . . And in the next moment, the moment after I was sixteen and could forget your hair, I was sixteen and I wanted your hair in my mouth, in my eyes, all over me. I wanted to catch you swimming naked in your pond. . . . I hopped over to that pond like every frog in every fairy tale my mother ever read me, and you kissed me, and I believed. I remember that kiss, I can still taste the butterscotch sucker I took out of your mouth to have that kiss, and I'm still dizzy and hot all of a sudden, and I remember loving you [*TD* II:62].

The relationship between Sam and his father contains the unique bitterness of a father and son who are temperamentally alike and intellectually opposed. Both have been compulsively absorbed in their callings; both have been God-figures trying to save souls or bodies by performing their respective kinds of miracles. But their quarrel does not have the close-to-the-bone intensity of Jessie's quarrel with her mother because it is more a battle of views than of individuals. Although Sam blames his father's neglect of his mother for her death (just as Stephen now blames Sam for Mavis's death), the blame lacks the passion of the personal. It seems more like an illustration of one of the stages in Sam's rejection of religion.

The most schematic use of a personal relationship is in the explanation of Mavis's unfaltering devotion to Sam. When Mavis was a child hanging around Everett's church (her father was the custodian), Everett did magic tricks to amuse her. Sam quickly saw how they were done; unlike Mavis, he was not fooled. Glory repeats Mavis's last words in the hospital, telling why she has loved Sam all these years:

> It was only one thing he did really. We were ten years old, and Everett had this magic trick and Sam knew how it worked and he showed me.... He knew it wasn't magic, and he knew it didn't always work, and he wasn't afraid to know. Tell him that's why I loved him. He wasn't afraid to know [*TD* II:68].

This is one of the chief arguments of the play: magic (faith) and medicine (reason) do not always work, and it is important that we know that and face it. But it strains credulity to suggest that this occurrence meant so much to the ten-year-old Mavis that it accounted for her unconditional adoration of Sam for the next 30 years.

The other principal argument is symbolized by a geode, a rock with a formation of crystals at its center. When Stephen wants to crack open the geode to examine the crystals more closely, Sam restrains him, quoting his mother's old admonition that "it was better for it to be safe than for you to know what it was exactly" (*TD* II:72). The notion of the geode as the apple of knowledge reiterates the ancient fear that we will be punished if we probe too deeply into the mysteries of the universe.

This leads to an ending of general reconciliation and more metaphors. The last of them is the "other verse" of "Twinkle, Twinkle Little Star," Sam's mother's favorite, now recalled by Sam and Everett:

> As your bright and tiny spark
> Guides the traveler in the dark
> Though I know not what you are
> Twinkle, twinkle little star [*TD* II:81].

No longer a potential subject for Sam's scientific inquiry, the star is purely a symbol of faith: the guide whose presence we travelers in the dark celebrate and whose mystery we need not try to explain.

Because this is a play by Marsha Norman, there are many passages of fluent and engrossing dialogue, lively characters (Everett is shadowy, but Sam, Glory, and Stephen are quite distinctly drawn), and moments of high drama leavened by humor. But Norman would have served her art better by focusing, as she has in the past, on the personal dilemma rather than the philosophical issue.

There is a puritanical quality to Norman's writing. Each of the plays raises a moral question: *Getting Out* weighs the temptations of crime against the limitations of "going straight"; *'Night, Mother* examines reasons for choosing to live or die; *Traveler in the Dark* is about embracing humanism or theism. The characters preoccupied with these questions, although as confused and alienated as their counterparts in much of contemporary American writing, are far less self-indulgent. "Getting out" in the context of these plays requires the courage to face up to one's life, to decide how it must be changed, and to act. And the action proceeds to its conclusion without diversion: there are no star turns or displays of verbal fireworks.

There are no visual diversions, either. The ruined garden in *Traveler in the Dark* is the most beguiling of the environments inhabited by Norman's characters. They are more likely to be found in cramped apartments or dreary laundromats or seedy pool halls or nondescript houses filled with objects that have the melancholy banality of items for sale in a K Mart.

Norman is able to convey the horror that is present in the everyday domestic world: the numbing tyranny of household tasks, the loneliness of family life (Glory reports her mother's seemingly paradoxical comment at her husband's funeral: "I'm never going to be lonely again"), the contrast between the blandness of surroundings and the acuteness of despair enclosed in them (*TD* I:25). Her spare writing, bleak landscapes, and spiritually improverished lives are reminiscent of the fiction of American "minimalist" writers like Raymond Carver, Frederick Barthelme, and Bobbie Ann Mason (who also writes about Kentucky people). But Norman's characters are at a critical point, when events of the past intersect with events of the present to bring about the need for a change in direction for the future. In that change lies the possibility of their redemption.

Interview with Marsha Norman

My interview with Marsha Norman took place in December 1986 at a popular (and clamorous) bar-restaurant in the Theater District in New York. I had originally asked for an interview several months earlier, but her agent explained that Ms. Norman would not have time even to consider my request until after the completion of four momentous events that were to occur in rapid succession over the next few months: her divorce, her move to a new home in New York, the release of the film version of 'Night, Mother, for which Norman wrote the screenplay, and the delivery of her first novel to Random House.

Norman is small, dark-haired, and blue-eyed, with the kind of expressive face that oscillates within seconds between ordinary and beautiful. She is friendly and chatty and laughs frequently with the slight but unmistakable hoarseness of the serious cigarette smoker. She was generous about the interview, which lasted over two hours, offering to do it again, via written questions and answers, if the din of the restaurant—her suggested meeting place—interfered with the taped recording.

ESTHER HARRIOTT: What kind of formative role did the Actors Theatre play? Do you think you would have been a playwright, rather than another kind of writer, if that theater hadn't been in Louisville?

MARSHA NORMAN: I always knew the theater was the form I was most interested in. I had the great good fortune of going to the theater as a child. When I was a teenager, my mother, who was an inveterate driver, got the idea that she and I should go to the theater together. She had never been to the theater before that and hasn't really been much since, but she did take me, when I was 12, up the stairs to this tiny loft-like theater that was the beginning of Actors Theatre in Louisville. They were doing *The Glass Menagerie*. So I think that the fact that that theater was in existence in the city when I was a young teenager was perhaps more important than the valuable friendships that I made there later. When I got ready to write, I knew that I wanted to write for the theater. It would have been so much harder, had there not been a world-class theater in my town.

HARRIOTT: What was there about the theater that especially drew you to it?

NORMAN: That was the place I felt most alive. That was where I had the feeling "I could do that." In college I was involved in productions and was always around the edges of theater. What I never did was believe, until I was almost 30, that I could support myself that way. I didn't come from a writer's family, my parents weren't readers—they still aren't. They didn't know what a Pulitzer Prize was until I won it.

HARRIOTT: They didn't disapprove, did they?

NORMAN: I never said to anybody that that's what I wanted to do. One of the things that I'm pretty cagey about is not saying what I want to do until it's done, until it's too late. I don't want those sympathetic looks or "Oh, poor dear" or anybody worrying about how terribly I'm going to fare in this adventure. I didn't really say to anybody, "Oh, I want to write a novel," until Kate Medina was standing there with a contract, and then I said, "Oh, fine, I'll write a novel." And it's going to be published this spring and it's fine and they like it. I didn't lounge around for years mooning about, "Oh, what I always wanted to do was write." I always thought that what I would have to do was work, and I didn't know exactly what work that would be. It's very hard for me to stay in one place for eight hours because somebody says, "This is when you start and this is when you stop." I can stay in my house for three solid days, if that's required, writing. But let anybody tell me I have to be someplace from 9 to 5 and I get crazy. Fortunately there were people who hired me all those years to do really interesting things, although I wasn't able to do them for very long—I had five jobs over the course of ten years.

HARRIOTT: Some of them included writing, didn't they, for a paper?

NORMAN: Yes. I was never a full-time employee, but I had a children's section, "The Jellybean Journal," for which they paid me $100 a week, the continuing income that allowed me to write *Getting Out*. I would go through all the jokes that the kids sent in and I would devise puzzles and do stories.

HARRIOTT: You were doing all this very jolly stuff and writing the searing play at the same time.

NORMAN: Right.

HARRIOTT: To backtrack for a minute, you say that you always wanted to write for the theater, and now you've just finished writing a novel.

NORMAN: Yes. There are seven or eight reasons for that, but it was also a great surprise to me when I arrived at a day when I did want to write a novel. I had never thought about it. I say that and then have to confess that when I had my lunch with Kate Medina, I had in my purse a three-page scene

149

based on an idea that I knew was too big for a play. So while I say that I never consciously thought about a novel, here were these three pages of dialogue about a fortune-teller and on the basis of that she gave me a contract to do the book.

HARRIOTT: Writing the novel must have been a very different kind of experience for you, because one of the striking things about your plays is that they never diverge for an instant from what is absolutely necessary to the action. They are scrupulously faithful to the unities. Was writing fiction a kind of release?

NORMAN: It was wonderful to have a bigger piece of paper. The questions are still the same: When can you go astray and when can you not? There is such a thing as pace in a novel, which I had to learn. In the first draft there was this great, fat middle section that just went rambling off into all these wonderful details just for the sheer joy of writing. I had to cut the book down from 980 double-spaced pages to 650. That's virtually three plays I cut out of the novel!

HARRIOTT: How much time does that represent in your writing?

NORMAN: Two and a half years. That part I'm most amazed by is that I was able to devote two and a half years. It was an act of faith that I could stay interested in something for that long. Nothing in my life would lead you to believe that I could stay interested in anything for much longer than eight or nine months.

HARRIOTT: Is that the longest time that it's taken you to write any of your plays?

NORMAN: Yes, and most of them didn't take that long. I wrote 'Night, Mother in about four months and then, when we went into rehearsals, I did further work, so that from the first moment I began to write it to the moment it arrived on Broadway, it was two and a half years. But the actual writing of it was not that long at all.

HARRIOTT: Are there certain things that you write about for the theater that wouldn't lend themselves to novels?

NORMAN: The requirements for the theater are pretty strict. You have to be able to find two hours of time in the life that you are talking about from which you can see the entire life. You have to find that critical moment around which the life balances, that sort of fulcrum of the life. And you have to be able to look all the way back to the beginning and look forward to the inevitable end. You have to know the whole story. I believe that in all lives there is that moment when you can see why the person is the person they are—whether it's a decision about something or an opportunity that's missed or one that's made to happen. I think that the theater requires that kind of dramatic moment from which all things are visible.

Interview

HARRIOTT: When you write fiction, do you have as much of an idea of what's going to happen, or is there a lot more of the process of discovery?

NORMAN: In my plays I always know. In the novel I hadn't a clue.

HARRIOTT: Was that more fun?

NORMAN: Oh, yes. And there's an enormous social issue in the novel, which I had no idea about. Enormous, controversial, hot issue. I swear I didn't know it was there. I just began to write about a fortune-teller and her old lover, this detective who works down the block at the police station, and her daughter, and I had no idea that this other thing . . . I mean, it's abortion, that's how serious it is. It happens that in the book there is a terrorist act by an anti-abortion group, which act Fay, the fortune-teller, is called on to help the police department solve. I didn't start out to do that, but I knew from the beginning that the book was about how we inevitably lose our children. "Missing" them is probably clearer than "losing" them. But if you had said to me, "Marsha, look, if you say this book is about how we miss our children, here are some of the things you could run into in this book — children dying, children being kidnapped, and abortion," you would think that somebody in the back of my mind knew that it was on the list. But I didn't know that.

HARRIOTT: You say that you started writing about a fortune-teller and a detective. Is that the usual genesis of your work — picking your characters?

NORMAN: Yes. It's someone this is a flashy way of saying it — someone I would really like to nominate for memory. I'd like to say, "Let's everyone remember this person and what they did" — almost the wax museum approach to writing. [Laughs]

HARRIOTT: Except that the wax museum remembers famous people. You seek out and celebrate the invisible ones.

NORMAN: Exactly. I don't consider myself a terribly courageous person — I'm certainly a physical coward. And yet it's courage that I respond to most strongly. It doesn't matter that the life hasn't been glorious or seemingly interesting. It's then my role to give them their voice.

HARRIOTT: How do you give them that voice? How do you get inside their consciousness, because you don't pick people from your own social class or milieu, do you?

NORMAN: It's a voicing process that I've come to love and trust, which just involves carrying around notebooks and having pieces of paper by every chair. In that pre-writing stage before I'm actually sitting at the typewriter, I would be aware of when phrases come to mind. I'm sure it's like

151

composers when they begin to hear melodies. You begin to hear the way somebody talks.

HARRIOTT: You're saying that you hear it literally?

NORMAN: Yes, literally. I'll begin to hear lines of dialogue. And the question gets to be "Who's speaking?" At that point, it's like that old TV show "This Is Your Life"—isn't that the one where they had someone speaking behind the scrim? So at that moment I'm the person sitting there in the chair, thinking, "I hear this voice, I know that's somebody that I know. Who is it?" And then once you get it "voiced," once you know how the characters talk, the writing can begin.

HARRIOTT: You make it sound so simple, but I'm struck by how authentic your characters sound and I wonder, just to take one example, how you know how Shooter [in *Third and Oak: The Pool Hall*] would speak?

NORMAN: That's very easy to explain. I spent some four years teaching film in an integrated alternative school that went from kindergarten to senior high, so there I was all day with black kids, from little kids to seniors, and you just pick up that language. And I do have that kind of ear—in seeing, they call it an eidetic memory or photographic memory. That's the kind of aural memory I have.

HARRIOTT: But you don't just have an aural memory for the way your characters speak. You seem to have an empathy for what's going on inside their consciousness.

NORMAN: Yes. But Shooter Stevens was based on the way Joe Morton talks. Joe Morton was around the theater at the time and said, "Why don't you write a play for me?" I would never have written *The Pool Hall*, never written a role for a young black man, had Joe Morton not invited me to do it.

HARRIOTT: Is that the only play that you've written for a specific actor?

NORMAN: No, *Getting Out* was written for Susan Kingsley.

HARRIOTT: I thought that Arlene in that play was based on a person you had met.

NORMAN: Yes, but that girl was 11 at the time I knew her. And I couldn't write about anybody who was 11—it isn't interesting. They don't need a play to solve their problems; they just need to get older.

HARRIOTT: I'm trying to figure out what attracts you to characters, apart from their being underdogs and survivors. Is it that they are clear-eyed?

NORMAN: Yes, it's people who need ultimately and finally to find out what the truth is, and who are willing to know it, whatever it costs them.

They are not interested in suffering, they are not interested in pretending, and they want to know how things are. They want the real story.

HARRIOTT: And yet in your last play, *Traveler in the Dark*, Sam's insistence on a clear-eyed view turns it into blindness to the poetry or mystery in life.

NORMAN: Yes.

HARRIOTT: And you're certainly not championing his point of view.

NORMAN: No. I had great sympathy for him. I have this theory that there's an analogue between how the play is written—the spirit, the frame of mind, the time—and how it's received into the world. If it's written at great speed and focus, chances are that's what will project out of it. What I am suggesting about the problem in the public reception of *Traveler in the Dark* is that I had great sympathy for Sam, and my sympathy for him was what went out to the audience. He may have played for my sympathy and I gave it to him. He played for the sympathy of the audience and they didn't care. [Laughs]

HARRIOTT: Do you feel that it's not one of your best plays?

NORMAN: I don't know. I think it has some of the best writing I've ever done. I think the play makes people mad. It makes critics mad in particular. It suggests that intelligence is not always useful. It challenges the rule of the rational.

HARRIOTT: If you admire people who "cast a cold eye," it's interesting that in this play you disapprove of having too much knowledge, and of people who try to have a life without any mystery in it.

NORMAN: Once you get to Jessie in 'Night, Mother, there's no other way to go. If you follow Jessie's path, you get this cold-eyed, clear reasoning that means you have to kill yourself. If you follow Jessie's argument all the way, you have to go with her. I didn't want to do that. I didn't want to die or quit writing. But I didn't know what to do. I was feeling at that moment that my intelligence was not enough. In lots of cases I still feel it. I think that I'm probably not at my best when I'm thinking about things. I have a wonderful analytic mind, but that's not the best part of me. It's the easiest part to use. It's like quick draw, like that's my sharpshooter. But the temptation is to use your mind and nothing else. One of the moments that really gets me in 'Night, Mother is when Mama suggests that Jessie could plant some begonias up the walk and maybe get enough rain for them all summer. Mama's idea is that you could make it to next summer just on the idea of the begonias maybe getting enough rain. At the end of 'Night, Mother, I was where Mama was: Yeah, that's right, let's hold on for the begonias and see if they get enough rain. I was ready to believe in something. Faith was my only choice. Writing 'Night, Mother moved me around. Maybe I should've lived a whole career before writing 'Night, Mother. Somebody even suggested at the time that what I should do is put 'Night, Mother away and have it published posthumously. [Laughs]

HARRIOTT: The play was an extraordinary achievement. Was that in itself a kind of problem? You were so young to have written a play like that. Was it an almost impossible act to follow?

NORMAN: I have to come to terms with 'Night, Mother just as everybody else does. It was very shocking to me in the reception to Traveler in the Dark that, in fact, everything I wrote was now going to be compared to 'Night, Mother. I was surprised at the hostility of the critics to the play. Even people whom I felt I had a personal relationship with thought it was somehow O.K. to attack me now, without understanding that I was perhaps more vulnerable at that moment than I had been before 'Night, Mother. The moment after a big success is precisely what determines whether someone is going to continue in the theater or whether they're going to be silenced for another ten years. One of the things that is just staggering in the American theatrical world is the number of writers who have been silenced by critics. Shut down. Critics have banished them.

HARRIOTT: Banished them by vitriolic criticism or by premature conferring of a mantle on them?

NORMAN: I think that the vitriolic criticism is worse than the mantle. The mantle is hard, but it's the viciousness of the attacks and the consequences of the attacks. And yet critics will say to you, "Oh, what power do we have?"

HARRIOTT: That's nonsense.

NORMAN: It is nonsense. A perfect example is a number of years ago New Dramatists gave a luncheon at which they honored Pulitzer Prize winners. There were 23 of us on the platform, going back to Charles Gordone, who wrote No Place to Be Somebody. Not one person on that podium was currently working on a play. Not one. The current critical establishment has assumed that writers ought to be able to take it and that plays ought to be fair game for a kind of consumer criticism. There's been a kind of brutishness about it and a feeling that it is fair to say anything.

HARRIOTT: Why is that the case with drama more than with the other forms? Drama criticism can be vicious in a way that fiction and poetry criticism rarely are.

NORMAN: Because novels and poetry are reviewed by people who also write them.

HARRIOTT: Not necessarily.

NORMAN: No, but in the theater it never happens, at least not up to now—this is something we are all trying to work on. It never happens that reviews are written by people who know what it takes, or what's really helpful in criticism. My personal feeling is that most criticism is written by people who harbor a secret desire to do it and so there's a jealousy that's really terrible.

HARRIOTT: But you could say that about any kind of criticism. Theater criticism is unique not just because it can be vicious, but because it's so powerful.

NORMAN: It could be that there's something about the enforced confinement in the theater that makes critics mad. John Leonard goes to an art show and he can walk away. Ada Huxtable goes to a building and she can get out of there. If somebody hates a book, they can slam it shut.

HARRIOTT: What about dance? It's a performing art held in a confined space that doesn't seem to bring out critical viciousness.

NORMAN: I don't know. The other thing that's real interesting about theater criticism is that it's about using a language that critics use, too. Everybody feels proficient in spoken English, as opposed to critics who know, for example, that they couldn't paint like that or dance like that. Everybody thinks they can talk or explain or tell jokes. So there's sort of an assumed mastery of the form that causes critics to feel superior real fast.

HARRIOTT: Do you feel that you've been discriminated against at all as a woman?

NORMAN: I don't feel that, but that doesn't mean it isn't so. Part of that is my temperament, which is that the last thing I'm likely to feel is that I'm a victim. I don't want to feel that. I will do almost anything, even to the point of not seeing it [laughs] in order not to feel victimized. It takes me a long time to realize that someone has taken advantage of me or has treated me badly. That's the difference between my characters and me—my characters pick up on those things much faster. I think that it's taken a while in the American theater for the managements—the directors and producers—to become interested in issues that are basically in the realm of women's secret knowledge. To put mother-daughter on stage all by themselves was new. We'd seen father-son on stage for centuries. What I do know is that there was a whole generation of writers who preceded me, who broke that ground. I think of feminist writing like *For Colored Girls*, for example, that said, "Our problems with men are significant problems. It's not just whining and complaining 'poor me.' They are real problems." And the early insistence on the part of feminist activists that writing grants be given for work by women. I benefited from that. I did not have to come in and break the doors down to write about a woman who's just gotten out of prison. The doors were open.

HARRIOTT: Would you call yourself a feminist writer?

NORMAN: If it's feminist to care about women's lives, yes, I'm a feminist writer. I don't have political points to make, although they are certainly made by the plays.

HARRIOTT: Does your great admiration for Lillian Hellman have more to do with her craft than with her subjects?

NORMAN: Yes, and with her sense of style. You have to understand that I didn't know her as a human being until one afternoon very, very late in her life. What I had from a great distance was this wonderful, looming model, this great, vibrant, feisty, swearing lady who had managed to make a life in that world. And a kind of glamor at a distance that really carried, so that her voice got all the way to Kentucky.

HARRIOTT: Getting back to 'Night, Mother, although I responded very much to Jessie, I felt that she was being cruel, that it was a night of vengeance for her, too. Does that go against what you feel about her?

NORMAN: I certainly don't feel that, but it's very hard for me to have any kind of external view. I wrote two points of view—Mama's and Jessie's. Mama would no doubt say, "This is the most obscene thing that I've ever heard of anybody doing." If Agnes's daughter did this to Agnes, Mama would be ready to go hang the girl. But Jessie approaches this out of a sense of "I'm just trying to help Mama." Jessie may be totally wrong about that, but that *is* what she thinks. So I see it from Jessie's side and from Mama's side and I'm not really called upon to take that triangular position and say, "O.K., here's what I get from both of these people." I've always felt that Jessie was true to herself and so was Mama, and so in that way it seemed fair to me, a fair contest. I knew Jessie was enormously powerful. I did not put Jessie up against nobody, you know, a weakling. Mama is not aware of her strength and when you first see Mama, you have no idea that she would be able to fight this battle. But in fact she is the best match Jessie will ever get. That's all I'm responsible for. I'm responsible for clarity of point of view and fairness that you don't put somebody in the ring with somebody helpless.

HARRIOTT: No, it *is* an equal match, but I guess I had read somewhere that you did not feel—is this right?—that she was punishing her mother.

NORMAN: I feel from Jessie's point of view that this is not why she's doing this. I accept from her that, from the inside, however it seems, she does not intend to do that. Obviously, we all have effects that we don't intend to have.

HARRIOTT: She's so fully realized as a character that a number of contradictory things ring true. She's cruel and she's heartbreaking. That line when she describes herself...

156

NORMAN: "I am what became of your child"? It was real interesting to wage that last part of the battle with them because Mama says all that she knows to say. You fight this battle one punch at a time, one little piece of footwork, another little piece of footwork, somebody goes against the ropes. And at that moment when Mama says, "You are my child," that's not a refutable statement. It carries with it enormous weight in the world of connective relationships. It's like "That's why you can't do this to me. I gave you your life. You can't take it." It's clear that Mama perceives that Jessie's life belongs to her. At that moment when Mama says, "You are my child," I wrote that down and then I literally walked the streets for three days until Jessie figured out what to say back. Another irrefutable statement.

HARRIOTT: How did you feel when you finished writing that play? It seems to me that you would be absolutely strung out.

NORMAN: I don't actually remember the finishing of it. I remember that I was terribly cold all the time I was writing it. It was summer and hot outside, and yet I was cold all the time and sitting in the room in sweaters and socks. I finally accepted that there was death in the room. Now, death does not happen to be a thing that I'm afraid of, so it didn't scare me to have it there. Since *'Night, Mother* I've learned a little bit more about death. I consider it to be a more fearsome presence than I did at the time and I don't know now how I would write about it again. But at the time I had Jessie's attitude of "It's exactly what I want—it's dark and quiet." [Laughs] Somebody even accused me of writing about death as though it were the New City.

HARRIOTT: The New City?

NORMAN: You know, the great place—where you go to get everything you want.

HARRIOTT: I just saw a documentary about Marlene Dietrich in which Maximilian Schell asked her if she was afraid of death, and she said, "Oh, no, death's not frightening. What's frightening is life."

NORMAN: I think that's a real difference between women and men. I think that women are not, on the whole, afraid of death.

HARRIOTT: I've never thought of that. I thought that was just a human response, not sexually differentiated.

NORMAN: I think for men it's kind of a contest. If you live, you win; if you die, you lose. Men don't like to lose. It's like a battle where they don't think about dying, they think about losing. Women are pretty comfortable with loss.

HARRIOTT: They're used to it.

NORMAN: Absolutely. It's basically what we know—that most of the time you lose anyway. In relationships, in efforts, in everything. I don't think men think about that.

HARRIOTT: Why did you pick a man to voice those views, then, in *Traveler in the Dark?* Also, you apparently feel very comfortable writing in a man's voice.

NORMAN: I really enjoyed it. Sam is much smarter than I am and it was really quite fun to write him. Lanford Wilson and I had a chat about that—that, in fact, you *can* write about people who are smarter than you are, because you can keep up with them for ten minutes at a time. Which is all you need. You write them for ten minutes and then you stop and write somebody else. And then you can come back and keep up with them again.

HARRIOTT: You make it sound as though your characters take on a life of their own.

NORMAN: Sure. That's why you do it. Somebody once told me that the people in the plays are all the folks Mother wouldn't let me play with as a kid. I think there's some of that—getting the people around you that you want to spend some time with. And I think one of the frustrations of writing for the theater is that your writing life can be so much more vivid than your personal life. For example, I write these great fights that people have—it's one of my skills—these horrible arguments. I never have them. I'm totally incapable of taking that risk with human beings.

HARRIOTT: But isn't that one of the functions of writing?

NORMAN: It's certainly one of the things that produces wonderful writing. Jimmy Kirkwood and I had this funny conversation about how to produce a writer, because we were at a cocktail party and a woman was saying, "I have these two little daughters and I would just love it if they would grow up to be writers." Jimmy and I almost fell over laughing about how you would do it. Basically, you would lock the kid away so there was nobody to talk to, so they didn't develop any social skills. They would never truly be comfortable with other people and would have to resort to paper, and you basically denied them access to any expression of their feelings. You would have to create an emotional cripple of a kind. Of course, Jimmy and I were just being perverse, but I do think that people are writers for a reason and that if they had any other way to say what it is that they write, they would say it. Nobody is going to listen to me for two and a half years talk about the world of fortune-tellers and astrology and palm reading, but the paper will.

HARRIOTT: The paper is the companion. Did you have to do research on fortune-telling? I wondered in *Getting Out*, for example, how much research you had done. Even for something like the announcements that preceded each act.

NORMAN: That's a thing that I believe in, that if I'm going to write, whatever else the work is, it is the actual truth about the subject matter.

Interview

In *Getting Out* I was assisted by a person at the Kentucky Prisoners Support Council who was able to put me in touch with various people who were former inmates, and also set up interviews for me. I spent a lot of time at this institution called Pee Wee Valley, where you're sitting there talking to a prisoner and listening, and you just pick it all up. All institutional announcements are the same. I love it that the play begins with "All kitchen workers report to the kitchen." For the fortune-teller I did an enormous amount of research based on visits to various psychics, and simple reading. There's been a lot written on the tarot—a lot of people have been fascinated by it.

HARRIOTT: Including the United States government.

NORMAN: Yes? How?

HARRIOTT: There have been articles recently about how officials in the State Department have consulted fortune-tellers—not very good ones apparently [laughs]—and how this is a sign of a widespread rebellion in this country against super-rational, super-scientific theory.

NORMAN: I think that's where it is, absolutely. And I think that that's what I would have said about *Traveler in the Dark*, but I didn't really want to say it. What I am hoping to do next, and I don't want to talk too much about it, is a real investigation of a biblical character, and so I am interested.

HARRIOTT: Which biblical character?

NORMAN: I'm interested in Sarah, Abraham's wife.

HARRIOTT: Why does she interest you? What was said about her in the Bible other than that she was barren?

NORMAN: Until she was 100. She was married to Abraham for 109 years. I don't want to talk about it too much.

HARRIOTT: Will it be a play?

NORMAN: Yes. The other project I'm doing is a screenplay based on the book *Medicine Women* by a woman named Lynn Andrews, the story of a woman who goes on a search for an Indian marriage basket and ends up in a teepee full of ancient Sioux medicine women in Manitoba, who, in the process of her first meeting with them, turn into bears and wolves and dogs. There is an ancient spirituality on this continent that we came in and covered up. We laid down the concrete and laid down the Protestantism. I think that work as religion is not satisfying, and that all of America seems to be coming to an understanding of that all at once.

HARRIOTT: It seems to me that very little has been made of the humor in your plays.

NORMAN: I know. People seem to be so reluctant to understand that I am funny and the plays are funny. I don't know why they are so eager to have me be so serious. *Traveler in the Dark* is hysterically funny, I think.

159

HARRIOTT: Is it the funniest?

NORMAN: *The Holdup* is the funniest. That's the one that doesn't ever get done.

HARRIOTT: What happened to *The Holdup* and to *Circus Valentine?*

NORMAN: *Circus Valentine* has never been done again after its initial production and I sort of keep it in the closet.

HARRIOTT: Are you not as fond of it as the others?

NORMAN: I think it doesn't quite work, but it has good stuff in it. *The Holdup* I pulled because I didn't want that to be anybody's first experience with my work. I had a really bad production that the reviews, which I took pretty seriously, just said, "O.K., let's stop." It's going to be published soon though, so that should help. *The Holdup* is based on stories of my grandfather's and I wrote it really to thank him. He was one of the great storytellers of the world and I grew up listening to him.

HARRIOTT: Speaking of storytellers, do you consider yourself a Southern writer? I always think that Southern writers are storytellers.

NORMAN: I think that I absolutely am. I didn't inherit the Gothic Southern style, but in terms of people having time to talk through something, that's certainly Southern. That thing about "You're going to sit on this porch and rock until this is straightened out." I think the quality that allows Southern writing to exist is the idea that you can't escape family, because people are always going to know whose boy you are.

HARRIOTT: What a contrast with New York. Do you write differently here?

NORMAN: I don't think so. *'Night, Mother* was written here. The novel is perhaps most Southern of all in terms of its voice. It begins almost as if a chatty neighbor from across the street was saying, "Fay Morgan never had any money." What I did, just because I didn't know any better, was to treat that narrator as another character. I know how this narrator talks and I know the things that she knows, and this is how she would express herself about this or that, this is how she feels about Fay, this is how she tells a story. That part was enormously satisfying—the old yarn-spinner aspect. I have that real desire to entrance, to charm, to mesmerize.

HARRIOTT: I was reading an interview with Joan Didion recently, and her interviewer said, "You wanted to be an actress originally. How is it that you became a writer?" And Didion said, "Same impulse. I wanted to entertain, to perform."

NORMAN: Absolutely. And I think it's also the desire to see how it would be to be somebody else. I can accept my own physical cowardice by writing Arnie Campbell.

HARRIOTT: You seem to stress your physical cowardice. Is it an important factor in your life, like being afraid to get on an airplane?

NORMAN: No. Darkness is something I've had problems with. Sounds in the street. I've always felt physically vulnerable.

HARRIOTT: You've been quoted as saying that you feel vulnerable because you're short. Since I'm two inches shorter than you are, I was especially interested.

NORMAN: I know that I have felt the need to protect myself in various ways. I certainly don't think that I would survive in any kind of physical combat. Now, endurance is another question. If we're talking about how long you have to do something, I can do it, whatever it is—if I have to—forever.

HARRIOTT: How did Robert Brustein come to produce 'Night, Mother?

NORMAN: We sent the play to three people. The other two, who are quite well-known in the world of theater, didn't even respond. Brustein called and said, "When can I do this?" One of the two others did respond finally and said, "I'm sorry, but this just isn't what we're doing right now." Nobody thought 'Night, Mother had a chance. I had seen it with a Circle Rep audience—we had done it as a reading at Circle Rep—and it was so funny and the audience was able to laugh. Not until that point did I know the audience would be able to take it.

HARRIOTT: How is it that Circle Rep didn't produce it?

NORMAN: Circle Rep has requirements about working in their company, and that includes what directors and actors are used. I felt that Tom Moore, who's not in the company, was the right person to direct the play, and that Anne Pitoniak and Kathy Bates were the right ones to play it, and they were not in the company, either. They were very helpful, but because of this rule, I had to take the play someplace else.

HARRIOTT: How did you feel when the play went to Broadway?

NORMAN: Obviously it changed my life forever. And I think it's a good lesson. It's not a play that you would ever design as a success, that you would sit down and say, "Gee, how can I write a hit play? Well, how about if you have two people on stage, and one of them says, 'I'm going to kill myself, Mama.'" I was very angry at the theater at the time. I didn't care if anybody ever saw it, ever acted in it, ever produced it. I just had to get this straight for me. I think there's something about blocking out the audience and just straightening something out for a record. It's a good way to write.

HARRIOTT: Can you write that way again?

NORMAN: That's what's hard. I can in a novel. I could say, "Look, I don't know how to write novels. Nobody is expecting me to write a decent novel. I'm just going to sit down and do this because I want to."

161

HARRIOTT: What did you think of the movie of 'Night, Mother?

NORMAN: The movie is simpler than the play. I think it's sadder than the play—the play is not sad. The movie is more inevitable than the play. You don't have quite the sense of struggle. I think the play keeps you on the edge of your seat, and the movie somehow doesn't do that. Jessie's death seems a foregone conclusion in the movie. It may have something to do with the form of the film, the fact that it's already on celluloid and you know beyond a shadow of a doubt that it's already over by the time you get there.

HARRIOTT: Part of the tension in the play comes from the sense of enclosure, which is harder to sustain in a movie, isn't it?

NORMAN: Right. There's also a tactile reaction that people have to the play. They grab at the person next to them, they open their purses—they're physically involved because Mama and Jessie are physically involved. They touch each other, you see them handling the objects, there's a physical reality to a play that you don't have in the movies. When you see Robert Redford sitting on the grass in Africa, you don't *feel* the wind, you *look* at it. Whereas in Fugard's plays, I promise you, you feel the wind. You know that you are there because you *can't* watch it. It's a different temperature. It's just hotter in the theater.

HARRIOTT: In McLuhan's sense?

NORMAN: Yes, exactly. Grappling with things is what the theater does best.

HARRIOTT: In writing the novel, did you miss the collaborative process of the theater?

NORMAN: No, that was one of the things I wanted a break from. I wanted to be able to write a sentence that said, "Edith blinked," and know that Edith, by God, was going to blink every time it came around to it. She was going to blink then, right on cue, no fuss, not a special blink tonight, not a shrug of the shoulder, but a blink.

HARRIOTT: Do actors keep changing the play?

NORMAN: Oh, yes. They have to stay alive up there, so they try other things. You have that real luxury with a novel—total control. It's your own little play in your own backyard and you're doing everything. That's the real pleasure of it. There are a number of other pleasures, too. You can say what they're thinking, and you can say what they remember. In the theater, you can't deal with memory. The audience doesn't want to hear anybody say, "I remember when..."

HARRIOTT: And you can do landscape. Do you do that in your novel?

NORMAN: No, but description is certainly a thing I had to work on consciously, and people who have read the novel say it's the single strongest

162

factor in the book—the incredible visual sense. But I learned that in the theater, that's not something I have naturally. I have been trained by the best people in the world about how things should look. Working with costume designers you learn what it means that there's a French shawl over somebody's table, and you learn what to do with it. But descriptions of how people get in and out of doors—I never had to write that. I never had to write a sex scene, which there are plenty of in the novel, and they're the hardest thing in the world to write.

HARRIOTT: Why is that?

NORMAN: I've blamed it on English, because English is the greatest language in the world to tell you how to put something together, a language that's real strong on mechanics and geography. But if you reduce sex to mechanics and geography, you're sunk. It took me months to write the love scenes.

HARRIOTT: Maybe you'll write love scenes in the theater now.

NORMAN: I do know that the continuing strong reaction to a character in the novel is to Arnie Campbell, this detective. Women are saying, "Where is this man? This is the most wonderful man I've ever read. This relationship between Fay and Arnie is so fabulous."

HARRIOTT: It's very short, in terms of the novel, but the speech that Sam makes in *Traveler in the Dark* about the kiss is a very sexy speech. Maybe in your next play you'll write more of that.

NORMAN: I had forgotten about that speech and I loved writing it. Yes, maybe I can write some sex for the theater. Sarah and Abraham certainly had some, didn't they!

New York City
December 1986

Afterword

Playwrights in America face more obstacles than other writers, beginning with the unlikelihood of having a play produced in the first place. The theater is a business enterprise and, since it is an unusually costly and risky one, producers are looking for marketable commodities, not works of art. A formula comedy, flashy musical, or proven hit imported from Britain is a safer commercial bet than a serious exploration of human experience written by a new playwright. Books are commodities, too, but publishers are more likely to gamble on an unknown writer: there is less financial investment at stake. (For example, David Mamet's *Glengarry Glen Ross*, a play with a small cast and Spartan sets and costumes, cost $900,000 to produce on Broadway in 1984. In order to break even, it needed a box office revenue of $97,000 a week.)[1] The failure of a novel hurts the novelist and the publisher; a failure in the theater is a business disaster for the playwright and the producer, as well as for the director, actors, designers, and technicians. In this atmosphere of market pressure, a serious playwright, no matter what he or she wishes to say, must first of all please a broad audience. It's as though a serious novelist had to make sure of writing a best-seller, too.

It follows that reviews serve the function of best-seller lists. The public reads them not for the discussion of the play, but to find out whether or not to go to it (the prohibitive price of tickets in New York theaters makes that caution understandable), and this gives the critic a formidable power over the life or death of the production. At the same time, the drama critic, unlike the critic of fiction and poetry, must judge the play on the basis of one performance. And, also unlike the literary critic, the drama critic has to review virtually everything that is produced. Consequently, faced with largely mediocre work, the drama critic often overpraises the promising, creating unreasonable expectations of a beginning playwright, or, conversely, may write a disproportionately harsh review that is more a reflection of general frustration with the state of the theater than a reaction to the specific play. Besides demolishing, if only temporarily, the playwright's ego, hyperbolic scorn demolishes the production. Then any hope of the play's publication—never a good prospect, with only a few houses

165

publishing plays to begin with—is obliterated. Writing for the theater can be more ephemeral than writing for a newspaper: it's easier to dig up an old newspaper file than old copies of typed play scripts.

Its ephemeral nature is reinforced by the paucity of published drama criticism. Unlike contemporary American fiction and poetry that have spawned a cottage industry of criticism, with the structuralists, semioticians, and deconstructionists, Freudians, Lacanians, and Marxists all producing their exegeses, contemporary American drama is rarely discussed beyond the original review. When critics do write books about playwrights, the playwrights are either European or dead. Drama is not regarded as part of literature in this country.

Actors and directors can be another kind of obstacle. While today's directors for the most part do not take the same radical liberties with the text as did their predecessors in the sixties, their interpretations can nonetheless alter the effect or even the intention of the written work. Bad acting simply destroys it; the realization of the play becomes the irreconcilable conflict between the playwright's imagination and the actors' representation. There is an additional problem for stage actors in an age of cinema: their "realism" seems artificial. Ionesco maintained that he began to write for the theater because he hated the realistic drama that he was seeing. "The playing of the actors disturbed me," he wrote. "I was embarrassed for them. The playing of film actors did not provoke in me that indefinable uneasiness, that embarrassment produced by a theatrical performance. Why could I not accept theatrical reality?... I believe now that what disturbed me in the theater was the presence on the stage of characters of flesh and blood. Their material presence destroyed the fiction."[2] Novels, music, painting—none of these contained anything outside their nature, Ionesco claimed. Nor did film, which was a series of images, not a written play to be interpreted by actors and thus changed and made impure.

If realistic acting in the theater seems artifical compared to the movies, realistic settings can't compete at all. A play is unable to produce a movie's visual effects, not only its spectacles and sweeping landscapes, but its interiors. On stage, a set that consists of one drab room, for example, can create an unpleasant feeling of claustrophobia that would be mitigated in a movie by the movement of the camera. (Sometimes, of course, the "opening up" by the movie can ruin the intended effect of confinement.) Even the most static mise-en-scène comes alive in the movies because of the constant flow of images, the rapid shifts of perspective, and the sensuous color. Indifferent movies are easier to watch than indifferent plays because they are visually diverting. The medium itself is hypnotic.

It is a cliché to speculate that the theater won't survive movies or television. But predicting the theater's imminent demise has been a pastime for years. I agree with critic Eric Bentley's contention that, while "the movie industry can threaten the theater industry, the one *art* cannot be threatened by the other. So long as an art is alive it will be cherished and kept going by the minority that is interested..."[3] Photography did not kill painting, but it led painters to work in different ways. Painting became non-representational, acknowledging that a landscape or a face could be represented with more fidelity by a photograph than by a brush on canvas. The movies and television, like photography, can do realism better. The theater must do what they cannot do.

As we become used to watching footage of the world's wars on TV every night, the theater is no longer able to represent these horrors to us with equal impact. It must transfigure the literal events in ways that cannot be done on television. As an illustration, here is George Steiner's description of the Berliner Ensemble's production of Brecht's *Mother Courage:*

> Her children bestially, uselessly done to death in a wasteland, Courage harnesses herself to her wagon. The stage begins to turn in an accelerating vortex of crazed misery. She opens her gaunt mouth as if to scream—as if to scream her anguish to the ends of the inhuman world. No sound comes; or, rather, what knifes across the theater is the same cry that comes from the torn mouth of the horse in Picasso's "Guernica."... Her cry is the loudest silence that art has known since the broken scream of Cassandra in the House of Atreus.[4]

This tableau, if filmed, would not have the same force. Mother Courage's scream is raw and unmediated by the camera. It speaks to the heart of the theatrical experience, which is the vibration of the live presence.

Because of that live presence we feel exposed in the theater. That may be why Ionesco was embarrassed rather than simply bored or annoyed. There is anonymity not only for the actors in a movie, but for the audience, too, sitting in the dark and watching the huge figures up there on the screen, grand and remote like archetypes. The theater is a more intimate experience: we are looking at actors who are our size, and we are looking them in the eye. We and they go through the performance together. The theater provides the unique experience of watching the play take place as we sit there, not the completed artifact as in a movie, but the act or process of its creation. It gives us the excitement of human possibility; or perhaps it is the possibility of failure in a live performance that makes the moments of triumph especially thrilling. The physical illusion of growing taller that actor-mime Bill Irwin created in his Off Broadway show *The Regard of Flight* was lost in the taped version subsequently shown on TV. Accustomed as we are to the illusions so easily produced by the camera, the uncanny transformation in Irwin's stage performance was reduced on television to a commonplace of technology.

Television critic John J. O'Connor, writing about the TV adaptation of the British theatrical masterpiece *Nicholas Nickleby*, praised the camera's ability to show closeups and "small details that might have been lost in the lively whirl of the stage presentation." But he mourned the priceless missing ingredient. "Surprisingly enough," he wrote, "there are moments when the presence of an audience is missed. The comic scene involving a performance of 'Romeo and Juliet' falls slightly flat without the sound of laughter. The laugh track does, evidently, have its legitimate uses. In the end, this version of 'Nicholas Nickleby' comes nowhere near capturing the theatrical experience of the original event, but it will give you a fairly good idea of what all the shouting was about."[5]

The particular kind of expectation that accompanies the theater's "dimming of the lights" is missing from television, too. There is no sense of removal from dailiness in order to participate in a ceremony. I am devoted to the reruns of "The Mary Tyler Moore Show," whose tight structures, fidelity of characterization, witty and moving dialogue, absorbing action, and flawless ensemble acting ought to be the envy of every playwright. But television cannot provide the theater's sense of occasion. Movies come closer to it than television, with the darkened movie house and the freedom from interruption by commercials, telephones, and chatting family members. Still, the theater is a public event. You get dressed for it—even if you wear jeans, it is a conscious decision—and you make plans to go with someone. You will drop into a movie dressed as you are, perhaps alone, scarcely aware of the other patrons. It is the theater that is related to the communal rituals of papal masses and royal weddings, bullfights and Olympic games, with their sense of performers and spectators sharing the moment.

Perhaps the most basic appeal of the theater is that it tells a story. Movies and television tell stories, too. But the theater can use language in all of its lively possibilities. Film is a visual medium in which words are secondary. The cutting process is rapid, moving the viewer around the subject; perspectives are held for only minutes or seconds. In the theater, uninterrupted by cuts to action, we can concentrate on and savor a long speech. It is the only medium that offers us the pleasure of listening to torrents of rich language. Of course, to write language well in a country that regards it with little esteem or affection can be another obstacle. We live in a visual society: the image, not the word, has prestige. At the same time, we are bombarded by the media with language that becomes quickly shopworn, and that is further debased by the proliferating jargon and neologisms of bureaucratic, technocratic, and academic diction. In any case, Americans place a premium on action, not on sitting around in English country houses making epigrammatic conversation, or in Irish pubs telling stories, or in French cafés arguing about art. We do not have a tradition of delight in the spoken word: eloquence is "elitist" in our egalitarian society.

Perhaps the greatest obstacle faced by the playwright is the theater's role in America where, unlike the museum or the symphony orchestra or the dance company, it is treated as a commercial enterprise rather than a cultural institution. Although subsidized non-profit theaters exist—and, significantly, each of the playwrights in this book is or has been attached to one of them—they receive nothing like the support of the national theaters in England and Europe that sustains and makes affordable a theater that interests serious audiences and that, less in thrall to box office and reviews, can experiment with new works. Above all, it makes it possible to develop a cohesive company of actors, directors, and playwrights. What would the works of the great American choreographers—Balanchine, Martha Graham, Merce Cunningham—look like if, for each new work, a group of dancers auditioned, then rehearsed for a few weeks? Playwrights are seldom given the equivalent of the choreographers' opportunity to make the dance on the dancer. Dance companies, chamber music groups, symphony orchestras rehearse together year in and year out. The only collaborative art in America rarely allowed to evolve over a period of time is the theater.

The writer whose inclination for expression leads him or her to the theater will have chosen a more difficult road than the novelist, poet or screenwriter. It is not surprising that so many promising playwrights abandon the stage for other forms. But some keep on, if only because they cannot help themselves. The English director Peter Brook once said, "There is no deep inevitable need for theater on the part of society. If theater completely disappeared, it would take weeks for most people to notice. No, theater exists because there are a number of individual people who could not survive without making one."[6] The playwrights in this book are among them.

References

Introduction

1. Antonin Artaud, *The Theater and Its Double* (New York: Grove Press, 1958), p. 89.
2. David Mamet, *Sexual Perversity in Chicago* (New York: Samuel French, 1977), p. 32.
3. Mamet, *American Buffalo* (New York: Grove Press, 1976), p. 11.

Sam Shepard: Inventing Identities

1. Sam Shepard, "Red Cross," in *Five Plays by Sam Shepard* (Indianapolis: Bobbs-Merrill, 1967), pp. 122, 123.
2. Shepard, "Icarus's Mother," in *Five Plays*, pp. 58, 59, 60.
3. Shepard, "Melodrama Play," in *Five Plays*, p. 157.
4. Shepard, "Note to the Actors," "Angel City," in *Angel City & Other Plays* (New York: Urizen Books, 1981), p. 6.
5. Christopher Lasch, *The Culture of Narcissism* (New York: Warner Books, 1979), p. 35.
6. Lasch, p. 59.
7. Ibid.
8. Shepard, "Back in the 1970s," *Hawk Moon* (New York: Performing Arts Journal Publications, 1973), p. 12.
9. Shepard, "Cowboy Mouth," in *Mad Dog Blues and Other Plays* (New York: Winter House Ltd., 1972), p. 100. Hereafter cited as CM, all references to the work will appear in the text.
10. Kenneth Chubb, "Interview: Metaphors, Mad Dogs and Old Time Cowboys," *Theatre Quarterly*, 4 Aug. 1974, p. 12.
11. Shepard, "The Tooth of Crime," in *Seven Plays* (New York: Bantam Books, 1981), p. 231. Hereafter cited as TOC, all references to the work will appear in the text.
12. Shepard, "The Curse of the Raven's Black Feather," *Hawk Moon*, p. 47.
13. Chubb, *Theatre Quarterly* interview, p. 16.
14. Shepard, "Curse of the Starving Class," in *Seven Plays*, pp. 174, 175. Hereafter cited as CSC, all references to the work will appear in the text.
15. Shepard, "Buried Child," in *Seven Plays*, p. 110. Hereafter cited as BC, all references to the work will appear in the text.

References

16. Shepard, "True West," in *Seven Plays*, p. 9. Hereafter cited as *TW*, all references to the work will appear in the text.

17. Shepard, *Motel Chronicles* (San Francisco: City Lights Books, 1982), p. 56.

18. Nan Robertson, "The Multidimensional Sam Shepard," *New York Times*, 21 Jan. 1986, Sec. C, p. 15.

19. Ed Fisher, Cartoon in *The New Yorker*, 6 Jan. 1986, p. 29.

20. Shepard, *Seduced* (New York: Dramatists Play Service, 1979), p. 44.

21. Heinz Lichtenstein, M.D., "The Dilemma of Human Identity: Notes on Self-Transformation, Self-Objectivation, and Metamorphosis," *Journal of the American Psychoanalytic Association*, Vol. II, 1963, p. 215.

Lanford Wilson: To Vanish Without a Trace

1. Lanford Wilson, *Balm in Gilead and Other Plays* (New York: Hill and Wang, 1967), pp. 26–27. Hereafter cited as *BG*, all references to this work will appear in the text.

2. Wilson, *The Gingham Dog* (New York: Dramatists Play Service, 1970), p. 7. Hereafter cited as *GD*, all references to this work will appear in the text.

3. Wilson, *Lemon Sky* (New York: Dramatists Play Service, 1970), p. 7. Hereafter cited as *LS*, all references to this work will appear in the text.

4. Wilson, *The Hot l Baltimore* (New York: Dramatists Play Service, 1973), p. 62. Hereafter cited as *HlB*, all references to this work will appear in the text.

5. Wilson, *The Mound Builders* (New York: Hill and Wang, 1976), p. 4. Hereafter cited as *MB*, all references to this work will appear in the text.

6. Wilson, *Serenading Louie* (New York: Dramatists Play Service, 1976), p. 17. Hereafter cited as *SL*, all references to this work will appear in the text.

7. Wilson, *Brontosaurus* (New York: Dramatists Play Service, 1978), p. 18. Hereafter cited as *B*, all references to this work will appear in the text.

8. Wilson, *Talley's Folly* (New York: Hill and Wang, 1979), p. 4. Hereafter cited as *TF*, all references to this work will appear in the text.

9. Wilson, *Angels Fall*, TS, 1:30. Hereafter cited as *AF*, all references to this work will appear in the text.

David Mamet: Comedies of Bad Manners

1. Richard Gottlieb, "The 'Engine' That Drives Playwright David Mamet," *New York Times*, 15 Jan. 1978, Sec. II, p. 4.

2. David Mamet, *A Life in the Theatre* (New York: Grove Press, 1977), pp. 57, 58.

3. Gottlieb, p. 4.

4. Mamet, *Lakeboat* (New York: Grove Press, 1980), pp. 24, 25. Hereafter cited as *L*, all references to this work will appear in the text.

5. Mamet, *The Duck Variations* (New York: Samuel French, 1977), p. 65. Hereafter cited as *DV*, all references to this work will appear in the text.

6. Mamet, *Sexual Perversity in Chicago* (New York: Samuel French, 1977), p. 40. Hereafter cited as *SPC*, all references to this work will appear in the text.

7. Mamet, *American Buffalo* (New York: Grove Press, 1976), pp. 72, 73.

8. Martin Gottfried, "'Buffalo' Is a Rare Broadway Coin," *New York Post*, 17 Feb. 1977, p. 22

9. Ross Wetzsteon, "David Mamet: Remember That Name," *The Village Voice*, 5 July 1976, p. 103.

10. Robert Storey, "The Making of David Mamet," *The Hollins Critic*, Oct. 1979, p. 6.

11. John Ditsky, "'He Lets You See the Thought There': The Theater of David Mamet," *Kansas Quarterly*, Fall 1980, p. 29.

12. Jack V. Barbera, "Ethical Perversity in America: Some Observations on David Mamet's 'American Buffalo'," *Modern Drama*, Sept. 1981, p. 274.

13. Harold Clurman, "Theater," *The Nation*, 12 March 1977, p. 313.

14. Richard Eder, "'Water Engine' Is Uptown," *New York Times*, 7 March 1978, Sec. I, p. 42.

15. T.E. Kalem, "Trickle," *Time*, 20 March 1978, p. 84.

16. Eder, "David Mamet's New Realism," *New York Times*, 12 March 1978, Sec. VI, p. 42.

17. Eder, "Mamet's 'The Woods' Redone at Public," *New York Times*, May 1979, Sec. C, p. 15.

18. Edith Oliver, "Too Many Trees," *The New Yorker*, 7 May 1979, p. 144.

19. Michael Feingold, "Mamet a Trois," *The Village Voice*, 7 May 1979, p. 103.

20. Mamet, *The Woods* (New York: Grove Press, 1979), p. 38.

21. Frank Rich, "Theater: Mamet's 'Edmond' at the Provincetown," *New York Times*, 28 Oct. 1982, Sec. C, p. 20.

22. Walter Kerr, "Two New Plays That Focus on the Male Loner," *New York Times*, 7 Nov. 1982, Sec. H, p. 3.

23. Mamet, *Edmond* (New York: Grove Press, 1983), pp. 91, 92. Hereafter cited as *E*, all references to this work will appear in the text.

24. *Author's note*: As this book goes to press, Mamet's most recent full-length play is *Speed-the-Plow*.

25. Mamet, *Glengarry Glen Ross* (New York: Grove Press, 1984), p. 105. Hereafter cited as *GGR*, all references to this work will appear in the text.

26. David J. Blum, "David Mamet's Wealth of Words," *The Wall Street Journal*, 9 April 1982, p. 23.

Charles Fuller: The Quest for Justice

1. Alain Locke, "The Negro and the American Theater," in *The Black Aesthetic*, ed. Addison Gayle, Jr. (New York: Doubleday & Co., 1972), p. 251.

2. James V. Hatch, "A White Folks Guide to 200 Years of Black & White Drama," *The Drama Review*, Vol. 16, No. 4, Dec. 1972, p. 16.

3. Errol Hill, ed., *The Theater of Black Americans* (Englewood Cliffs, N.J.: Prentice-Hall, 1980), p. 210.

4. Stark Young, *Immortal Shadows* (New York: Charles Scribner's, 1948), p. 122.

5. Douglas Turner Ward, "American Theater: For Whites Only?" *New York Times*, 14 Aug. 1966, Sec. D, p. 3.

6. Personal interview with Charles Fuller, 6 May 1982.

7. Charles Fuller, *Zooman and the Sign*, TS, 2:17. Hereafter cited as *ZS*, all references to this work will appear in the text.

8. Fuller, *A Soldier's Play*, TS, 1:38–39. Hereafter cited as *SP*, all references to this work will appear in the text.

Marsha Norman: Getting Out

1. Marsha Norman, *Getting Out* (New York: Dramatists Play Service, 1979), p. 19. Hereafter cited as *GO*, all references to this work will appear in the text.

2. Norman, *Third and Oak: The Laundromat* (New York: Dramatists Play Service, 1978), p. 11. Hereafter cited as *L*, all references to this work will appear in the text.

3. Norman, *'Night, Mother* (New York: Dramatists Play Service, 1983), p. 11. Hereafter cited as *NM*, all references to this work will appear in the text.

4. Norman, *Traveler in the Dark*, TS, I:9. Hereafter cited as *TD*, all references to this work will appear in the text.

Afterword

1. Samuel G. Freedman, "Prize Aids 'Glengarry'," *New York Times*, 24 April 1984, Sec. C, p. 15.

2. Eugene Ionesco, "Discovering the Theater," in *Theater of the Twentieth Century*, ed. Robert W. Corrigan (New York: Grove Press, 1963), pp. 77–78.

3. Eric Bentley, *The Playwright as Thinker* (New York: Meridian Books, 1957), p. 16.

4. George Steiner, "Arts of Survival," rev. of *Brecht: A Biography*, by Klaus Volker, *The New Yorker*, 19 March 1979, p. 150.

5. John J. O'Connor, "TV: Nicholas Nickleby Week Begins," *New York Times*, 10 Jan. 1983, Sec. C, p. 18.

6. Peter Brook, as quoted in Lawrence Weschler, "Louisiana in Denmark," *The New Yorker*, 30 Aug. 1982, p. 60.

Selected Bibliography

Primary Sources

Fuller, Charles. *The Brownsville Raid*. TS. Negro Ensemble Co., New York. Copyright 1975.
_____. *A Soldier's Play*. TS. Negro Ensemble Co., New York. Copyright 1981.
_____. *Zooman and the Sign*. TS. Negro Ensemble Co., New York. Copyright 1979–80.
Mamet, David. *American Buffalo*. New York: Grove Press, 1976.
_____. *Edmond*. New York: Grove Press, 1983.
_____. *Lakeboat*. New York: Grove Press, 1981.
_____. *A Life in the Theatre*. New York: Grove Press, 1977.
_____. *The Poet and the Rent*. New York: Samuel French, 1981.
_____. *Reunion and Dark Pony*. New York: Grove Press, 1979.
_____. *The Revenge of the Space Pandas*. Chicago, Illinois: Dramatic Publishing Co., 1978.
_____. *Sexual Perversity in Chicago and The Duck Variations*. New York: Samuel French, 1977.
_____. *Short Plays and Monologues*. New York: Dramatists Play Service, 1981.
_____. *The Water Engine and Mr. Happiness*. New York: Grove Press, 1978.
_____. *The Woods*. New York: Samuel French, 1979.
Norman, Marsha. *Getting Out*. New York: Dramatists Play Service, 1979.
_____. *'night, Mother*. New York: Dramatists Play Service, 1983.
_____. *Third and Oak: The Laundromat*. New York: Dramatists Play Service, 1978.
_____. *Third and Oak: The Pool Hall*. New York: Dramatists Play Service, 1978.
_____. *Traveler in the Dark*. TS. American Repertory Theater, 1984.
Shepard, Sam. *Action and The Unseen Hand*. London: Faber & Faber, 1975.
_____. *Angel City and Other Plays*. New York: Urizen Books, 1976.
_____. *Buried Child and Seduced and Suicide in B♭*. New York: Urizen Books, 1979.
_____. *Five Plays*. Indianapolis: Bobbs-Merrill Co., 1967.
_____. *Fool for Love*. New York: Bantam, 1984.
_____. *Four Two-Act Plays*. New York: Urizen, 1980.
_____. *Hawk Moon*. New York: Performing Arts Journal Publications, 1981.
_____. *A Lie of the Mind*. New York: Dramatists Play Service, 1986.
_____. *Mad Dog Blues and Other Plays*. New York: Winter House, Ltd., 1972.
_____. *Motel Chronicles*. San Francisco: City Lights Books, 1982.
_____. *Rolling Thunder Logbook*. New York: Viking Press, 1977.
_____. *Seven Plays*. New York: Bantam, 1981.
_____. *The Tooth of Crime and Geography of a Horse Dreamer*. New York: Grove Press, and London: Faber & Faber, 1974.

Selected Bibliography

————. *The Unseen Hand and Other Plays*. Indianapolis: Bobbs-Merrill, 1971.

Lanford Wilson. *Angels Fall*. TS. Circle Repertory Theatre, New York. Copyright 1982.

————. *Balm in Gilead and Other Plays*. New York: Hill and Wang, 1965.

————. *Brontosaurus*. New York: Dramatists Play Service, 1978.

————. *5th of July*. New York: Dramatists Play Service, 1978.

————. *The Gingham Dog*. New York: Dramatists Play Service, 1969.

————. *The Great Nebula in Orion and Three Other Plays*. New York: Dramatists Play Service, 1973.

————. *The Hot l Baltimore*. New York: Dramatists Play Service, 1973.

————. *Lemon Sky*. New York: Dramatists Play Service, 1970.

————. *The Mound Builders*. New York: Hill and Wang, 1976.

————. *The Rimers of Eldritch and Other Plays*. New York: Hill and Wang, 1967.

————. *Serenading Louie*. New York: Dramatists Play Service, 1976.

————. *A Tale Told*. TS. Circle Repertory Theatre, New York. Copyright 1981.

————. *Talley's Folly*. New York: Hill and Wang, 1979.

Secondary Sources—Books

Artaud, Antonin. *The Theater and Its Double*. New York: Grove Press, 1958.

Beckett, Samuel. *Waiting for Godot*. New York: Grove Press, 1954.

Bentley, Eric. *The Dramatic Event*. Boston: Beacon Press, 1954.

————. *In Search of Theater*. New York: Alfred A. Knopf, 1953.

————. *The Life of the Drama*. New York: Atheneum, 1974.

————. *The Playwright as Thinker*. New York: Meridian Books, 1957.

————. *The Theatre of Commitment*. New York: Atheneum, 1967.

————. *Theatre of War*. New York: Viking Press, 1954.

————. *The Theory of the Modern Stage*. Harmondsworth, Middlesex, England: Penguin Books, Ltd., 1968.

————. *What Is Theatre?* New York: Atheneum, 1968.

Bernstein, Samuel J. *The Strands Entwined*. Boston: Northeastern University Press, 1980.

Brustein, Robert. *Critical Moments*. New York: Random House, 1980.

Buchner, George. *Complete Plays and Prose*. Trans. Carl Richard Mueller. New York: Hill and Wang, 1963.

Bullins, Ed. *Four Dynamite Plays*. New York: William Morrow & Co., 1972.

Chinoy, Helen Krich and Linda Walsh Jenkins, eds. *Women in American Theatre*. New York: Crown Pub., 1981.

Clurman, Harold. *The Divine Pastime*. New York: Macmillan, 1974.

————. *The Naked Image*. New York: Macmillan, 1958.

————, ed. *Nine Plays of the Modern Theater*. New York: Grove Press, 1981.

Cohn, Ruby. *Currents in Contemporary Drama*. Bloomington and London: Indiana University Press, 1971.

_____. *New American Dramatists*. New York: Grove Press, 1982.

Croyden, Margaret. *Lunatics, Lovers and Poets*. New York: McGraw-Hill, 1974.

Cruse, Harold. *The Crisis of the Negro Intellectual*. New York: William Morrow and Co., 1967.

Fiedler, Leslie. *Waiting for the End*. New York: Dell Pub. Co., 1964.

Garreau, Joel. *The Nine Nations of North America*. Boston: Houghton Mifflin, 1981.

Gassner, John. *Directions in Modern Theatre and Drama*. New York: Holt, Rinehart and Winston, 1966.

_____. *Dramatic Soundings*. New York: Crown Pub., 1968.

_____. *Masters of the Drama*. New York: Dover Pub., 1954.

_____. *Theater at the Crossroads*. New York: Holt, Rinehart and Winston, 1960.

_____. *The Theatre in Our Times*. New York: Crown Pub., 1954.

Gayle, Addison, Jr., ed. *The Black Aesthetic*. New York: Doubleday & Co., 1972.

Gilman, Richard. *Common and Uncommon Masks*. New York: Vintage Books, 1972.

_____. *The Making of Modern Drama*. New York: Farrar, Straus and Giroux, 1972.

Gordone, Charles. *No Place to Be Somebody*. Indianapolis: Bobbs-Merrill, 1969.

Hatch, James V., and Omanii Abdullah, eds. *Black Playwrights 1823–1977*. New York & London: R.R. Bowker Co., 1977.

Hill, Errol, ed. *The Theater of Black Americans*. 3 vols. Englewood Cliffs, N.J.: Prentice-Hall, 1980.

Houghton, Norris. *The Exploding Stage*. New York: Dell Pub., 1971.

James, Henry. *The Scenic Art*. New Brunswick: Rutgers University Press, 1948.

Jones, LeRoi. *Dutchman and The Slave*. New York: William Morrow and Co., 1964.

Kauffman, Stanley. *Theater Criticisms*. New York: Performing Arts Journal Pub., 1983.

King, Woodie, Jr. *Black Theater: Present Condition*. New York: Publishing Center for Cultural Resources, 1981.

Lahr, John. *Up Against the Fourth Wall*. New York: Grove Press, 1970.

Lasch, Christopher. *The Culture of Narcissism*. New York: Warner Books, 1979.

Leverett, James, ed. *New Plays U.S.A.* New York: Theater Communications Group, 1982.

McCarthy, Mary. *Mary McCarthy's Theatre Chronicles*. New York: Farrar, Straus and Co., 1962.

MacNicholas, John, ed. *Dictionary of Literary Biography: Twentieth Century American Dramatists*. Detroit, Mich.: Gale Research Co., 1981.

Malpede, Karen. *Women in Theatre*. New York: Drama Book Pub., 1983.

Marranca, Bonnie, ed. *American Dreams: The Imagination of Sam Shepard*. New York: Performing Arts Journal Pub., 1981.

177

Selected Bibliography

——————— and Gautam Dasgupta. *American Playwrights: A Critical Survey*. New York: Drama Book Specialists, 1981.

Marx, Leon. *The Machine in the Garden: Technology and the Pastoral Ideal in America*. New York: Oxford University Press, 1972.

Matthews, John F., ed. *Shaw's Dramatic Criticism (1895–98)*. New York: Hill and Wang, 1959.

Mitchell, Loften. *Black Drama*. New York: Hawthorn Books, 1967.

Moore, Honor, ed. *The New Women's Theatre*. New York: Vintage Books, 1977.

Moritz, Charles, ed. *Current Biography 1978*. New York: H. Wilson Co., 1978.

———————, ed. *Current Biography 1979*. New York: H. Wilson Co., 1979.

Mottram, Ron. *Inner Landscapes: The Theater of Sam Shepard*. Columbia, Missouri: University of Missouri Press, 1984.

Nathan, George Jean. *Passing Judgments*. New York: Alfred A. Knopf, 1935, 1972.

New York Theater Critics' Reviews. New York: Critics' Theater Reviews, 1940–.

Olauson, Judith. *The American Woman Playwright: A View of Criticism and Characterization*. Troy, New York: Whitston Publishing Co., 1981.

O'Neill, Eugene. *The Emperor Jones*. New York: Modern Library, 1921, 1948.

Patterson, Lindsay, ed. *Black Theater*. New York: Dodd, Mead & Co., 1971.

Salem, James M. *A Guide to Critical Reviews*. Metuchen, N.J.: Scarecrow, 1973.

Shewey, Don. *Sam Shepard*. New York: Dell Publishing Co., 1985.

Simon, John. *Singularities*. New York: Random House, 1964, 1975.

Steiner, George. *The Death of Tragedy*. New York: Hill and Wang, 1961.

Young, Stark. *The Flower in Drama and Glamour*. New York: Charles Scribner's, 1955.

———————. *Immortal Shadows*. New York: Charles Scribner's, 1948.

———————. *The Theatre*. New York: Hill and Wang, 1954.

Secondary Sources—Articles

Bachman, Charles R. "Defusion of Menace in the Plays of Sam Shepard." *Modern Drama*, Dec. 1976, pp. 405–415.

Barbera, Jack V. "Ethical Perversity in America: Some Observations on David Mamet's *American Buffalo*." *Modern Drama*, Sept. 1981, pp. 270–275.

Berkvist, Robert. "Lanford Wilson—Can He Score on Broadway?" *New York Times*, 17 Feb. 1980, Sec. 2, p. 1.

Blau, Eleanor. "How Lanford Wilson Writes With Actor in Mind." *New York Times*, 27 Jan. 1983, Sec. C, p. 15.

Blum, David J. "David Mamet's Wealth of Words." *Wall Street Journal*, 9 April 1982, p. 23.

Bruckner, D.J.R. "The Play's Not the Thing." *New York Times Book Review*, 26 Dec. 1982, p. 23.

Brukenfeld, Dick. "A Fresh Look at Black Manhood." *The Village Voice*, 13 June 1974, p. 81.

———————. "Theatrical Nembutal." *The Village Voice*, 10 Feb. 1975, p. 1.

Brustein, Robert. "The Crack in the Chimney." In *Images and Ideas in American Culture*. Ed. Arthur Edelstein. Hanover, N.H.: University Press of New England, 1979.

178

_____. "The Theater of Middle Seriousness: A Report on the Broadway Season." *Harper's*, March 1959, pp. 56–63.

_____. "Two Couples." *The New Republic*, 5 April 1980, pp. 28–29.

_____. "Why American Plays Are Not Literature." *Harper's*, Oct. 1959, pp. 167–172.

Chubb, Kenneth. "Fruitful Difficulties of Directing Shepard." *Theatre Quarterly*, Aug. 1974, pp. 17–25.

_____. "Interview: Metaphors, Mad Dogs and Old Time Cowboys." *Theatre Quarterly*, Aug. 1974, pp. 3–16.

Clurman, Harold. "Theater." *The Nation*, 25 Dec. 1976, p. 70.

_____. "Theater." *The Nation*, 18 Nov. 1978, p. 557.

_____. "Theater." *The Nation*, 12 March 1977, p. 313.

_____. "Theater." *The Nation*, 26 Nov. 1977, p. 571.

_____. "Theater." *The Nation*, 24 Feb. 1979, pp. 221–222.

Cohn, Ruby. "Sam Shepard." In *Contemporary Dramatists*, ed. James Vinson. New York: St. Martin's Press, 1977.

Crouch, Stanley. "American Perfection." *The Village Voice*, 2 Nov. 1982, p. 85.

Croyden, Margaret. "The Playwright Vanishes: Reflections on Today's Theater." *New York Times*, 20 June 1982, Sec. H, p. 33.

Dasgupta, Gautam, Michael Earley and Bonnie Marranca. "The American Playwright: A Life in the Theater?" *Performing Arts Journal*, Feb. 1979, pp. 33–50.

Denby, David. "Stranger in a Strange Land: A Moviegoer at the Theater." *The Atlantic Monthly*, Jan. 1985, pp. 37–50.

Ditsky, John. "'He Lets You See the Thought There': The Theater of David Mamet." *Kansas Quarterly*, Vol. 12, No. 4, Fall 1980, pp. 25–33.

Donahue, Walter. "American Graffiti: The Pulsating World of Sam Shepard." *Plays and Players*, April 1974, pp. 14–18.

Duberman, Martin. "The Great Gray Way." *Harper's*, May 1978, pp. 79–87.

Dunne, John Gregory. "Hollywood's Hessians." *New York Review of Books*, 19 Nov. 1981, pp. 34–37.

Eddy, Bill. "Four Directors on Criticism." *The Drama Review*, Spring 1974, pp. 24–28.

Eder, Richard. "David Mamet's New Realism." *New York Times*, 12 March 1978, Sec. 6, pp. 40, 42, 45, 47.

_____. "Mamet's 'The Woods' Redone at Public." *New York Times*, 1 May 1979, Sec. C, p. 15.

_____. "'Water Engine' Is Uptown." *New York Times*, 7 March 1978, Sec. L, p. 42.

Feingold, Michael. "American Playwriting: The State of the Art, the State of the Union." In *New Plays U.S.A.*, ed. James Leverett. New York: Theatre Communications Group, 1982.

_____. "And Suicide Is Confession." *The Village Voice*, 12 April 1983, p. 81.

_____. "Is There Hope in Soap?" *The Village Voice*, 17 May 1976, p. 123.

_____. "Mamet a Trois." *The Village Voice*, 7 May 1979, p. 103.

_____. "A Soldier's Play." *The Village Voice*, 20 Dec. 1981, p. 105.

_____. "The Way We Are." *The Village Voice*, 9 Nov. 1982, pp. 81, 82.

_____. "Wilson's Waltz." *The Village Voice*, 3 March 1980, pp. 77–79.

Flatley, Guy. "Lanford Is One 'L' of a Playwright." *New York Times*, 22 April 1973, Sec. D, pp. 21, 24.

Fox, Terry Curtis. "Lively Fossil, Spoilt Song." *The Village Voice*, 7 Nov. 1977, pp. 84, 86.

Selected Bibliography

Fraser, C. Gerald. "Integrity—Not Jive." *New York Times*, 3 Dec. 1976, Sec. C, pp. 1, 11.

_____. "Mamet's Plays Shed Masculinity Myth." *New York Times*, 5 July 1976, Sec. II, p. 7.

Freedman, Samuel G. "Sam Shepard's Mythic Vision of the Family." *New York Times*, 1 Dec. 1985, Sec. 2, pp. 1, 20.

Gill, Brendan. "Events Before Mass." *The New Yorker*, 31 Jan. 1983, p. 101.

_____. "Missouri Circus." *The New Yorker*, 17 Nov. 1980, pp. 172–173.

_____. "No News from Lake Michigan." *The New Yorker*, 28 Feb. 77, p. 54.

_____. "A Soldier's Play." *The Nation*, 23 Jan. 1982, pp. 90–91.

Glore, John. "The Canonization of Mojo Rootforce: Sam Shepard Live at the Pantheon." *The Drama Review*, Winter 1972, pp. 53–64.

Gottfried, Martin. "'Buffalo' Is a Rare Broadway Coin." *New York Post*, 17 Feb. 1977, p. 22.

Gottlieb, Richard. "The 'Engine' That Drives Playwright David Mamet." *New York Times*, 15 Jan. 1978, Sec. II, pp. 1, 4.

Gregory, André, and Wallace Shawn. "Wally and André Dissect the Theater." *New York Times*, 17 Jan. 1982, Sec. C, pp. 1, 26.

Gussow, Mel. "Negro Ensemble Stages Fuller's 'Deepest Sleep'." *New York Times*, 5 June 1974, Sec. B, p. 54.

_____. "Sam Shepard Revisits the American Heartland." *New York Times*, 15 Dec. 1985, Sec. H, pp. 3, 7.

_____. "Stage: Mamet Explores the Fall of 'Edmond'." *New York Times*, 17 June 1982, Sec. C, p. 17.

_____. "Stage: Shepard's 'West' Revived and Restored." *New York Times*, 18 Oct. 1982, Sec. C, p. 18.

_____. "Theater: 'The Tooth of Crime' at La Mama Annex." *New York Times*, 2 March 1983, Sec. C, p. 11.

_____. "Theater: Wilson's 'Mound Builders'." *New York Times*, 3 Feb. 1975, Sec. L, p. 35.

_____. "Women Playwrights: New Voices in the Theater." *The New York Times Magazine*, 1 May 1983, pp. 22–40.

Hall, Trish. "Sam Shepard: Theater's Reluctant Star." *Wall Street Journal*, 8 April 1983, p. 23.

Hamill, Pete. "The New American Hero." *New York*, 5 Dec. 1983, pp. 75–102.

Hatch, James V. "A White Folks Guide to 200 Years of Black and White Drama." *The Drama Review*. Vol. 16, No. 4, Dec. 1972.

Hill, Errol. "Black Theater in Form and Style." *The Black Scholar*, July–Aug. 1979, pp. 29–31.

Holmberg, Arthur. "Long Before 'Cats,' Eliot Wooed the Theater." *New York Times*, 21 Nov. 1982, Sec. 2, pp. 1, 4.

Ionesco, Eugene. "Discovering the Theater." In *Theater in the Twentieth Century*. Robert W. Corrigan, ed. New York: Grove Press, 1963, pp. 77–93.

Kakutani, Michiko. "Myths, Dreams, Realities—Sam Shepard's America." *New York Times*, 29 Jan. 1984, Sec. 2, pp. 1, 26.

_____. "The New Writer vs. Hollywood." *New York Times*, 25 April 1982, Sec. D, pp. 1, 30.

Kalem, T.E. "Blind Injustice." *Time*, 20 Dec. 1976, p. 83.

_____. "Color Line." *Time*, 18 Jan. 1982, p. 87.

_____. "Transient Souls." *Time*, 23 April 1973, p. 94.

_____. "Trickle." *Time*, 20 March 1978, p. 84.

Kauffman, Stanley. "On Theater." *The New Republic*, 13 June 1970, pp. 18, 31.

Kellman, Barnet. "The American Playwright in the Seventies: Some Problems and Perspectives." *Theatre Quarterly*, No. 29, 1978, pp. 45–58.

Kerr, Walter. "An Absorbing New Drama and a Superb Performance." *New York Times*, 21 Dec. 1980, Sec. H, p. 3.

_____. "'The Brownsville Raid' Plays Fair with History." *New York Times*, 12 Dec. 1976, Sec. D, pp. 5, 18.

_____. "A Fine New Work from a Forceful Playwright." *New York Times*, 6 Dec. 1981, Sec. D, p. 3.

_____. "The Hazards and Pains Plaguing an Actor's Life." *New York Times*, 3 Feb. 1983, Sec. C, p. 15.

_____. "Playwrights Are Growing Articulate Again." *New York Times*, 31 Oct. 1981, Sec. H, pp. 3, 17.

_____. "Playwrights Need to Be Nurtured." *New York Times*, 18 April 1982, Sec. D, p. 18.

_____. "Two New Plays That Focus on the Male Loner." *New York Times*, 7 Nov. 1982, Sec. H, p. 3.

_____. "Where Has Sam Shepard Led His Audience?" *New York Times*, 5 June 1983, Sec. H, pp. 3, 16.

Klein, Julia M. "Charles Fuller Sat Down to Write a Black *Billy Budd*—and Wound Up with a Pulitzer." *People*, 28 June 1982, pp. 85–86.

Kroll, Jack. "Anatomy of a Murder." *Newsweek*, 21 Dec., p. 77.

_____. "The Muzak Man." *Newsweek*, 28 Feb. 1977, p. 79.

_____. "Who's That Tall Dark Stranger?" *Newsweek*, 11 Nov. 1985, pp. 68, 74.

Lahr, John. "Black Theater: The American Tragic Voice." *The Evergreen Review*, April 1969, pp. 55–63.

_____. "On-Stage." *The Village Voice*, 22 March 1974, p. 64.

Lamb, Margaret. "Feminist Criticism." *The Drama Review*, Spring 1973, pp. 46–50.

Lawson, Carol. "Broadway Is in Its Worst Slump in a Decade." *New York Times*, 3 Jan. 1983, Sec. A, p. 1 and Sec. C, p. 13.

_____. "Interview: Charles Fuller 'Stunned' On Winning Pulitzer." *New York Times*, 14 April 1982, Sec. C, p. 11.

Lewis, Patricia and Terry Browne. "David Mamet." In *Twentieth Century American Dramatists, Part 2*. John MacNicholas, ed. Detroit, Mich.: Gale Research Co., 1981.

Lion, John. "Rock 'n' Roll Jesus with a Cowboy Mouth." *American Theatre*, April 1984, pp. 4–8.

Lippman, Amy. "Rhythm & Truths: An Interview with Sam Shepard." *American Theatre*, April 1984, pp. 5, 28.

Mamet, David. "First Principles." *The Drama Review*, Fall 1980, pp. 51–52.

_____. "A 'Sad Comedy' about Actors." *New York Times*, 16 Oct. 1977, Sec. D, p. 7.

_____, and Ted Talley. "Playwrights on Resident Theaters: What Is to Be Done?" *Theater*, Vol. 10, 1979, pp. 82–84.

Mazzocco, Robert. "Heading for the Last Roundup." *The New York Review of Books*, 9 May 1985, pp. 21–27.

Medley, Cassandra. "Interview: A Soldier's Playwright." *Other Stages*, 22 April 1982, pp. 3, 18.

Miner, Michael D. "Grotesque Drama in the '70's." *Kansas Quarterly*, Vol. 12, No. 4, Fall 1980, pp. 99–109.

Mitgang, Herbert. "The Dramatists Defend Their Own." *New York Times*, 11 July 1982, Sec. H, pp. 3, 16.

Moore, Gaylen. "Ellen Stewart: The Mama of La Mama." *Ms.*, April 1982, pp. 48, 52, 54, 56.

Nightingale, Benedict. "For Lanford Wilson, Drama Begins at the Crossroads." *New York Times*, 12 Feb. 1984, Sec. H, pp. 5, 28.

Novick, Julius. "Affirmative Actions." *The Village Voice*, 22 Oct. 1982, p. 103.

_____. "How to Write a Play, Dully." *The Village Voice*, 20 Dec. 1976, pp. 111, 112.

_____. "Legends and Vignettes." *The Village Voice*, 29 Oct. 1979, pp. 83–84.

_____. "Mamet: Some Life in His Theater." *The Village Voice*, 31 Oct. 1977, p. 83.

_____. "The Real Perversity Is Fear." *The Village Voice*, 16 Aug. 1976, p. 95.

_____. "Wooden Indians." *The Village Voice*, 25 June 1979, p. 105.

O'Connor, John J. "TV: 'Nicholas Nickleby' Week Begins." *New York Times*, 10 Jan. 1983, Sec. C, p. 18.

Oliver, Edith. "At the Boathouse." *The New Yorker*, 5 April 1980, pp. 84, 86.

_____. "News from Off Off." *The New Yorker*, 6 Nov. 1978, p. 82.

_____. "Off Broadway." *The New Yorker*, 17 June 1974, p. 84.

_____. "Off Broadway." *The New Yorker*, 20 Dec. 1976, p. 84.

_____. "Off Broadway." *The New Yorker*, 15 June 1982, p. 81.

_____. "Off Broadway." *The New Yorker*, 8 Nov. 1982, p. 160.

_____. "A Sergeant's Death." *The New Yorker*, 7 Dec. 1981, pp. 110–111.

_____. "Too Many Trees." *The New Yorker*, 7 May 1979, p. 144.

O'Neal, John. "Motion in the Ocean." *The Drama Review*, Summer 1958, pp. 70–78.

Pasolli, Robert. "Theater: Uptown and the Calico Cat." *The Village Voice*, 1 May 1969, p. 64.

Press, Aric. "'The Verdict': A Legal Opinion." *Newsweek*, 28 Feb. 1983, p. 51.

Quintero, Jose. "Where Are All the New Directors?" *New York Times*, 28 Nov. 1982, Sec. 2, pp. 1, 23.

Rich, Frank. "'Fool for Love,' Sam Shepard Western." *New York Times*, 27 May 1983, Sec. C, p. 3.

_____. "New Angry Playwrights Are Taking Center Stage." *New York Times*, 3 Jan. 1982, Sec. H, pp. 1, 24.

_____. "Play: 'Angels Fall,' Lanford Wilson's Apocalypse." *New York Times*, 16 Oct. 1982, Sec. C, p. 15.

_____. "Play: New Fuller Drama, 'Zooman and the Sign'." *New York Times*, 8 Dec. 1980, Sec. C, p. 13.

_____. "Stage: Negro Ensemble Presents 'Soldier's Play'." *New York Times*, 27 Nov. 1981, Sec. C, p. 16.

_____. "Theater: Mamet's 'Edmond' at the Provincetown." *New York Times*, 28 Oct. 1982, Sec. C, p. 20.

_____. "'A Lie of the Mind,' by Sam Shepard." *New York Times*, 6 Dec. 1985, Sec. C, p. 3.

_____. "Where Writers Mold the Future of Theater." *New York Times*, 1 Aug. 1982, Sec. H, pp. 1, 4.

Robertson, Nan. "The Multidimensional Sam Shepard." *New York Times*, 21 Jan. 1986, Sec. C, p. 15.

Rogoff, Gordon. "Review of Mamet's *American Buffalo*." *Saturday Review*, 2 April 1977, pp. 37–38.

Sainer, Arthur. "Lanford Wilson." In *Contemporary Dramatists*, James Vinson, ed. New York: St. Martin's Press, 1977.

————. "A Liaison with Energy." *The Village Voice*, 21 May 1970, p. 45.

Sarris, Andrew. "The Selling of Sam Shepard." *The Village Voice*, 10 Dec. 1985, p. 59.

Searle, Judith. "Interview: Four Drama Critics." *The Drama Review*, Vol. 18, No. 3, 1963, pp. 5–23.

Shewey, Don. "David Mamet Puts a Dark New Urban Drama on Stage." *New York Times*, 24 Oct. 1982, Sec. 2, pp. 1, 4.

————. "The Regrouping of American Theater." *The Village Voice*, 10 Dec. 1985, pp. 14, 15, 17, 18, 20, 21.

————. "Where Plays Are Born and Tried in Tranquility." *New York Times*, 25 July 1982, Sec. H, pp. 4, 20.

Simon, John. "Ideals Lost – and Found." *New York Magazine*, 7 Feb. 1983, pp. 57–58.

————. "Likeable But Unlikely Transplant." *New York Magazine*, 15 May 1978, pp. 77–78.

————. "Soldiers and Sisters." *New York Magazine*, 7 Dec. 1981, p. 159.

Smith, Michael. "Theatre Journal." *The Village Voice*, 8 Feb. 1973, p. 61.

Steiner, George. "Books: Arts of Survival." *The New Yorker*, 19 March 1979, pp. 144, 147–150.

Storey, Robert. "The Making of David Mamet." *The Hollins Critic*, Vol. XVI, No. 4, Oct. 1979, pp. 1–11.

Stout, Kate. "Marsha Norman: Writing for the 'Least of Our Brethren'." *Saturday Review*, Oct. 1983, pp. 29–33.

VerMeulen, Michael. "Sam Shepard: Yes, Yes, Yes." *Esquire*, Feb. 1980, pp. 79–86.

Ward, Douglas Turner. "American Theater: For Whites Only?" *New York Times*, 14 Aug. 1966, Sec. D, pp. 1–3.

Weales, Gerald. "American Theater Watch 1980–81." *Georgia Review*, Fall 1981, pp. 597–607.

Weschler, Lawrence. "Louisiana in Denmark." *The New Yorker*, 30 Aug. 1982, pp. 50–60.

Wetzsteon, Ross. "David Mamet: Remember That Name." *The Village Voice*, 5 July 1976, pp. 101–104.

————. "Unknown Territory." *The Village Voice*, 10 Dec. 1985, pp. 55–56.

Wilkerson, Margaret B. "Redefining Black Theater." *The Black Scholar*, July–Aug. 1979, pp. 32–42.

Winer, Linda. "Milwaukee Cast Floats a Winner from Mamet Trunk." *Chicago Tribune*, 1 May 1980, Sec. 2, p. 2.

————. "Wilson, Mason: The Duet Is in Perfect Stage Harmony." *Chicago Tribune*, 27 Aug. 1978, Sec. G, pp. 4, 10.

Index

Action 4
Actors Conservatory Theatre 130
Actors Theatre 130, 148
The Advocate 96
The Alternate 96
American Buffalo xiv, 63, 67–68, 74, 75, 83
American Repertory Theatre 130
Angels Fall 33–35, 40, 42, 49, 51, 52, 55
Aristotle 80, 93
Arkin, Alan 95
Artaud, Antonin xi

Back Bog Beast Bait 11
Balm in Gilead 20, 25, 27, 39, 42
Barbera, Jack V. 68
Barth, John 5
Barthelme, Donald 5
Barthelme, Frederick 147
Bates, Kathy 161
Beckett, Samuel xi, 61, 68
Benny, Jack 87
Bentley, Eric 167
Berezin, Tanya 20, 52, 54, 55
Berle, Milton 87
Berliner Ensemble 167
Berman, Shelly 95
Billy Budd 107, 108, 110, 123
The Birth of a Nation 101
Bishop, John 46
Black Theater Movement 102
Brecht, Bertolt 167
Brigadoon 42
Brontosaurus xii, 30–31, 40, 52
Brooks, Mel 65

The Brownsville Raid 103–105, 107, 110
Bruce, Lenny 64, 73, 87
Brustein, Robert 90, 161
Bryden, Bill 83
Buried Child 4, 9, 11–13, 15
Bus Stop 57
Butch Cassidy and the Sundance Kid 50

Café La Mama xi, 19
Caffe Cino xi, 19, 36
Carmen Jones 101
Carver, Raymond 147
Cather, Willa 86
Chekhov, Anton 29, 30, 51, 80
Cherry Lane Theatre 63
Chicago Sun-Times 90, 96
Chicago Tribune 90, 96
Christiansen, Richard 90
Cino, Joe 19
Circle Repertory Theater 20, 36, 37, 38, 161
Circus Valentine 130, 160
The Clansman 101
Clarke, Martha xii
Clurman, Harold 68
Cohan, George M. 83
Collins, Bill 96
"Come Back Ag'in to the Raft, Huck Honey" 49
Compass Players 95
Congreve, William 83
Connelly, Marc 101
Cook, Ralph 5
Country 15
Cowboy Mouth xv, 7
Cowboys 6

Index

Cowboys #2 6
Craig's Wife 52
Crouse, Lindsay 52, 63, 95
The Culture of Narcissism 5
"The Curse of the Raven's Black Feather" 9
Curse of the Starving Class 9–11, 15

Days Ahead 20
Days of Heaven 15
The Death of a Salesman 42
Deathtrap 53
Dedalus, Stephen 102
The Desperate Hours 53
Detective Story 94
Dickens, Charles 51, 56
Ditsky, John 68
Dixon, Thomas 101
Downey, Roger 90
Drama Critics Circle Award 63
Dramatists Guild Quarterly 94
Dreiser, Theodore 86
DuBois, Blanche xii
The Duck Variations 63, 64–66, 67, 70, 74

Eder, Richard 69, 70
Edmond xiv, 62, 63, 72–74, 80–81, 85
Ellison, Ralph 113, 120
The Emperor Jones 101
Equus 134
Esquire magazine 95
Euripides 114

The Family Continues 20, 36
Faulkner, William 58
Feingold, Michael 70, 90
Fiedler, Leslie 49, 74
5th of July xii, 31–32, 56
Fitzgerald, F. Scott 5, 58
Fool for Love xv, 15
For Colored Girls 155
Forster, E.M. 58

Frances 15
Freud, Sigmund 123
The Front Page 94
Fugard, Athol 39, 162
Fuller, Charles xi–xv, 101–111, 112–125 (interview)

Gardner, Herb 82
Gate Theater 102
The Genius and the Goddess 57
Getting Out 129, 130–135, 149, 152, 158, 159
Gide, André 50
Gill, Brendan 84
The Gingham Dog xii, 20, 22–24, 32, 37, 39, 41, 49, 53, 58
Ginsberg, Allen 40
The Glass Menagerie 41, 148
Glengarry Glen Ross 63, 74–75, 77, 78, 79, 81, 83, 94, 165
Goodman Theater 61, 63, 88
Gordone, Charles 103, 154
Gottfried, Martin 68
The Great Gatsby 57
The Great Nebula in Orion 38
The Green Pastures 101
Gussow, Mel 96

Hamlet 123
Hammerstein, Oscar 101
Harlem Renaissance 101
Hawk Moon 9
Hawthorne, Nathaniel 9
Hedda Gabler 62
Hellman, Lillian 156
The Hold-up 130, 160
The Hollins Critic 68
The Holy Ghostly 11
Holy Modal Rounders 7
Home Free! 20, 55
The Homecoming 12
Horizon magazine 94
The Hot l Baltimore 20, 26–27, 28, 36, 37, 39, 49, 51, 56

Index

Hughes, Howard 16
Huxley, Aldous 57

Iago 9, 52, 123
Ibsen, Henrik 80
Icarus's Mother 3–4
Iceman 95
Ikke Ikke Nye Nye Nye 38
In the Deepest Part of Sleep 103
Inge, William 57, 79
Ionesco, Eugene xii, 166, 167
Irwin, Bill 167

Jagger, Mick 9
Jong, Erica 5
Jory, Jon 130
Joseph Jefferson Award 63
Joyce, James 101
Judson Theater xi

Kalem, T.E. 69
Kansas Quarterly 68
Kerr, Walter 72, 90
Kingsley, Susan 152
Kirkwood, James 158

Lahr, John 86, 96
Lakeboat xiv, 63–64, 67, 74, 79, 82
Lange, Jessica 15
Lasch, Christopher xv, 5
The Laundromat see also; *Third and Oak: The Laundromat* 129, 135–138
Lee, Gypsy Rose 84
Lemon Sky 19, 20, 24–25, 32, 33, 37, 43, 44, 47, 48–49
Lichtenstein, Heinz 16
A Lie of the Mind xv, 15
Life magazine 94
A Life in the Theatre 61–62, 70, 83, 89
Living Theatre xi
Locke, Alain 101

Loman, Willy xii, 74
Louisville Times 130
Luce, Claire Booth 84
Ludlow Fair 20

Mabou Mines xii
McCarter Theater 102
The Madness of Lady Bright 20
Mailer, Norman 9
Mamet, David xi–xv, 61–76, 77–97 (interview), 165
Mark Taper Forum 42, 130
Mary Hartman, Mary Hartman 62
Mason, Bobbie Ann 147
Mason, Marshall 20, 37, 38, 42, 43, 46
May, Elaine 61, 87, 95
Melodrama Play 4, 8
Melville, Herman 107, 110, 123
Men in White 94
Miller, Arthur 74
Milwaukee Repertory Company 63
Modern Drama 68
Mondrian, Piet 91
Morton, Joe 152
Motel Chronicles 14
Mother Courage 167
The Mound Builders xiv, 19, 20, 27–29, 38, 44, 54, 55

The Nation 68
National Endowment for the Arts 130
National Theatre 77, 83
Negro Ensemble Company 102, 103, 117
New York Film Festival 15
New York Post 68
New York Times 15, 61, 63, 69, 72, 96
The New Yorker 16, 70
Next Time I'll Sing for You 39
Nicholas Nickleby 168
Nichols, Mike 61, 87, 95
'Night, Mother 129, 130, 138–142, 150, 153, 154, 156, 157, 160, 161, 162
The Night of the Iguana 57

Index

Nightingale, Benedict 96
No Place to Be Somebody 154
Norman, Marsha xi–xv, 129–147, 148–
    163 (interview)

Obie award 20, 63
O'Connor, John J. 168
Odets, Clifford 79
Oedipus 93
Oliver, Edith 70
O'Neill, Eugene 51, 79, 80, 101
Open Theatre xi
Orwell, George 56, 85
Othello 123, 124
Our Mutual Friend 56
Our Town 22
Outer Critics Circle awards 130

Pacino, Al 83
The Paris Review 84
Paris, Texas 15
Partisan Review 50
The Perfect Party 102
Performance Group xi
The Petrified Forest 57
Philadelphia Inquirer 96
Phoenix Theatre 130
Pinter, Harold xi, 12, 50, 61, 84
Pitoniak, Anne 161
Playwrights Company 95
Poetics 80
The Pool Hall 152; see also Third and
    Oak: The Pool Hall
Powell, Michael Warren 55
Prairie de Chien 82
Pulitzer Prize 15, 20, 63, 77, 103, 112,
    118, 130, 149, 154

Rabb, Ellis 61
Raggedy Man 15
Red Cross 3
The Regard of Flight 167
Reiner, Carl 65

Resurrection 15
Reunion 83, 84
Rice, Thomas Dartmouth ("Daddy")
    101
Rich, Frank 72, 90, 96
Richard, Keith 9
The Right Stuff 15
The Rimers of Eldritch 21–22
Rock Garden 6–7
Rolling Stones 9
Roth, Philip 5, 40

Sahl, Mort 87
St. Nicholas Company 63
Sardou, Victorien 53
Saunders, James 39, 58
Schneider, Alan 37
Second City 61, 95
Seduced 16
Serenading Louie 29–30, 37, 44, 45–
    48, 51, 52, 54, 55
Sexual Perversity in Chicago xiii, 63,
    66–67, 70, 71, 75
Shaffer, Peter 134
Shakespeare, William 50, 83, 123, 124
Shepard, O-lan 7, 9
Shepard, Sam xi–xv, 3–16, 89
Sheridan, Richard Brinsley 83
Sills, Paul 95
Silvers, Phil 87
Smith, Michael 6
Smith, Patti 7
So Long at the Fair 19, 55
A Soldier's Play 103, 107–110, 112, 116,
    120, 121, 122, 123, 124
A Soldier's Story 103, 112
Sophocles 114
Stanislavski, Konstantin 78, 93
Steiner, George 167
Stoop 20
Storey, Robert 68
Stowe, Harriet Beecher 101
Suicide in B♭ 9
Syse, Glenna 90

A Tale Told 41, 42, 52
Talley & Son 31, 32–33; see also A Tale Told
Talley's Folly 20, 31, 39, 49, 51, 58
Tavel, Ronald 39
The Tempest 57
Theater Genesis xi, 6
Theatre de Lys 130
"Theatre of Cruelty" xi
Theatre Quarterly 7
The Theory of the Leisure Class 168
Third and Oak: The Laundromat 129, 130; see also The Laundromat
Third and Oak: The Pool Hall 129, 130, 152; see also The Pool Hall
Thirkield, Rob 20
This Is the Rill Speaking 20, 22
Three Journeys 5
The Threepenny Opera 21, 43
Time magazine 69
Tolstoy, Leo 89, 96
The Tooth of Crime 4, 8–9
Traveler in the Dark xv, 129, 130, 142–147, 153, 154, 158, 159, 163
True West 4, 13–15

Uncle Tom's Cabin 101
The Unseen Hand 4

Veblen, Thorstein 68
Village Gate 5
The Village Voice 6, 68, 70, 90, 112
Vivian Beaumont Theater 63

Waiting for Godot 68
Wall Street Journal 76
Wandering 20, 38
Ward, Douglas Turner 102, 117
The Water Engine 68–69
Weaver, Fritz 55
Wetzsteon, Ross 68
Wilder, Thornton 22
Williams, Tennessee 57
Wilson, Lanford xi–xv, 19–35, 36–58 (interview), 158
Wilson, Robert xii
The Women 94
The Woods 62, 69–72, 84
Woyzeck xiv
Writers at Work 84

Young, Stark 101

Zooman and the Sign xiii, 103, 105–107, 109, 116, 117, 119
Zweig, Paul 5